Metaphor

"Metaphor," a form of figurative language in which one thing or idea is expressed in terms of another, is becoming an increasingly popular area of study, as it is relevant to the work of semanticists, pragmatists, discourse analysts, and also those working at the interface of language and literature, and in other disciplines such as philosophy and psychology. This book provides a summary, critique, and comparison of the most important theories on how metaphors are used and understood, drawing on research from linguistics, psychology, and other disciplines. In order to ground the discussion in actual language use, the book uses examples from discourse, including casual conversations, political speeches, literature, humor, religion, and science. Written in a non-technical style, the book includes clear definitions, examples, discussion questions, and a glossary, making it ideal for graduate-level seminars.

L. DAVID RITCHIE is Professor in the Department of Communication at Portland State University.

KEY TOPICS IN SEMANTICS AND PRAGMATICS

'Key Topics in Semantics and Pragmatics' focuses on the main topics of study in semantics and pragmatics today. It consists of accessible yet challenging accounts of the most important issues, concepts, and phenomena to consider when examining meaning in language. Some topics have been the subject of semantic and pragmatic study for many years, and are re-examined in this series in light of new developments in the field; others are issues of growing importance that have not so far been given a sustained treatment. Written by leading experts and designed to bridge the gap between textbooks and primary literature, the books in this series can either be used on courses and seminars, or as one-stop, succinct guides to a particular topic for individual students and researchers. Each book includes useful suggestions for further reading, discussion questions, and a helpful glossary.

Already published in the series:
Meaning and Humour by Andrew Goatly

Forthcoming titles:
The Semantics of Counting by Susan Rothstein
Modification by Marcin Morzycki
Game-Theoretic Pragmatics by Anton Benz
Imperatives by Mark Jary and Mikhail Kissine
Speech Act Theory by Savas L. Tsohatzidis

Metaphor

L. DAVID RITCHIE

CAMBRIDGE
UNIVERSITY PRESS

CAMBRIDGE UNIVERSITY PRESS
Cambridge, New York, Melbourne, Madrid, Cape Town,
Singapore, São Paulo, Delhi, Mexico City

Cambridge University Press
The Edinburgh Building, Cambridge CB2 8RU, UK

Published in the United States of America by Cambridge University Press, New York

www.cambridge.org
Information on this title: www.cambridge.org/9781107606661

First published 2013

Printed and bound in the United Kingdom by the MPG Books Group

A catalogue record for this publication is available from the British Library

Library of Congress Cataloguing in Publication data
Ritchie, L. David.
    Metaphor / L. David Ritchie.
        p.   cm.
    Includes bibliographical references and index.
    ISBN 978-1-107-02254-6 – ISBN 978-1-107-60666-1 (pbk.)
    1. Metaphor.   I. Title.
    P301.5.M48R5776 2012
    808.032–dc23
    2012027102

ISBN 978-1-107-02254-6 Hardback
ISBN 978-1-107-60666-1 Paperback

To my mother, Lois Brannan, in honor of her lifelong love of language and her vocation as a teacher

Contents

Figures

Acknowledgments

There is a widespread misconception that writing is a solitary activity; my own experience has been quite different: For me both thinking and writing are decidedly social. Much of the thinking that has gone into this book has been shaped by interactions with Ray Gibbs, Jr., editor of *Metaphor and Symbol*, and with a series of anonymous reviewers for that journal. Conversations over the years with Lynne Cameron and other participants in workshops and seminars generously sponsored by the Research Council of the United Kingdom and hosted by Dr. Cameron in the United Kingdom have been quite important in shaping my thinking about metaphor and related topics – conversations with Alice Deignan, Graham Low, and Elena Semino in particular come to mind.

I am indebted to Helen Barton, the Cambridge University Press editor who looks after the series, for her support, encouragement, and many useful suggestions, and to two anonymous reviewers for their critiques of earlier drafts and suggestions for improvement.

As always, I am deeply indebted to my wife, LaJean Humphries, for her unfailing support and encouragement.

I am indebted to my niece, Laura Garcia, for inspiring me to begin thinking about this project when she reacted to my first book on metaphor theory by asking, "Why don't you write something I can read?" I am indebted to the students in my introductory metaphor classes at PSU, who read and provided useful feedback on the first and second drafts of the book, and in particular to the following students who generously made detailed suggestions for making the book more readable, and who helped me find and correct many errors and omissions, some minor and some not so minor: Summer Ali, Erin Block, Andrew Hedinger, Meagan Johnson, and Ryan Stroud.

All remaining errors and omissions are, of course, my own responsibility.

1 Introduction

"We the people, in order to form a more perfect union."
    Two hundred and twenty one years ago, in a hall that still stands across the street, a group of men gathered and, with these simple words, launched America's improbable experiment in democracy … The document they produced was eventually signed but ultimately unfinished. It was stained by this nation's original sin of slavery, a question that divided the colonies and brought the convention to a stalemate until the founders chose to allow the slave trade to continue for at least twenty more years, and to leave any final resolution to future generations.
(Barack Obama, "A More Perfect Union,"
Philadelphia, Pennsylvania, March 18, 2008)

This dramatic passage opens a speech given by then-Senator Barack Obama at a crucial moment in his first campaign for the US presidency. Obama's pastor and long-time friend, Reverend Jeremiah Wright, had made a series of remarks, in sermons and interviews, which were construed by many who heard them as unpatriotic. (A notable example occurred in a sermon critical of government policies and actions, in which Reverend Wright quoted the patriotic song, "God *bless* America," then substituted "God *damn* America.") The furor over Reverend Wright's harshly worded criticisms of US policies threatened to undermine Obama's support among moderate and independent voters, key constituencies in his election campaign. The immediate purpose of the speech was to defuse this controversy before it derailed the entire campaign.

The broader issue Obama faced was the role of "race" in the election. He had to address the issue of race relations in a way that would prevent it from becoming the central theme of his campaign. In this opening passage, Obama began with a reference to a defining event in US history, and then quickly narrowed the focus to a particular aspect of that event. The language in this passage set the stage for much of what follows, including a detailed discussion of the more recent history of the civil rights struggle in the United States, his own campaign, and the controversy over Reverend Wright's remarks.

Now consider an example from another, very different political speech. In spring 2005, in Gateshead, an industrial city in northern England, then-Prime Minister Tony Blair addressed the annual conference of his party. The Labour party was badly divided, in large part over a series of controversial decisions Blair had made, decisions which many voters regarded as dangerously mistaken and potentially destructive to the good of the nation. In the face of widespread hostility within the party toward these policies and decisions, Blair's task was to unite the party in preparation for elections later that year. His address included the following passage, in which he began with a description of the early days of his tenure as prime minister following the initial Labour victory that brought him to power, and recounted the history leading up to the current situation:

> So after the euphoria, came the steady hard slog of decision-making and delivery. And the events that tested me. And the media mood turning, and friends sometimes being lost as the big decisions mounted, and the thousand little things that irritate and grate, and then all of a sudden there you are, the British people, thinking: you're not listening and I think: you're not hearing me. And before you know it you raise your voice. I raise mine. Some of you throw a bit of crockery. And now you, the British people, have to sit down and decide whether you want the relationship to continue. If you decide you want Mr. Howard, that is your choice. If you want to go off with Mr. Kennedy, that's your choice too. It all ends in the same place. A Tory Government not a Labour Government. (Blair, 2005; for a detailed discussion see Deignan and Semino, 2010; Ritchie, 2008a)

Both of these passages come from speeches delivered at crucial times in the speaker's political career, but the speakers faced very different political situations. Not surprisingly, the speeches also reflect very different ways of using language. In particular, they reflect different ways of using and developing metaphors and stories. Both passages include some conventional phrases, which might not be classified as metaphorical at all, depending on how *metaphor* is defined. Examples from Obama's speech include "*divided*" and "*brought to a stalemate.*" In addition to "*steady hard slog,*" "*decision-making,*" and "*delivery,*" examples from Blair include "the media mood *turning,*" "friends being *lost,*" "the *big* decisions *mounted,*" and "the thousand *little things* that *irritate and grate.*" In Blair's speech, the entire story about throwing crockery functions as a metaphor.

What accounts for the expressive power of these passages? How do the metaphors in Obama's opening lines prepare the hearers to understand (and, Obama hoped, accept) the remainder of the speech? What does Blair's metaphorical story about a quarrel between spouses tell his listeners about the situation facing the Labour Party in 2005? How do listeners or readers make sense of these metaphors, and how do they contribute to meaning? These are a few of the questions that will be addressed throughout this book.

WHAT IS A METAPHOR?

Before taking up questions about how metaphors work and how they are used, it is important to establish what we are talking about – what is a metaphor? How is a metaphor related to other uses of language? It is impossible to understand the results of metaphor research, compare different studies, or even think systematically about metaphors without having a clear understanding of what a metaphor is, and knowing how each researcher defines and identifies metaphors.

The question "what is a metaphor?" is not easy to answer. At one extreme are the eloquent and colorful literary metaphors, such as the oft-quoted lines, "All the world's *a stage*, and all the men and women merely *players*" (William

> **Notation:** I use the convention of marking metaphorical phrases by placing the metaphorical elements in italics and the entire phrase within quotation marks.
>
> Invented examples will be placed within single quotation marks ('*rising* prices') to contrast them with attested examples from actual discourse ("*stained by*"), which will appear in double quotation marks. Following Richards (1936) I will refer to the concept that is described or expressed by the metaphor (in the case of "*stained by*," the moral feelings aroused by treating human beings as property) as the *topic* of the metaphor, and the metaphorical words or phrase (in this case, "*stain*") as the "*vehicle*." I will introduce other notational conventions as they are needed.

Shakespeare, *As You Like It*, Act 2, Scene 7, lines 139–140). Virtually everyone would recognize these words, "*stage*" and "*players*" as metaphors, especially in the context of the scene, which takes place between the exiled Duke and Jaques, a member of his retinue.

In the following lines Jaques develops and expands the metaphor, describing the "seven ages of man" as "*acts*," beginning with "the infant / Mewling and puking in the nurse's arms," proceeding through "the lover / Sighing like furnace, with a woeful ballad / Made to his mistress' eyebrow" and ending with the "Last scene of all, / That ends this strange eventful history, / ... second childishness and mere oblivion, / Sans teeth, sans eyes, sans taste, sans everything."

Many other familiar phrases are based on the "*stage*" metaphor. We speak of 'the journalist's *role* in a democracy.' A person known for frequent emotional outbursts is a '*drama queen*.' A person who exaggerates his own contribution to a project is '*hogging* the *spotlight*.' (Notice that this phrase combines the "*stage*" metaphor with a common animal metaphor, 'being greedy is *being a pig*.') In a song written by Paul Anka (1969), Frank Sinatra and others sing about "When I *face the final curtain*." Goffman (1959) analyzed social interactions in terms of '*front-stage performance*' and '*back-stage* preparations' and Meyrowitz (1985) developed the '*front-stage/back-stage*' metaphor into a critique of television content.

At the other extreme are familiar idioms such as '*rising* prices,' '*icy* greeting,' '*close* relationship,' and '*dead-end* job'. These phrases are certainly not *literal*, since prices are not objects located in or capable of moving through space, and a greeting is not an object or substance that can have a temperature. But they are so commonly used and so readily understood that they may not seem metaphorical at all. Even more problematic are words like '*salary*,' with a metaphorical origin that would be recognized only by a specialist. ('*Salary*' comes from Latin *sal*, salt; at one time Roman soldiers were paid with a monthly allotment of salt, which at that time served as a medium of exchange. The idiom '*not worth his salt*' probably derives from the same vehicle.) In between these extremes are phrases like Obama's "*brought* the convention to a *stalemate*" (this phrase also combines two distinct metaphors) and Blair's "*end in the same place*."

"Metaphor" has been variously defined in terms of substituting one word for another word with an apparently different meaning, comparing one idea to another, or creating an implicit analogy or simile. For example, the *Oxford English Dictionary* (unabridged) defines metaphor as both transfer and analogy: "the figure of speech in which a name or descriptive term is transferred to some object different from, but analogous to, that to which it is properly applicable." Aristotle regarded a metaphor as an implicit comparison, based on rules of analogy. According to this definition, Obama's phrase, "the *original sin* of slavery," implicitly compares slavery to Adam and Eve's sin of disobedience to God, and Tony Blair's "some of you *throw a bit of crockery*" implicitly compares accusing the prime minister of betraying party principles in a political dispute to throwing dishes in a marital dispute. Kövecses gives a similar definition: "metaphor is a figure of speech in which one thing is compared to another by saying that one is the other" (2002, p. vii). In this definition, metaphor can be thought of as a simile with the comparison term (e.g. *like)* dropped. To use Kövecses' example, which appears frequently in the philosophy and linguistics literature, 'Achilles is *like* a lion' becomes 'Achilles *is* a lion.' Achilles, or more precisely Achilles' character (the topic) is compared to a lion (the vehicle) with respect to specific qualities they have in common, such as fierceness and courage. (The qualities that provide a basis for comparison are often referred to as the *'ground'* or *'grounds'* of the metaphor.) As Kövecses points out, in this traditional view, metaphor is a figure of speech, based on qualities common to the two entities that can be identified and compared, and used primarily for aesthetic or rhetorical purposes.

A definition in terms of comparing topic to vehicle would seem to apply readily to metaphors composed of two nouns linked by *to be* or a similar verb. In 'Achilles is *a lion*,' Achilles exhibits moral or personality characteristics such as *bravery* that are commonly attributed to lions. Thus, 'Achilles is *a lion*' seems to be merely a fancy way of saying 'Achilles is *brave like a lion*,' and that explanation seems to capture most of what is meant by the metaphor. Some metaphors that do not include *to be* can be changed to this form without loss of meaning; for example the idiom, *'beanpole*,' is often used in a phrase like "that child is a *beanpole*," in which the qualities of being tall and thin are attributed to a fast-growing child, and the comparison definition seems to capture most or all of the intended meaning.

At first glance, the implicit comparison explanation seems to fit "*the world is a stage*," but when we read the entire passage in which Jaques elaborates on this metaphor, it appears that Shakespeare meant something more than simply comparing social performance to theatrical performance (see also Black, 1993). Even greater difficulties arise when we attempt to apply this definition to metaphors like Blair's "some of you *throw a bit of crockery*" and adjective-based metaphors like "*incendiary* language," from Obama's speech. In order to analyze these metaphors in terms of implied simile it would be necessary to change the syntax of each statement in ways that would, arguably, also change their meanings in context. Each of these metaphors has a complex relationship with its context that defies translation into a simple "A is B" statement. "Some of you *throw a bit of crockery*" does not merely compare a political quarrel to a comically violent quarrel between spouses; among other things it implies something about the respective roles of Mr. Blair and the party dissidents, and about the intellectual weight of their disagreements. Ordinarily "*incendiary* language" might be taken as a simple description of the emotional intensity of Reverend Wright's language, but in the context of race relations in the United States, where language ("burn baby burn") actually has led to urban riots and arson-caused fires, the metaphor takes on a resonance that extends well beyond a simple comparison.

Going beyond the more traditional definitions, Kenneth Burke (1945) defined metaphor as "a device for seeing something in terms of something else." Yanow (2008) defines metaphor as "the juxtaposition of two superficially unlike elements in a single context, where the separately understood meanings of both interact to create a new perception of each and especially of the focus of the metaphor." Along slightly different lines, Semino (2008, p. 1) defines metaphor as "the phenomenon whereby we talk and, potentially, think about something in terms of something else." Applying Semino's definition, "*incendiary* language" would be considered a metaphor because the vehicle, "*fire*" is used to talk and think about an abstract quality of certain very emotional language. "*Throw a bit of crockery*" would be considered a metaphor because the vehicle is used to talk and think about the way certain Labour Party members and other citizens had recently criticized Mr. Blair.

Although these definitions mark an improvement over the more traditional idea of a simile with the word *like* omitted, they remain rather vague – what does it mean to *see* words used in a sermon in terms of *fire*? And what is it that we do when we talk or think about *words from a sermon* in terms of *fire*? What do we do when we talk or think about an intra-party quarrel in terms of *throwing crockery*? These remarks are not intended to criticize these definitions (I don't think I can offer anything better) so much as to underscore the difficulty of formulating a satisfactory definition of this complex phenomenon. One might be tempted to follow the example of US Supreme Court Justice Potter Stewart's definition of pornography: "I know it when I see it."

Note that we find ourselves relying on metaphors even as we attempt to define metaphors. 'Metaphor *vehicle*' is itself a metaphor, expressing the idea that a metaphorical word or phrase '*carries*' some meaning associated with the topic. '*Detachment*' and '*disengagement*' also seem to be metaphorical: they express *practical affairs* as an object of some sort to which more practical-minded people are '*attached*' or not. So the attempt to explain how "*incendiary*" or "*throw a bit of crockery*" qualifies as a metaphor leads to use of other metaphorical language.

In Burke's definition of metaphor as "a *device* for *seeing* something in terms of something else," "*device*" refers literally to a *machine* or *tool* of some sort, and carries an implication of passivity – the activity is performed by the *user* of the device. *"Seeing"* refers literally to one mode of perception, vision, but here it may also be understood as a *metonym* (using a term designating one concept to refer to related concepts). A reader *sees* a metaphor but a listener *hears* it. If we change Burke's phrase to *"perceiving* something in terms of something else" it will become apparent that *perceiving* can itself be understood as referring to the sequence of processes through which language is perceived and comprehended. '*See*' and '*hear*' are both often used as metaphors for *understand*, although they usually express different aspects of understanding.

At this point, it seems evident that Semino's definition has much in common with Burke's – but the differences are worth noticing because they are theoretically important. Burke refers to *seeing*, which implies an emphasis on the audience rather than the speaker or writer; Kövecses and Semino refer to *talking*, which implies an emphasis on the originator, the speaker or writer. Burke refers to a

> **Notation:** When discussing what Lakoff and Johnson (1980) call "conceptual metaphors" I will mark the broader metaphorical concept underlying the vehicle – in this case, MORE IS UP – by small capital letters.

"device," and Semino refers to a "phenomenon." *Device* places emphasis on the agency of the perceiver, and *phenomenon* places more emphasis on the metaphor itself as a locus of activity independent of either the speaker or the listener. Both Burke's and Semino's definitions differ from Kövecses' definition, which simply refers to a figure of speech and the comparison it makes.

Semino's stipulation that we "potentially think about something in terms of something else" extends the definition in a way that suggests a cognitive aspect to metaphor: it suggests that metaphor may be an attribute of thought. Conceptual metaphor theory (Lakoff and Johnson, 1980) introduces a way of thinking about metaphor that extends this implication even further (Chapter 4). Lakoff and Johnson define metaphor as not merely *thinking* about something in terms of something else, but actually *experiencing* something *as* something else. When we speak of a '*warm* relationship,' according to Lakoff and Johnson we experience the emotion of affection as actual physical temperature (EMOTION IS TEMPERATURE). When we understand Obama's description of Wright's language as "*incendiary,*" we experience the emotional intensity of the language as if we were experiencing sensations associated with physical *fire* (PASSION IS HEAT). When we hear Blair's characterization of the intra-party policy disputes, we experience them as an actual dish-throwing squabble between spouses. Semino's claim is somewhat less extreme than that of Lakoff and Johnson (and somewhat less precise as well). She does not claim that "*incendiary* language" is experienced *as* fire, but merely that it is experienced *in terms of* fire – by which she seems to mean that we experience some of the emotional, intellectual, and perhaps perceptual responses associated with fire as we process the metaphor.

In the next several chapters it will become apparent that definitions of "metaphor" and advice for identifying metaphors tend to be associated with theories about how metaphors are used and understood. This is why it is important to be clear about what a researcher or theorist means by *metaphor*: the definition itself may imply assumptions about metaphors that will constrain the kind of theory that can be expressed. A second reason why definitions are important is that, if two writers use different definitions, they are likely to be discussing different things. When this happens, what appears to be a theoretical difference may actually be the result of looking at different phenomena.

For the present, I will continue to follow the definitions proposed by Burke and Semino, and understand metaphor as seeing, experiencing, or talking about something

> **Definition:** For the present, "metaphor" is defined as *seeing, experiencing, or talking about something in terms of something else.*

in terms of something else. However, Yanow's qualification is also important: to qualify as a metaphor, the topic and the vehicle must be "superficially unlike." In the most straightforward instances, the topic and the vehicle will be from entirely different realms of experience. Thus, "*incendiary* language" is a metaphor because *language*, a system of regularized sounds used to express meanings, is presented to be understood in terms of *fire*, a physically hot and destructive process of combustion. "Grief is a *journey*" (Obst, 2003) can be classified as a metaphor because grief, a variety of emotional response, is described as a *journey*, a form of extended motion through space.

In other commonplace examples, however, topic and vehicle appear to belong to closely related realms of experience, for example, "white is *the new black*" and "he's *another Jackie Chan.*" *White* and *black* are two (opposite) shades, so "white is *the new black*" would seem merely to state a falsehood. However, the trope shifts attention from the realm of color to the realm of fashion, thus implicitly invoking an entirely different realm of experience. In "he's *another Jackie Chan,*" the shift is between two aspects of identity, requiring something like Yanow's criterion of "superficially unlike."

Even with Yanow's qualification, this simple definition is not as straightforward as it might seem. In the first place, this definition suggests that expressions are either metaphorical or not, and there are many examples for which a clear and simple classification is not easy to determine. A frequently discussed example is a group of metaphors such as '*win*' or '*lose* an argument,' '*attack* an opponent's argument,' '*defend a position* in an argument and so on, all of which Lakoff and Johnson cite as evidence for an underlying metaphor, ARGUMENT IS WAR. As their critics have pointed out and Lakoff and Johnson acknowledge, both *argument* and *war* are associated with a more general concept, *conflict*, and hence might reasonably be considered to belong to the same broader realm of experience. If words and phrases such as '*win*,' '*defend*,' and '*attack*' pertain to the more general concept, *conflict*, then applying them to *argument* would be an example of metonym, not metaphor.

A different sort of problem arises from ambiguous phrases that appear to be intended metaphorically even though they are literally applicable, and phrases that can be understood either literally or metaphorically, or both at once. In the United States, a person may refer to a friend who behaves in a crude or unmannerly way as "an *animal*," a characterization that is literally true in a biological sense but is used metaphorically to express an attitude toward the friend's behavior. In "Stopping by Woods on a Snowy Evening," Frost (1923) ends with the line, "And miles to go before I sleep," repeated for emphasis. Closing a poem about riding home on horseback, the line is literally true, but coming after "I have promises to keep," it is also a metaphor for Frost's life, drawing on the commonplace metaphors LIFE IS A JOURNEY and DEATH IS SLEEP; understanding the poem requires that the closing lines be understood as simultaneously literal and metaphorical.

In spite of these difficulties, at least for the present the definitions proposed by Burke and Semino provide a basis for classifying many of the phrases from Tony Blair's speech to the Gateshead Conference as metaphorical. For example, "*steady hard slog*" expresses the *process* of decision-making in terms of *motion through space* and "*end in the same place*" describes the election process as *motion through space*, which

> **Terminology:** '*Mapping*' generally refers to a process in which particular words are connected with meanings. In metaphor theory it refers to a process in which certain attributes of a metaphor vehicle are associated in a systematic way with ('*mapped onto*') comparable attributes of the topic.

appears to draw on the same JOURNEY vehicle used by Obst (2003) to describe the grieving process, and frequently used to express many abstract experiences. We often speak of the '*beginning*' of life, '*goals* in life,' and '*direction*' in life; '*beginning*' a project and '*making progress*' or '*coming to a dead-end*.'

Metaphor might also be defined in terms of what it is not, and metaphorical language contrasted with literal language. However, the concept of *literal* poses its own difficulties (Gibbs, 1994). *Literal* derives from the same root as *letters* and *literacy*, and originally refers to a *letter-by-letter* reading of a text such as the Bible or another religious text (unabridged *Oxford English Dictionary*). Moreover, '*literal*' is itself frequently used in a clearly metaphorical sense, as in 'My mother will *literally kill me* if I'm not home by midnight,' in which '*literally*' serves to intensify '*kill*,' which itself might be understood as either metaphor or hyperbole (exaggeration used for emphasis or humor).

Literal ordinarily implies a code-like one-to-one *mapping* of words with meanings. Very few words afford such a direct mapping; the precise meanings '*conveyed by*' words are usually strongly influenced by context (Gibbs, 1994; Wilson and Sperber, 2004). Accordingly, it may be more accurate to think of a continuum that ranges from what we think of as literal language (*feather-pillow*) through hyperbole ('*feather-weight*') to what would be universally recognized as metaphor ('*feather-brain*'). This issue is itself of some theoretical importance, and it will be discussed throughout the book.

A note about terminology

As explained earlier in this chapter, I refer to the concept that is described or expressed by the metaphor as the *topic* of the metaphor, and the metaphorical word or phrase as the '*vehicle*.' In Tony Blair's "*steady hard slog* of decision-making," the task of making decisions or, more precisely, Blair's feelings about the task, is the topic, and "*steady hard slog*" or, more generally, '*marching*,' is the vehicle. To look at a more complicated example, '*put your thoughts into words*' implies 'thoughts are *objects*,' 'words are *containers*,' and 'speaking or writing is *putting objects into containers*.' *Expressing one's thoughts* is the implicit topic of the overall statement and '*putting objects into (something)*' is the vehicle. *Words* is the topic of a related metaphor that is implied by the phrase, with '*container*' as the implied vehicle.

Many other terms have been used to describe the parts of a metaphor. What I call the *topic* is sometimes called the *tenor* and sometimes the '*target*' (a metaphor that implies perhaps that the meaning is '*aimed at*' what is being discussed). What I call the '*vehicle*' is also sometimes called the *basis*. I like '*vehicle*' because it specifies that the metaphorical word or phrase '*carries*' the meaning. I like *topic* because it seems clear and intuitive. But, like *target*, *topic* is not free of problems. In particular, in many instances it is not at all easy to identify a specific meaning that is the *topic* of a metaphor and can be expressed without simply paraphrasing the metaphor. Even in "All the world's *a stage*," it is not easy to specify the topic – the form of the sentence suggests the topic is *world*, but that is clearly not what is intended. *World* itself seems to serve as a metaphor (or perhaps a metonym) for *society*, but even that clarification is not fully satisfactory.

The attributes that provide a basis for comparing vehicle to topic are sometimes referred to as the '*ground*' of the metaphor. In "All the world's *a stage*," the '*ground*' would appear to be something like *theatrical conventions*. In "*steady hard slog* of decision-making," the '*ground*' is *marching* or, more generally, *a journey*. Note that '*ground*' itself is metaphorical and could be taken to imply something '*solid*' or '*fundamental*,' attributes that we might not wish to associate with metaphorical interpretations. It is unlikely that any set of terms is entirely free of problems and hidden assumptions.

Identifying metaphors

It is probably apparent that procedures for identifying metaphors will themselves depend on how "metaphor" is defined, which in turn depends on the underlying theoretical perspective. The definition of metaphor as an implicit comparison between two different sorts of event or object, consistent with Aristotle and Kövecses, would lead the analyst to look for words and phrases that imply just such a comparison. A definition of metaphor as perceiving, talking, thinking about, or experiencing something in terms of something else, consistent with Semino and Burke, would require the analyst to adopt some other strategy.

The Metaphor Analysis Project's website (Cameron, 2006) provides a relatively flexible identification procedure. A metaphor vehicle is identified as "a word or phrase that somehow contrasts with (is incongruous or anomalous with) the topic of the ongoing text or talk," but can be connected with the topic. A word or phrase is classified as a metaphor if it can be interpreted in context, but its apparent contextual meaning is incongruous with the basic or customary meaning. (For a more precise – and more complicated – procedure see Pragglejaz, 2007.) Thus, in a common idiom, "justice is *blind*" applies a concept, "*blind*" for which the basic or usual meaning (severely visually impaired) is clearly different from its meaning in context:

justice, an abstract concept, is not the sort of entity that can be visually impaired. Tony Blair's "*throw a bit of crockery*" describes an action that might possibly have occurred at a Labour Party conference, but is clearly different from what actually happened, and thus from the meaning of the phrase in context. (If objects of any sort were thrown at the Labour Party conference the news media were uncharacteristically silent about it.) In "Stopping by woods on a snowy evening," *distance traveled* ("*miles to go*") is used to describe *time yet to live*, and "*sleep*" is used to describe *death*. In both cases, the metaphorical meaning is expressed by violating the basic, customary meaning: *miles to go* basically refers to physical distance, and *sleep* basically refers to a condition from which one expects to awaken. These examples also illustrate another important point: it is not enough to look for anomalous usage; it is also necessary to look for potential meanings that are inconsistent with the primary or basic meaning of a word or phrase, even if the primary or basic meaning makes sense in context.

Finally, it is also necessary to consider whether a sensible interpretation is possible. Noam Chomsky's famous example, "Colorless green ideas sleep furiously" (1957, p. 15) fits the criterion of using words in a way that violates the basic, customary meaning, but it would be difficult to arrive at a meaningful

> **Terminology:** Metaphors such as '*warm* relationship' and '*rising* inflation' are often identified as *lexicalized*, because the metaphorical meaning has come to be regarded as one of the word's basic definitions, and thus part of the *lexicon* or dictionary.

interpretation in any reasonable context. Nonsense verse often has a similar quality (see Chapter 7). Thus, it is useful to add the criterion that, for a word or phrase to be identified as a metaphor, it must be possible to arrive at some sensible interpretation independent of the basic, customary meaning.

This approach obviously allows for greater individual discretion in interpretation, but it still permits a research team to specify precise coding rules and compute a measure of how closely two or more members of a research team agree about the identification of metaphors in a passage (this is called *inter-coder reliability*). The reliability or consistency in metaphor identification and interpretation can also be checked by consulting people who participated in a communication event or other members of the same speech community about the coding, and by comparing the metaphor coding with the way other researchers have coded other samples. By comparing how different researchers define and identify metaphors, it is often possible to explain why they come to different conclusions about them.

Varieties of metaphor

It has probably already become apparent that metaphors differ from each other in many ways. One set of differences is in how familiar they are to a "typical" listener or reader, how conventional they are and the extent to which the metaphorical meaning has become *lexicalized*, and as a consequence how readily they are recognized as metaphorical. As noted in the preceding discussion, words and phrases that might potentially be classified as metaphorical range from phrases such as *salary* or *pedigree* that are no longer recognized as metaphorical through phrases like 'warm relationship' that are commonly regarded as literal but have a recognizable metaphorical origin, to phrases everyone would recognize as metaphorical, such as "All the world's *a stage*." Words like '*salary*' and '*pedigree*' are often referred to as '*dead* metaphors.' More commonplace expressions like 'warm reception' or '*distant* relative' are sometimes called 'tired or sleeping metaphors.' *Affectionate* is usually regarded as simply a secondary literal meaning of *warm* and *close*, and *unfriendly* as a secondary literal meaning of *cold* and *distant*. Chapter 2 will describe the "*career of metaphor*" theory, which holds that metaphors progress from fully metaphorical through partially lexicalized to fully lexicalized metaphors as they are encountered with increasing frequency and become increasingly familiar. However, Lakoff and Johnson (1980; 1999, discussed in Chapter 4) treat even almost completely lexicalized metaphors as fully metaphorical, and there is evidence that these words and phrases are, at least under some circumstances, processed as metaphors.

Another way of classifying metaphors is in terms of the part of speech. Examples that have already been discussed include several parts of speech that are used metaphorically:

> noun: "The world is *a stage*"
> adjective: "*incendiary* language"
> verb: "*brought* the convention," "*ends in*"
> narrative: "*Some of you throw a bit of crockery*"

Lakoff and Johnson argue that prepositions are also often metaphorical. In "It all *ends in the same place*," "*in*" is used in a way that suggests a physical location, consistent with the noun "*place*," and thus according to Lakoff and Johnson would also be classified as a metaphor. According to this analysis, '*in* love' and '*in* despair' would also be metaphorical.

In Cameron's (2003) data from conversation in an elementary school classroom, 63 percent of the metaphors are verbs or verb phrases, and only 22 percent are "nominative metaphors" – nouns or noun phrases. Cameron reports that prepositions, adverbs, and adjectives are also frequently used as metaphors. Often parts of speech are combined, as in "*go back to* your memory" (Cameron, 2003, p. 200) in which the verb "*go*" combines with the adverb "*back*" and preposition "*to*," all used metaphorically to express "think about it again." Cameron (2008) also notes that metaphors can be classified in terms of whether they are used deliberately or automatically, and whether they are novel or conventional.

METAPHORS AND OTHER FORMS OF FIGURATIVE LANGUAGE

The word *metaphor* is sometimes used as a general term for figurative, or non-literal, language; Miller (1982, cited in Schneider, 2008) identifies seven kinds of metaphor: analogy, translation, exchange, contradiction, synecdoche, metonymy, metaphor proper. Often it is difficult to determine whether a word or phrase should be understood metaphorically or not. In this section I will discuss some other forms of figurative language that may be used in combination with metaphor, or may be used metaphorically.

Metonym

Metonym refers generally to the use of a word to reference another closely related concept. Metonyms include part for whole ('could you *lend me a hand*,' where '*hand*' is a metonymic reference to the addressee's entire body; this is also referred to as *synecdoche*, from the Greek for *receiving together*). Another form of metonym is whole for part, as in 'the *White House* issued a statement on the controversy,' in which the statement was actually uttered by the Press Secretary or some other designated official. But this could also be understood as an 'institution for process' metonym, if '*White House*' is intended to stand for the discussion among the President and his advisers from which the statement originated. '*President Nixon bombed Cambodia*' can be understood as a "participant or leader for process" metonym.

Overstatement and understatement

Overstatement (hyperbole) is sometimes used for emphasis ('I have a *million* things to do today') and sometimes for ironic effect as, from a conversation among a group of scientists about communicating with non-scientists, "If we were better communicators we'd be *swimming in money*." This also illustrates the combination of overstatement with metaphor. Similarly, 'I have a *ton* of chores to finish up' combines overstatement with metaphor, in this case NUMBER IS WEIGHT. An example of overstatement combined with metonym is 'I have a *ton* of papers to grade,' where the weight of the papers is associated with the number of them. Understatement is often used ironically, as in 'we have a *little* problem here,' where understatement is combined with the metaphor, IMPORTANCE IS SIZE.

Idioms

Idioms, expressions that are commonly used within a speech community to express a consistent idea or experience, represent a special case. Some of these, like '*kick the bucket*' and '*take with a grain of salt*' have become thoroughly lexicalized, and even if they think of them as metaphorical, very few people could explain the 'metaphorical *mapping*,' why they have the meaning they do. Other idioms, however, have an easily recovered metaphorical origin. "*Ivory tower*," at least among academicians, is readily understood in terms of the idealistic purity of "*ivory*" and the isolation from worldly cares implied by "*tower*." "The *blood* of slaves and slave-owners," from Obama's speech, is based on an archaic understanding of reproductive biology, in which sperm was thought actually to convey some of the father's blood to the fetus. The origin of "*blood*" as a metaphor for ancestry is probably known only to a small share of those who heard Obama's speech (mainly people who have studied the history of science), but most hearers would recognize "*blood*" as a metaphor in this context, as well as in related metaphorical expressions such as '*full-blooded*' and '*blood* relatives.'

In some cases, like '*put through a wringer*,' even when the cultural practice (washing machines with rollers to squeeze out the water) on which an idiom is based has passed out of common experience, the underlying metaphor is still likely to be widely understood. In other cases, like '*warm his britches*,' research has shown that the underlying metaphor may be understood in a variety of ways. This expression most likely originated as a metonymic reference to the feeling of warmth caused by the flow of blood to the skin when a child was spanked, but Keysar and Bly (1999) report a range of interpretations, including "give him praise," which is quite the opposite of the original metonymic reference. This ambiguity may be a result of cultural and legal changes: the practice of spanking with an object such as a wooden paddle, which was common as recently as the 1960s, is now illegal in many localities, and spanking in any form is much less widely practiced than it was even a few decades ago (Pinker, 2011).

Consequently, many people under the age of fifty are unlikely to have personal experience of the metaphor vehicle.

Non-linguistic metaphors

Many theorists include *language* in their definition of metaphor, in which case describing a picture, gesture, or melody as a *metaphor* would be understood as a metaphor in itself, with *visual representation* or *musical passage* as the topic and *language* as the vehicle. However, some theories, conceptual metaphor theory in particular, permit any communicative actions, including pictures, gestures, sounds, and so on, to be analyzed as being metaphorical.

In the agricultural community where I grew up, when a speaker was telling an obviously exaggerated story, listeners would often mime using a pitchfork as if to throw manure-laden straw out of a cattle shed (many cultures have some version of the equivalent verbal metaphor). Listeners would also often respond by holding their hands up as if demonstrating the length of an improbably long fish; a related idiomatic verbal metaphor refers to 'a *fish tale*' or merely '*fishy*.' Sometimes when one person is complaining about something, a listener will mime playing a slow tune on a violin, metaphorically associating the complaint with sad music (Ritchie, 2009c). Pointing a finger toward one's open mouth can be understood as a metonymic expression of disgust if it is used in response to a food item, based on its connection with an action sometimes used to induce vomiting; if it is used in response to mention of a disliked person or idea it can be understood as a metaphor, similar to the verbal expression, 'don't *make me puke.*' Making a spiral gesture near one's temple is often interpreted as a comment on another person's sanity. This may be an example of a gestural expression for '*dizzy*,' based on the sensation of spinning associated with vertigo and disorientation or of a verbal metaphor, 'he has a *screw loose*,' based on the '*machine*' metaphor for the brain.

Visual metaphors are a staple of editorial cartoons. Every so often an editorial cartoon depicts the earth with an icepack on top and a cartoonish sad face. At the height of the Watergate scandal, cartoonist John Pierotti (1973) drew a cartoon image of Richard Nixon as Pinocchio, with a long nose labeled "Watergate"; the same metaphor was also developed in a comedy monologue by satirist David Frye (Grofman, 1989). Advertising photography is filled with visual metaphors and metonyms (Müller, 2008; Cienki and Müller, 2008). An example from several years ago was a whiskey ad featuring a woman wearing a black velvet evening gown, which visually echoed the brand name of the whiskey and emphasized the metaphorical association of tactile *smoothness* with '*smooth*' flavor as well as metonymically associating the brand with sophisticated nightlife.

Literary versus conventional and commonplace metaphors ▬▬▬▬▬

Traditional approaches to metaphor theory (e.g. Black, 1993) have often taken creative, novel metaphors as prime exemplars, and literary metaphors deserve close attention in their own right. An example of a creative and novel literary metaphor appears in Stephen Spender's (1955) poem, "Seascape": "There are some days the happy ocean lies / Like an unfingered harp, below the land." "The ocean is like *a harp*" is introduced as a simile, but in subsequent lines it is developed more fully as a metaphor. The vehicle, "*harp*," is familiar, but its use as a simile and then as a metaphor for the ocean is novel and creative. Toward the end of the poem, Spender introduces a "*sacrifice*" metaphor and then a metaphorical allusion to classical epic and myths: "What voyagers, oh what heroes, flamed like pyres / With helmets plumed" (see Chapter 10).

We usually think of literary metaphors in terms of a novel pairing of vehicle and topic like *ocean* with *harp*, or metaphors in which the vehicle is drawn from classical epics or myths, but writers and speakers often achieve striking effects with common and familiar metaphor vehicles. "All the world's *a stage*" was a common metaphor before Shakespeare gave it new meaning by developing and elaborating it. Emily Dickinson frequently used commonplace personification and JOURNEY metaphors, for example in "Because I could not *stop* for Death – / He kindly *stopped for* me" ([1890] 1960). Dylan Thomas combined common DAY/NIGHT and LIGHT/DARK metaphors for life and death in "Do not *go gentle into that good night / rage, rage against the dying of the light*" ([1951] 2011). Shakespeare's "When forty winters shall *besiege thy brow* / And *dig deep trenches in thy beauty's field*" combines commonplace metaphors of WAR and PLOWING in a novel commentary on aging. Each of these poets develops common metaphors in original ways to express ideas and feelings that resonate powerfully with readers' experience. Similarly, most of the metaphors in the speeches by Obama and Blair draw on familiar metaphor vehicles and use them in ways that resonate powerfully with ordinary experience.

On the other hand, as Müller (2008) points out, ordinary speakers also use conventional metaphors in ways that make them seem fresh, original, and very much '*alive.*' An example appears in a conversation among scientists discussed by Ritchie and Schell (2009). The scientists had been discussing the need to be continually concerned about how to fund their research when one participant commented that "there is no more *ivory tower*." A few lines later another participant referred to the metaphor with the remark that "I've never really *seen the ivory tower*," another participant asked "Is that what you *dream about, in the night*, Jim?" The brief exchange of quips led to a relatively long exchange in which the group developed the "*ivory tower*" metaphor into a story about the contemporary plight of theoretical science.

Complexities

Metaphors are often used in a way that can be understood as either literal or metaphorical, or both at once. The Robert Frost (1960) poem "The road not taken" starts with a literal journey through the woods, then this literal journey is transformed into a metaphor for the poet's life, so the lines "*Two roads diverged in a wood, and I, / I took the one less traveled by*" can be read simultaneously as a literal description of a particular journey and a metaphorical description of the poet's life (like "*miles to go before I sleep*"). In the passage from the conversation among scientists (Ritchie and Schell, 2009) discussed in the previous section, one participant made a joke about never having "*seen the ivory tower*" and another participant asked "Is that what you *dream about, in the night*, Jim?" Here, "*dream about in the night*" can be understood simultaneously as asking about the nature of Jim's literal dream life and as a metaphor for his unrealized yearnings (Chapter 8). In the Reconciliation Dialogues, analyzed by Lynne Cameron (2007), Jo Berry refers to her "*journey* of understanding," which can be understood both literally as a reference to her travels throughout England and Ireland and metaphorically as her process of cognitive and emotional develop-ment – which was facilitated by her literal journey (Chapter 8).

Assumptions about language

Müller (2008) argues that theories about metaphors are strongly influ-enced by underlying assumptions about language, and that current controversies about metaphors can be traced to contrasting views about language. Classic approaches to metaphor are based on the view that language primarily serves to represent objective facts about the world, and to report these facts to other persons. According to Searle (1993), a meaningful utterance makes an assertion about the world based on a set of assumptions or conditions such that the utter-ance is true only if all of the conditions are true; conversely, to under-stand an utterance is to understand its truth conditions and to believe an utterance is to accept the truth of its conditions. "I got a good hair-cut" implies something like the following truth conditions:

- There is a type of action, *haircut*, with a certain list of features.
- A *good* haircut is characterized by a certain list of qualities.
- The action I experienced had the features associated with a *haircut*.
- The haircut I received had the qualities associated with a *good* haircut.

To believe the statement is to accept the truth of each of these statements. Extending this approach to a beauty salon named '*A Cut Above*,' the literal meaning of the phrase establishes the following truth conditions:

- The purpose of the establishment is to cut something.
- The cutting happens above something.

The metaphorical meaning must establish a separate set of truth conditions, which may be taken from the colloquial meaning of the phrase, producing something like the following:

- Quality is like dividing or '*cutting*' a list of items that has been sorted by value.
- Better quality is like dividing the items higher in the list and thus separating the higher-ranking from the lower-ranking items.

These truth conditions entail a third truth condition asserted by the use of the phrase as a slogan or name:

- The establishment offers better quality services ('*above*' similar services available from other establishments).

To believe the literal meaning of the phrase is to believe that something is cut (e.g. hair) and that the cutting happens above something (e.g. the patron's face). To believe the metaphorical meaning of the phrase is, first, to accept the truth of the comparison of quality to '*cutting*' a list of items and, second, to accept as true the claim that the establishment offers better quality services.

According to the information transfer model, the purpose of language is to maintain and improve our representation of the world, where "representation" refers to the set of truth conditions we understand and know to be either true or false. This describes a "task-based" view of language, where language use is meaningful only if and to the extent that it serves the accomplishment of some informational task, such as inquiring, informing, persuading, commanding, and so on. To explain metaphors is to explain how they establish truth conditions and contribute to accomplishing informational tasks. Theories discussed in Chapters 2 and 3 are based on an information transfer model of language.

In later chapters I will discuss two other views of language, both of which are compatible with what Müller calls the "meaning construction" model. Perceptual simulation theory (Barsalou, 1999; 2007) focuses on the ability of language to activate simulations of actions and perceptions. Robin Dunbar (1996) has argued that language may have originally evolved, not in the service of informational tasks but rather in response to the social pressures of living in large complex social hierarchies. According to this view, language serves social needs, including building and maintaining coalitions (relationships) as well as negotiating the language user's position in social hierarchies. In this model language also serves an informational purpose, but much of the information exchanged in a typical conversation is about social structure, and in particular about other people's relationships. By implication, information about the environment external to the primary group is a secondary function of language. In support of this view, Dunbar cites evidence that, across a wide range of conversations, 65 percent of talk is about other people and their relationships. This view of language suggests that theories about the use and comprehension of metaphors and other figurative language must also account for their social and relational functions (see Chapter 7).

SUMMARY

Defining metaphor is not easy, and definitions vary according to theoretical perspectives. I have proposed a provisional definition of metaphor as "thinking, talking about, or experiencing one kind of thing in terms of another"; this definition and the underlying theoretical assumptions will be discussed again in later chapters. Identifying metaphors is similarly difficult and theory-dependent. At the extremes, most people will probably agree about the identification of indisputably literal words on the one hand, and the identification of original and creative metaphors on the other. Between these extremes, even experts often disagree about whether a word or phrase is metaphorical. This reflects the fact that some people may understand a phrase as metaphorical while others do not. What is crucial when reading essays about metaphor, both for the beginner and for the seasoned expert, is to be clear about what is meant by the term, *metaphor* and how the examples discussed are identified and classified. Failure to understand the definitions used by a researcher is likely to lead to confusion. It is also useful to be aware of the ways in which metaphors can differ from one another. Many types of metaphor will be discussed in this book, ranging from *"sleeping"* or *"dead"* metaphors, which may not be recognized by many researchers as metaphorical at all, to the original and creative phrases recognized as metaphors by almost everyone.

PREVIEW OF CHAPTERS

Gibbs (2006) has observed that metaphor is a very complex phenomenon, and predicted that no one theory is likely to explain all aspects of metaphor use in all situations. Consistent with this claim, in the first few chapters I will discuss several approaches to explaining how metaphors are used and understood, beginning with the least complex and most traditional accounts and proceeding to more complex and more recently proposed accounts. Although I will point out inconsistencies and gaps in these various accounts where these are important for understanding the relationships among the various theories, my primary concern is to show how each theory works and compare their implications by applying them to a common set of examples, including examples from actual discourse. I will also describe some of the research that has been based on each approach.

Chapter 2 begins with comparison and substitution theories, then proceeds with a discussion of some recent elaborations on these theories, structure mapping (Gentner, 1983; Gentner and Bowdle, 2001) and Giora's (1997; 2003) graded salience hypothesis. Chapter 3 discusses two approaches based on the idea that metaphors can best be understood as *category inclusion* statements. Glucksberg and colleagues have proposed that a metaphor creates an ad hoc category to which the topic is assigned, based on salient common attributes. Wilson and Sperber argue that metaphors are "loose language," in which the category identified with the vehicle is *expanded* to include the topic and *contracted* to exclude non-relevant attributes. Chapter 3 also introduces and discusses the "metaphor within metaphor" or "circularity" issue, arising from the claim that metaphor theories often assume a prior act of metaphorical interpretation (Ritchie, 2003a).

Chapter 4 introduces a quite different approach to metaphor theory, which is called conceptual metaphor theory (CMT) (Lakoff and Johnson, 1980; 1999; Lakoff and Turner, 1989). Müller (2008) explains that previous theorists such as Black (1993) took creative, nove metaphors as the prime exemplars of metaphors and dismissed highly conventionalized metaphors as "*dead*," but Lakoff and Johnson turn this argument upside down and take these conventionalized "*dead*" metaphors as their prime exemplars. Lakoff and Johnson start with phrases like '*rising* prices,' 'a *close* relationship,' and 'a *turning point* in the relationship,' and argue that these and other similar phrases express underlying "conceptual metaphors," in which relationships perceived in the physical world (adding more blocks to a stack causes the stack to grow higher) are used to understand less tangible experiences, such as changes in the price of consumer goods.

Lakoff and Johnson use the phrase *conceptual metaphor* as a technical term, in order to emphasize that metaphors connect not just words and phrases, but the ideas underlying words. They argue that virtually all of our intangible concepts, such as *love*, *duty*, and *price inflation*, are formed and understood through association with tangible concepts, such as *physical proximity*, *physical constraint*, and *physical height*. Thus, '*rising* prices' expresses an underlying conceptual metaphor, MORE IS UP, which originates in the experiences such as a child observing a pile of blocks growing higher as more blocks are added. Similarly, 'a *close* relationship' is based on INTIMACY IS PHYSICAL PROXIMITY and 'a *turning point* in the relationship' is based on LOVE IS A JOURNEY.

Chapter 5 discusses a theory of cognition and language processing that can be regarded as an extension of conceptual metaphor theory (Gibbs, 2006; Lakoff and Johnson, 1999), but can also stand on its own. According to perceptual simulation theory, language interpretation involves simulations whereby we imagine actions and perceptions referenced by the language. Thus, Obama's mention of "*incendiary* language" would activate perceptions associated with fire, and Blair's story about throwing crockery would activate perceptions associated with a marital fight, including emotions.

Chapter 6 discusses two other theoretical approaches that combine well with conceptual metaphor theory. One set of theories examines how language, including metaphors, can be used to '*frame*' a topic or interaction and thus influence how people react to the topic and the kinds of solutions that might be appropriate (Price, Tewksbury, and Powers, 1997; Thibodeau and Boroditsky, 2011), and the expectations they form regarding social roles and how they should react in a conversation (Tracy, 1997). Conceptual integration theory (CIT) and Turner, 2002) posits a process of integration or two or more concepts ("*mental spaces*") to explain how and metaphors as well as other figurative language

Closing out the discussion of how metaphors are comprehended, Chapter 7 discusses metaphors, distorted metaphors, and transformed metaphors in language play and humor as well as playful but meaningful forms such as tautologies ('boys will *be boys*'), metaphorical teases and insults ("they never did *let you in*, did they?" from the scientist's "*ivory tower*" conversation), and metaphorical puns (a beauty salon named '*A Cut Above*,' Carter, 2004). Chapter 7 also discusses the interaction of metaphors with storytelling, as in Blair's "*throwing crockery*" story.

The second section of the book addresses the relationship of metaphors to various forms of discourse. Chapter 8 discusses research on metaphor use in conversation, focusing on face-to-face conversation. Chapter 9 discusses research on metaphor use in political communication. Chapter 10 discusses metaphor use in the arts, focusing particular attention on poetry.

DISCUSSION

In high school we were all warned not to use "mixed metaphors." Yet Dylan Thomas mixes several metaphors in his lines, "Do not *go gentle into that good night | rage, rage against the dying of* the light." These include DEATH IS A JOURNEY, DEATH IS SLEEP, and LIFE IS LIGHT. Obama also mixes metaphors in many passages in his speech. How do these mixed metaphors affect the meaning of the passages in which they occur?

Do people need to be aware that a phrase is a metaphor in order to understand it metaphorically?

When do people think about whether a certain word or phrase is metaphorical or not?

Is it necessary to know what metaphors are in order to use them or understand them?

Are interesting metaphors encountered primarily in literary and journalistic texts, or are they also encountered in ordinary conversations?

SUGGESTED READINGS

At the end of most chapters I will recommend additional readings relevant to some of the ideas presented in that chapter. In general, I highly recommend browsing through back issues of the interdisciplinary journals, *Metaphor and Symbol* and *Metaphor in the Social World*. Although a few of the articles in these journals are rather technical, most are clearly written and accessible to the non-specialist. Browsing through back issues will provide a sense of how the field of metaphor studies has changed over the past couple of decades, and will provide a good sense of the range of topics and questions addressed by metaphor researchers. Articles include discussions of theoretical issues (Vervaeke and Kennedy, 1996), application of metaphor analysis to various topics such as emotions (Meier and Robinson, 2005), science (Al-Zahrani, 2008), and immigration (O'Brien, 2003), and research on metaphors using methods ranging from experimental research (Giora *et al.*, 2004) to textual analysis (Semino, 2010).

Following are a few additional readings that will supplement some of the discussions in Chapter 1:

- Cameron, L. J. (principal investigator) (2006). Procedure for metaphor analysis. *The Metaphor Analysis Project*. Milton Keynes, Bucks: Open University Press. This essay lays out a simple definition of metaphor and a clear method for identifying metaphors.
- Pragglejaz Group (2007). MIP: A method for identifying metaphorically used words in discourse. *Metaphor and Symbol, 22*, 1–39. This essay has an excellent and thorough discussion of the problems involved in defining and identifying metaphors.
- Reddy, M. J. (1993). The conduit metaphor: A case of frame conflict in our language about language. In Ortony, A. (ed.), *Metaphor and thought* (2nd edn.), Cambridge University Press, pp. 164–201. In this essay Reddy analyzes words and phrases commonly used to discuss language, such as '*put your thoughts into words*' and '*get your ideas across*' and argues that they reflect an underlying conceptual metaphor, language is a conduit, which constrains the way we think about language and limits the kinds of theories we are able to develop.

2 Understanding metaphors: substitution and property attribution theories

In a conversation among scientists about communicating with the public (Ritchie and Schell, 2009), a participant remarked, "if we were better communicators we'd be *swimming in* money." We all might suppose that if we were better communicators – or better investors or less addicted to the January clearance sales – we would be "*swimming in* money." Fans of Disney Comics may recall an image of "Uncle Scrooge" in his cubic-block-sized money bin, but even for comic book fans, "*swimming in* money" is readily identifiable as a metaphor, and the comic book money bin brings the metaphor humorously to life. But what does it mean to be "*swimming in* money"? How do we make sense of metaphors like this?

SUBSTITUTION, COMPARISON, AND PROPERTY ATTRIBUTION THEORIES

This chapter will begin with theories that focus on the lexical meanings, the "dictionary definitions" of the words used as topic and vehicle of a metaphor. These approaches begin with the assumption that a metaphor compares the topic to the vehicle by some attribute they hold in common, or that a metaphor simply substitutes a fancier word for a more common word and thereby '*dresses up*' a sentence. Most of the examples discussed by advocates of these approaches are nominative metaphors such as 'Achilles is *a lion*,' in which both topic and vehicle are nouns. In order to convert the scientist's metaphor to a nominative metaphor we must first identify the topic, which might be something like 'having great wealth.' Thus we get the nominative metaphor 'having great wealth *is swimming in* money.'

Substitution

Substitution models assert that a metaphor is created when a word or phrase from an apparently different area of experience is substituted for a word that expresses some attribute of the topic. In 'Achilles is *a lion*,' the noun phrase '*a lion*' is substituted for the adjective, *brave*, an attribute associated with both Achilles and lions. According to this view, comprehending a metaphor simply requires the hearer to substitute the associated attributes for the vehicle. "Oh. You mean to say Achilles is brave." Similarly, "we'd be *swimming in* money" is understood by substituting "have an abundance of" for "be *swimming in*." 'White is *the new black*' is understood by substituting a phrase related to the realm of fashion, yielding 'white is *the new fashionable shade*.'

Other examples of nominative metaphors, such as "All the world's *a stage*," are not so easily explained by substitution theory. What attributes could be substituted for *stage* to form a literal sentence that would capture the richness of Shakespeare's version? (In the play, the character Jaques develops and extends the metaphor for several lines, using additional metaphors that would also need to be accounted for by the substitution.) In "A More Perfect Union" Barack Obama spoke of "the idea that this nation is *more than the sum of its parts*," which is "*seared into my genetic makeup*." What attributes could be substituted for *more than the sum of its parts*, *seared*, and *genetic makeup* without changing the meaning of this passage? In each of these examples, a literal equivalent would require several sentences, and would probably still fail to express the same ideas. Even 'white is *the new fashionable shade*' doesn't seem to account fully for the commentary on the whims and contradictions of high fashion implied by 'white is *the new black*.'

Comparison

Comparison models treat metaphors as implicit comparisons or similes, with the word *like* omitted. In this view, 'Achilles is *a lion*' is equivalent to 'Achilles is *like a lion*' and "we'd be *swimming in* money" is equivalent to 'it would be *like* we were swimming in money.' The comparison/attribution view is easiest to apply to metaphors that link two concepts with similar behavioral characteristics, like the fighting prowess of *Achilles* and that of *a lion* or the thin body shape of a *young person* and the thin shape of a *willow* or *bean pole*. An apparent contradiction like 'white is *the new black*' is a little more complicated, in that it requires shifting from the apparent realm of visual hues and shades to the implied realm of fashion to yield 'white is fashionable this year *like* black was last year.'

Applying comparison theory to more complex metaphors, like "All the world's *a stage*" or "*original sin* of slavery," requires a more complex process of sorting out the attributes of the vehicle that are relevant to the topic and deciding which attributes of the vehicle provide a relevant basis for comparison. In the passage from *As You Like It*, in precisely what ways does Jaques mean to imply that all the world is *like* a stage? In the passages from Obama's speech, in exactly what way does Obama mean to imply that being easily remembered is *like* being seared into one's genetic makeup, or that slavery is *like* original sin?

In testing the comparison account, Chiappe and Kennedy (2001) report on experiments, using nominative metaphors, in which they varied the degree of similarity between vehicle and topic. Their research participants preferred the metaphor form ('*rumors are weeds*' and "*fog is a cat*") over the simile form ('rumors are *like* weeds' and "fog is *like* a cat") when the similarity between the topic (*rumors* or *fog*) and the vehicle (*weeds* or *a cat*) is high. When the similarity is lower (e.g. the earth and an apple both have a core and a skin but share little else in common), participants preferred the simile form ('the earth is *like* an apple') over the equivalent metaphor ('the earth *is an apple*').

Chiappe, Kennedy, and Smykowski (2003) tested the relationship between metaphors and similes by reversing topic–vehicle pairs. For example, the metaphor '*crime is a disease*' and the simile version '*crime is like a disease*' were reversed to produce '*disease is a crime*' and '*disease is like a crime*'. They showed one version of each pair (the original or the reversed version) to participants and asked them to rate how easy the phrase was to interpret, then write a paraphrase of what the speaker is attempting to say. Reversing the order in this way increased the difficulty of understanding the metaphor versions much more than it increased the difficulty of understanding the simile versions, and the metaphor versions were much more likely than the simile versions either to be rated as uninterpretable or given an entirely different interpretation. In a second experiment participants were requested to rate how apt and how conventional each phrase is. The rated aptness of the topic-vehicle pairing had a greater effect on preference for the metaphor version versus the simile version than the rated conventionality.

Chiappe and Kennedy (2001) propose that metaphors and similes are used to increase the momentary salience of certain features that are common to vehicle and topic, and thus to ensure that they are relevant for the moment. The property may be something known to be associated with the topic, or it may be something previously unsuspected. Thus Sandberg's description of fog as "*a cat*" increases the salience of certain features common to both phenomena (e.g. their quietness), and Blair's "*steady hard slog*" increases the salience of certain features common to marching through mud and reading a series of position papers in an air-conditioned office (e.g. a sense of tedium).

Attribution

Attribution models go beyond substitution and comparison models, by focusing on the attributes of the vehicle that are transferred to the topic. If an acquaintance remarks, 'Sam is a *pig*,' in a context in which eating is salient, qualities such as consuming more than his share of food or eating in a sloppy manner may be attributed to Sam. In a context in which orderliness or disorder is salient, qualities such as being slovenly may be attributed to Sam (Bortfeld and McGlone, 2001; Searle [1993]). Searle further points out that the properties need not be genuine properties of the vehicle, and in many cases the properties that are transferred are already culturally associated with the vehicle. Given suitable pens, pigs are generally not slovenly, but because they are often confined in small spaces in which it is difficult to clean themselves, the property of slovenliness and dirt have come to be culturally associated with pigs. Similarly, as Searle points out, gorillas are shy, sensitive vegetarians, but they have been culturally represented (e.g. in movies) as ugly, powerful, and uncontrollable. Because of these cultural associations, even if a hearer regularly watches *The Nature Channel*, 'Sam is a *gorilla*' is likely to transfer properties to Sam that are culturally associated with gorillas, such as *ugly*, *ungainly*, and *dangerous*. For an idiomatic metaphor of this sort, what matters is the culturally relevant properties, not the actual properties.

Summary

At least for the simple nominative metaphors most often used as examples, it appears that the substitution, comparison, and attribution approaches are all compatible with a common account of how metaphors are used and understood; they merely draw attention to different aspects of the process. Consistent with the substitution approach, 'Sam is a *pig*' can be said to substitute *pig* for *person who eats too much* or *person with slovenly personal habits*. Consistent with the comparison approach, the metaphor is effectively equivalent to 'Sam is like a pig.' The property attribution approach answers the potential question, 'in what way is Sam a pig' or 'in what way is Sam like a pig' by specifying the culturally salient attributes of *pig* that are transferred or attributed to *Sam*.

Applying the three approaches to an example from actual discourse, Tony Blair's "*steady hard slog* of decision-making" can be modified to a nominative metaphor, 'decision-making is a *steady hard slog*.' In this

Figure 2.1 Aligning the shared relation in structure mapping

form, the metaphor substitutes '*steady hard slog*' for *boring and tedious activity* (the substitution approach). 'Decision-making is a *steady hard slog*' can be further modified to a simile, 'decision-making is like a *steady hard slog*' (the comparison approach). It can also be analyzed as attributing properties of a *steady hard slog,* such as tedium, to *decision-making* (the property attribution approach). Which approach is better for a particular analysis depends on the question the analysis is expected to answer.

ANALOGICAL MODELS

Gentner and Bowdle (2001, p. 226) argue that "metaphor can be seen as a species of analogy" in that metaphors "establish links between conceptual systems in the target [topic] and base [vehicle] domains, in which relational correspondences are emphasized over correspondence between isolated object attributes." The most fully developed analogical model, *structure-mapping theory* (Gentner, 1983; Gentner and Bowdle, 2001), is based on the idea that metaphor interpretation begins by aligning representations of topic and vehicle in a "one-to-one mapping" with "parallel connectivity." Elements of the vehicle and relationships among elements are placed in correspondence with elements and relationships among elements of the topic. Only a limited number of elements from vehicle and topic are mapped, and no element of one domain is mapped onto more than one element of the other. This alignment process is also constrained by *systematicity*: "Alignments that form deeply interconnected structures, in which higher order relations constrain lower order relations, are preferred over less systematic sets of commonalities."

Gentner and Bowdle (2001) illustrate the structure-mapping processes with the metaphor "men are *wolves*." The process begins with alignment of the shared relation *prey on* (see Figure 2.1). Next, the nonidentical arguments of this identical relation are aligned by parallel connectivity: *wolves → men* and *animals → women* (see Figure 2.2).

An important way in which structure-mapping theory goes beyond other property-attribution models is that "once a structurally consistent

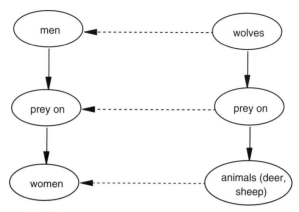

Figure 2.2 Aligning the non-matching elements in structure mapping

match between the target and base domains has been found, further predicates from the base [vehicle] that are connected to the common system can be projected to the target [topic] as *candidate inferences*" (p. 226). In the "men are *wolves*" example, Gentner and Bowdle's argument that the idea that wolves' predatory behavior is caused by instinct can be carried over to the topic (men), leading to an inference like "men instinctively prey on women" (see Figure 2.3). Similarly, effects of the primary relation of wolves to prey (the deer or sheep die) may be mapped onto effects of the primary relation of men to women (the women experience loss of social status and disruption of their life plans).

Following Gentner's approach, Blair's "*domestic spat*" metaphor maps *prime minister* onto *husband*, and *voters* (or *party members*) onto *disgruntled wives*. Additional relevant features of the vehicle include *reconciliation* or *divorce* and *re-marriage*, providing the basis for inferences that Blair spells out: "And now you, the British people, have to *sit down and decide* whether you want the relationship to *continue*. If you decide you want Mr Howard, that is your choice. If you want to *go off with* Mr Kennedy, that's your choice too. It all *ends in the same place*. A Tory Government not a Labour Government."

> *husband* → *Tony Blair*
> *aggrieved wife* → *party members; voters*
> *throwing crockery* → *criticizing harshly*
> *going off with another man* → *voting for another party leader*

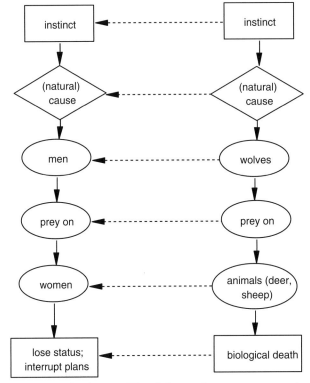

Figure 2.3 Projecting *candidate inferences* in structure mapping

This metaphorical story also invites other mappings (candidate inferences) that Blair does not call attention to and may not have intended:

> *unrepentant husband → unrepentant Prime Minister*
> *relatively helpless wife → relatively helpless voters*
> *future potential marital problems → future potential political problems*

As the "*throwing crockery*" example illustrates, the analogical model provides a useful tool for analyzing complex metaphors. However, it doesn't do as well with other examples, including some of the other examples we have discussed. For example, in '*Sally is a block of ice*' it is not apparent what relationship is transferred from '*a block of ice*' to *Sally*. There is no apparent "shared relation" between *Sally*, a living, breathing mammal, and *a block of ice*, a cube-shaped mass of frozen,

inert water. Something more is required to find the shared relation
that supports interpretation of this metaphor.

Even in Gentner and Bowdle's (2001) example, the hypothesized
shared relation is not explicitly present in the metaphorical phrase,
but must be inferred before the mapping can begin. It is apparent
how *preys on* pertains to *wolves and deer*: Deer are a staple of the wolf
diet, and, without wolves (or other predators such as human hunters)
to control their population, herds of deer will soon breed beyond the
carrying capacity of their forage and die of starvation in great num-
bers. On the other hand, aside from homicidal maniacs like the storied Hannibal Lecter, men do not actually *prey on* women. As with '*block
of ice*,' something else, some additional interpretive step, is needed
before *preys on*, or the *predator–prey* relationship, can provide a "shared
relation" between *men* and *wolves*. Useful as it is for metaphor analysis,
structure-mapping theory does not provide much help in identifying
this badly needed "something else," an additional interpretive step.

Moreover, an entirely different shared relation between wolves
and men might reasonably be identified, for example, *eats rapidly*
('*wolfs down* his food') or *enforces social hierarchy* ('he thinks he's the
alpha male'), leading to quite different (but equally plausible) structure
mappings. Along the same lines, Tourangeau and Rips (1991, p. 453)
interpret "men are *wolves*" as suggesting that "men are competitive
in their dealing with other men, a feature that does *not* characterize
wolves." Structure-mapping theory provides little guidance for determining when and why one shared relation rather than another is
deployed in the interpretation process. I will return to these issues in
Chapter 3 and later chapters.

Attribution versus analogy?

Bortfeld and McGlone (2001) observe that there appears to be a continuum between attributional metaphors and relational or analogical
metaphors. "Attributional metaphors such as 'Matt is a pig' highlight
the common attributes (e.g. gluttonous, slovenly, untidy, and so on)
of topic and vehicle concepts that do not have obvious analogical
similarities. In contrast, relational metaphors such as 'Memory is a
sponge' convey common analogical structures (e.g. information is to
memory as water is to a sponge) in topic and vehicle concepts that
do not have obvious attributional similarities" (p. 77). Intermediate
between these extremes are metaphors such as 'a lifetime is a day'
that can be interpreted either by seeking common attributes (e.g.
short) or by seeking "analogical conceptual structures (e.g. birth =
dawn, childhood = morning, etc.)."

Bortfeld and McGlone (2001) argue that the apparent contradiction between attribution and analogical or relational models can be explained by researchers' assumptions about metaphor processing and by the research strategies used to test these models. According to Bortfeld and McGlone, advocates of both attribution models and analogical or relational models assume that a single cognitive process must be able to explain the processing of all metaphors by all persons under every possible context. This common assumption has remained unchallenged because of the research strategies used to test these models. Previous researchers in both camps have tended to focus on examples from only one type of metaphor, from one or the other of a continuum of metaphor types. Previous researchers have also relied on indirect measures such as the time it takes readers to understand and respond to a metaphor, rather than direct measures such as the actual interpretations people provide, whether in writing, oral reports, or other forms.

Bortfeld and McGlone (2001) claim that Glucksberg and his collaborators have tended to focus on metaphors that might be used in conversations, in which time limitations preclude extensive processing and metaphors are likely to highlight a few characteristics relevant to a particular point, such as 'Sam is *a pig*' or 'Sally is *an icebox.*' In contrast, Bortfeld and McGlone claim, Gentner and her colleagues (e.g. Gentner and Bowdle, 2001; Gentner and Clement, 1988) often begin with a framework suited to scientific analogies such as 'an atom is *like the solar system*,' for which extensive cognitive processing is much more likely. Thus, according to Bortfeld and McGlone, researchers in one group draw metaphors almost entirely from attributional metaphors, researchers in another group draw metaphors almost entirely from analogical metaphors, and the results of response-time experiments by both sets of researchers support their respective theories.

Bortfeld and McGlone (2001) identify an intermediate point between the two extremes, giving the example 'A lifetime is *a day.*' In cases of this sort, they point out that differences in context may lead people to draw on quite different aspects of the vehicle as the grounds for their interpretation. Characteristics of '*a day*' that might be relevant under different circumstances include its relatively short duration on the one hand, and its predictable sequence of phases (dawn, morning, afternoon, evening) on the other. In a context in which the brevity of human life is most salient, the short duration might be attached to the topic, consistent with attribution, but in a context in which the stages of life are salient, the structure of a day might be mapped onto the structure of life, leading to thoughts about the '*morning,*' '*noontime*,' and '*twilight*' of life, and perhaps thoughts about the '*dawn of a new day*' that might be expected to follow the end of the present day. Which interpretation is most plausible can be determined only by considering the context. This insight might be tested by varying the context and asking for the thoughts that come to mind when research participants read the metaphor.

Processing set

In order to test further their claims that attributional and relational metaphors lie at opposite ends of a single continuum, Bortfeld and McGlone (2001) adapted the concept of a *processing set* from Bobrow and Bell's (1973) research on idioms. Bobrow and Bell demonstrated that ambiguous phrases like 'John *gave Mary the slip*' would be interpreted literally (John gave Mary an undergarment) if preceded by several unequivocally literal sentences, but would be interpreted metaphorically (John evaded Mary) if preceded by a series of unequivocally metaphorical idioms. A series of literal sentences instigates a tendency to think first of literal interpretations (a literal processing set); conversely, a series of metaphorical idioms instigates a tendency to think first of idiomatic metaphorical interpretations (a metaphorical processing set).

Following similar reasoning, Bortfeld and McGlone (2001) argue that exposing a person to a series of metaphors that are clearly attributional, such as 'Matt is *a pig*' or 'clouds are *marshmallows*' will prime a tendency to look for attributes common to both topic and vehicle (an attributional-processing set). Conversely, exposing a person to a series of metaphors that are clearly analogical, such as 'an atom is *a tiny solar system*' or 'sarcasm is *a veil*,' will prime a tendency to look for common analogical relationships (an analogical-processing set). When participants are subsequently exposed to ambiguous metaphors such as 'a lifetime is *a day*' that can be interpreted through either attribution or analogy, they will tend to interpret the ambiguous metaphor according to the processing set primed by the previously presented metaphors.

In order to test this idea, Bortfeld and McGlone (2001) selected one set of metaphors they believed to be unambiguously attributional (they describe physical properties shared by topic and vehicle) and another set of metaphors they believed to be unambiguously analogical (they describe a set of attribute correspondences common to the topic and vehicle but independent of the physical attributes). They pretested these with one group of students to confirm that they were perceived by the students as unambiguously either attributional or analogical. Then they asked a different group of students to read several series of metaphors. Each series began with several unambiguous metaphors that were either analogical or attributional, but not both, after which the participants were presented with hybrid metaphors such as 'life is *a day*' and asked to generate written interpretations of them. Other students were trained to code the responses as either attributional (descriptions of physical properties shared by topic and vehicle) or analogical (description of a set of attributes common to the topic and vehicle but independent of the physical attributes).

In the condition in which a series of attributional metaphors was followed by a hybrid target, common attributes were mentioned first in 67 percent of the interpretations of the hybrid target. In the condition in which a series of analogical metaphors was followed by a hybrid target, analogical commonalities were mentioned first in 83 percent. However, in the attributional condition, analogical interpretations were also mentioned after the attributional interpretations, and in the analogical condition, attributional interpretations were also mentioned after the analogical interpretations. Thus, inducing one interpretation set did not block interpretations consistent with the alternative approach, but the induced interpretation set did influence which sort of interpretations came to mind first.

Interaction of topic and vehicle

Tourangeau and Rips (1991) compare models of metaphor according to "which features, or predicates, of the vehicle determine the meaning of the metaphor." For property attribution theories, "the critical features are salient features of the vehicle that are less salient for the tenor [topic]." For Gentner's structure-mapping approach, the critical features "are shared predicates that convey 'the system of relations' in which the vehicle is embedded" (Tourangeau and Rips, 1991, p. 453). Tourangeau and Rips propose an alternative explanation, that "some features relevant to the interpretation characterize neither the tenor nor the vehicle, but 'emerge' from the metaphor" (p. 454).

One of the examples used by Tourangeau and Rips is "the eagle is *a lion among birds*." Asked to list features of lions, participants mentioned features like their color, size, identification with Africa, that they have manes, are the king of beasts, and are predators. Asked to list features of eagles, participants mentioned that they are an endangered species, that they fly, that they have feathers, that they are large, and that they are predators. When participants were asked to list features that characterize the meaning of the metaphor, "the eagle is *a lion among birds*," eight features that *were* listed as characterizing the meaning of the metaphor were *not* listed for either lions or birds; the most popular of these was "is respected." It is likely that most participants, if asked whether lions or eagles are respected, would answer *yes*, but this attribute was not sufficiently salient for either topic or vehicle to be mentioned until the juxtaposition of the two in the metaphor raised its salience: this is the basis for the claim that this interpretation '*emerged*' from the metaphor.

In order to test this proposition, Tourangeau and Rips (1991) invented twelve metaphors that take the form, 'the *topic* is a *vehicle* among *domain*,' by pairing birds, animals, objects, and people, for example 'the *eagle* is a *lion* among *birds*.' In a separate condition they left the topic blank: 'the *X* is a *lion* among *birds*.' Participants were asked to rate each metaphor for aptness, goodness, and comprehensibility, and then to list phrases describing what the metaphor attributed to its topic. Participants were separately asked to describe each of the topics, vehicles, and domains.

Only a few of the features included in the interpretation were shared by topic and vehicle, and fewer than half of these were included in the interpretation. For the *lion/eagle* example, as noted before, shared features not included in the interpretation included *large* and *predator*; *respected* was mentioned for neither *lion* nor *eagle* when presented alone but was the most popular feature associated with the metaphor. Across all twelve metaphors, over half of the features mentioned at least once as part of the interpretation were unique to the interpretation (not listed as an attribute of either topic or vehicle), and thus were classified as *emergent*. On the other hand, features shared by topic and vehicle were mentioned in a minority of the interpretations. *Has eyes* was frequently mentioned as a feature of both *lion* and *eagle* but was rarely mentioned as part of the interpretation. Participants readily interpreted the generic metaphors with the topic unspecified, and thus unavailable to furnish attributes for interpretation, such as 'the *X* is a *lion* among *birds*.'

An important implication of their findings about generic metaphor that is not discussed by Tourangeau and Rips (1991) is that people seem to be capable of holding generic metaphors and applying them to a variety of different topics. For example, it appears that people use '*journey*' and related words such as '*dead-end*' and '*cross-roads*' as vehicles for many topics, including *love* (Lakoff and Johnson, 1980) and *grief* (Obst, 2003). '*War*' and related words are used as a vehicle for topics including *argument* (Lakoff and Johnson, 1980) as well as *business*, *sports*, and even *love* (Ritchie, 2003b). These generally applicable metaphor vehicles might reasonably be grouped together as x is a journey and x is war. I will pick up this idea again in Chapter 4.

Tourangeau and Rips (1991) acknowledge that features common to vehicle and topic may play an important role in interpreting metaphors. However, based on the results of their experiments they conclude that emergent features, features that are not immediately associated with either topic or vehicle but that emerge from the metaphorical comparison itself, are also important in metaphor interpretation. Although Tourangeau and Rips differentiate their approach from Gentner's approach, it appears from Gentner and Bowdle's (2001) discussion of "men are *wolves*" that structure-mapping theory also supports the identification of entailments that might not be attributed to either topic or vehicle on its own, for example that men's '*predatory*' behavior toward women is instinctual. These added entailments might be considered '*emergent*' in much the same sense as the attributes identified in Tourangeau and Rips' research. Whether these features may reasonably be considered to be truly '*emergent*,' in the sense of stemming exclusively from the juxtaposition of topic and vehicle, and having no prior relationship to either topic or vehicle, is another and more tricky question.

Summary

The approaches discussed in this section all start with the metaphor vehicle and relevant qualities associated with the metaphor vehicle, and explain the metaphor in terms of how these are related to the topic. In the *substitution* approach, the vehicle term (*a lion*) is simply substituted for another term that denotes a quality associated with both vehicle and topic (*bravery* or *ferocity*). In the *comparison* approach, the topic (*Achilles*) is compared to the vehicle (*a lion*) with respect to some quality that they have in common (*bravery* or *ferocity*). In the *attribution* approach, one or more qualities associated with the vehicle (*bravery* or *ferocity*) are attributed to (or transferred to) the topic (*Achilles*). Each of these approaches focuses on a different aspect of what appears to be a single underlying account.

Analogical models emphasize relationships among attributes or elements of vehicle and topic; analogical models project or map relationships among elements of the vehicle onto relationships among elements of the topic. According to an attribution model, "men are *wolves*" would simply map some attribute of *wolves*, such as *fierceness*, onto *men*. According to analogical models, "men are *wolves*" maps *predators* onto *men*, *prey* onto *women*, and *predatory behavior* (the relationship between *predators* and *prey*) onto *stereotypical sexual behavior of men* (the relationship between *men* and *women*). For a simple metaphor like 'Achilles *is a lion*," for which these accounts are difficult to distinguish from one another, the attribution model might reasonably be preferred on the basis of simplicity. For more complex metaphors like "men are *wolves*" or '*love is war*,' structure-mapping theory provides the basis for a more comprehensive analysis, and for explaining the derivation of *candidate inferences* that go beyond the stated metaphor.

THE GRADED SALIENCE HYPOTHESIS

The theories discussed thus far treat the cognitive aspects of metaphor comprehension, what happens in the brain when a metaphor is encountered, as a '*black box*' that has no part in explaining how metaphors are understood. In 'Achilles is *a lion*,' *Achilles* activates knowledge about the person, *lion* activates relevant attributes of the animal, and they are combined to attribute the relevant attributes to Achilles. Exactly how the knowledge about Achilles and lions might be activated, how the relevant attributes are selected, and how the two sets of knowledge are combined plays little or no part in these theories. However, in recent years, aided by new research tools, language researchers have begun to develop and test theories of language comprehension based on processes in the brain itself. In this section I will discuss one of these cognitive theories; I will take up other cognitive theories in later chapters.

Giora (1997; 2003) argues that comprehension begins with initial activation of lexical information (word meanings), and that contextual information, including relevant background information (knowledge about relevant aspects of the world) is activated in a separate but parallel process. *Achilles* activates what the reader knows about Achilles, *lion* activates what the reader knows about lions, and the entire phrase activates background knowledge about the nature of mythical heroes, the discourse context in which the phrase appears, and so on. This initial activation is followed by integration processes that include selecting context-relevant word meanings and background information (lions are fierce, proud, and aggressive) and reducing the activation of less relevant meanings and information (lions have large manes, chase antelopes, and spend much of the day sleeping). Then the relevant meanings and information are combined, producing changes in the person's cognitive representations of the current context, facts about the world, and so on.

Giora (2003) argues that access to information, including lexical meanings, is dominated by salience. "The graded salience hypothesis assumes that the modular, lexical access mechanism is ordered: more salient meanings – coded meanings foremost on our mind owing to conventionality, frequency, familiarity, or prototypicality – are accessed faster than and reach sufficient levels of activation before less salient ones" (2003, p. 10). Because lexical and context processing are independent of one another, the most salient information is accessed first regardless of contextual relevance. Moreover, much of the lexical and background information activated at any one time is likely to be of limited or no relevance to the current context. If the facts that lions are carnivores and that male lions often kill the cubs of other male lions are most salient, they will be accessed first. If these facts are not relevant to the context, "suppression of the inappropriate meaning may occur via the enhancement of the selected appropriate meaning" (Giora, 2003, p. 43). If the non-relevant meaning interferes with meaning construction (e.g. *strict* with respect to *a firm bed*) it may be totally suppressed, but if it does not interfere with meaning construction (*solid* with respect to *a firm teacher*), the non-relevant or less relevant meanings may remain partially activated, and accessible for further processing if subsequently introduced information increases their relevance (p. 27).

Salience is itself influenced by several factors. More conventional and familiar meanings tend to be more salient, hence more readily accessed. More prototypical meanings tend to be more salient, hence more readily accessed: *lions are carnivores* is likely to be more salient than *lions spend most of the day sleeping*. More recently accessed information is usually more salient than less recently accessed information. For a person who has recently visited a zoo or wild animal park on a hot afternoon, *sleeping in the sun* may be a more salient attribute of *lion* than *carnivorous*. Since neither *carnivorous* nor *sleeping in the sun* is relevant in the immediate context of the metaphor, 'Achilles is *a lion*,' both will become less strongly activated compared to other, more contextually relevant, attributes such as *brave* and *fierce*. Because *carnivorous* does not interfere with constructing the *brave and fierce* meaning, it may remain weakly activated, but *sleeping in the sun* is more likely to interfere with meaning construction, so is likely to be more completely suppressed.

Based on a review of previous research, Giora (1999) argues in favor of modifying many of the assumptions of traditional metaphor theory. In particular, she argues that more salient interpretations are always more likely to be activated than less salient meanings, novel interpretations require more contextual support and involve a sequential process in which the initially salient meaning is rejected because it is irrelevant, and novel interpretations require more effort. On the other hand, non-relevant meanings are not fully suppressed unless they actually interfere with processing, and may remain activated to facilitate subsequent processing. This is especially important to Giora's account of humor, in which initially non-relevant meanings remain activated at a low level until information introduced in the punchline renders them suddenly relevant.

Consistent with Cameron's (2007) research on patterns of metaphor use in conversations (see Chapter 8), Giora observes that previous speech, by self or other participants, may increase the salience of certain information, including metaphor vehicles. "Time constraints make resonating with already retrieved salient meanings a more economical and plausible strategy than innovating … and should facilitate the discourse flow" (2003, p. 128). The same observation should also apply to speeches and other texts (see Chapters 6, 9, and 10). Thus, both lexical and contextual information may be continually (but separately) updated as a conversation or other discourse progresses.

SUMMARY

This chapter began by examining several closely inter-related models of metaphor processing, all based on attributes of the vehicle that are either common to vehicle and topic or attributed to the topic as a result of processing the metaphor. Then I examined an extension of these models in which various attributes associated with the vehicle may be "*mapped onto*" the topic. For the simple, invented metaphors often used in traditional discussions of metaphor, such as 'Achilles is *a lion*,' the more complex accounts such as structure-mapping theory add little if anything to substitution and attribute-transfer models. However, for examples like "men are *wolves*" and the "*crockery-throwing*" story from Tony Blair's Gateshead speech, relations among elements of the vehicle are also transferred to the topic, which requires a theory like structure mapping for a complete explanation. In Chapter 3 I will focus on a contrasting approach, in which attention is focused not on the attributes common to topic and vehicle, but rather on categories that are specified by these common attributes.

DISCUSSION

Much of the research on the theories covered in this chapter has involved designs using nominal metaphors that were invented to maximize consistency between conditions at the expense of failing to reflect the way people actually talk. How well do these theories apply to metaphors that people use in actual discourse?

If metaphor vehicles like '*gorilla*,' '*shark*,' '*pig*,' and '*wolf*' depend on attributes that are not actually typical of the animals in question, does this pose difficulties for attribute transfer and categorization theories?

Bortfeld and McGlone (2001) attribute some of the theoretical disagreements about metaphor to many theorists' habit of focusing on just one type of metaphor. How do some of the theories discussed in this chapter work if they are applied to very different sorts of metaphor?

SUGGESTED READINGS

- Bortfeld, H., and McGlone, M. S. (2001). The continuum of metaphor processing. *Metaphor and Symbol, 16* (1 and 2), 75–86. This essay provides a clear and very thorough discussion of attribution and relational theories of metaphor.
- Gentner, D., and Bowdle, B. F. (2001). Convention, form, and figurative language processing. *Metaphor and Symbol, 16*, 223–247. This article introduces and explains in detail two important theories, the structure-mapping theory discussed in this chapter and the career of metaphor theory that will be discussed in Chapter 4.
- Giora, R. (2003). *On our mind: Salience, context, and figurative language*. Oxford University Press. I have summarized only a few of the topics covered in this book, and I have not nearly done justice to the richness of Giora's exposition. The book is also worth reading for its discussion of humor, irony, and other forms of figurative language.

• Searle, J. R. (1993). Metaphor. In Ortony, A. (ed.), *Metaphor and thought* (2nd edn. [1st edn. 1979]). Cambridge University Press, pp. 83–111. In this essay, Searle lays out the conventional pragmatics view of metaphor in very clear and comprehensive form.

3 Categorization and relevance

'An apple is a fruit' tells us that *apple* belongs to the category, FRUIT. 'Sally is a sophomore' tells us that *Sally* belongs to the category, SOPHO- MORES. Both sentences are examples of what may be called *category inclusion statements*. Glucksberg and his colleagues (Glucksberg, Keysar, and McGlone, 1992) and Wilson and Sperber (2004; Sperber and Wilson, 2008) have proposed that a metaphor is another kind of category inclusion statement, which assigns the topic to a category specified by the vehicle. Thus, 'Achilles is *a lion*' tells us that *Achilles* belongs to a category specified by *lions*, something like ENTITIES THAT ARE BRAVE. Since Glucksberg's version of category-assignment theory is the most closely related to theories discussed in Chapter 2, I will begin with it.

The theories discussed in Chapter 2 emphasize the transfer of attributes, such as *brave* and *fierce* from the vehicle, *lion*, to the topic, *Achilles*. In contrast to these theories, Glucksberg and his colleagues argue that the vehicle, *lion*, refers to a more abstract category (ENTITIES THAT ARE BRAVE AND FIERCE) rather than to the more basic level category (LARGE PREDATORY FELINES), and the metaphor assigns *Achilles* to the more abstract category. With respect to a metaphor such as 'my lawyer is *a shark*,' for which a suitable pre-existing category is not readily identifiable, Glucksberg and Keysar (1990) claim that the metaphor creates what they call an ad hoc category, in this case something like PREDA- TORY ENTITIES*, with *sharks* as a prime example. In nominal meta- phors like 'my lawyer is *a shark*,' they argue that the vehicle ('*shark*') refers to this more abstract ad hoc category, PREDATORY CREATURES*, rather than to the more basic level category, A CARTILAGINOUS FISH.

> **Terminology:** Consistent with the practice of Glucksberg, Wilson, and Sperber and others, I will designate categories in small caps, for example FRUIT, and ad hoc categories in small caps followed by an asterisk (PREDATORY ENTITIES*). Similar notation is used for conceptual metaphors, but it is almost always evident from the context whether a category or a conceptual metaphor is intended.

In another example from Glucksberg and Keysar (1990), 'cigarettes are *time bombs*' creates an ad hoc category of OBJECTS THAT SEEM HARMLESS AT FIRST BUT ARE EVENTUALLY DEADLY*, with *time bomb* as a salient example, and places *cigarettes* into this category. In a third example, 'jobs are *jails*' places 'jobs' into "the category of things that the metaphor vehicle *jail* typifies – situations that are unpleasant, confining, difficult to escape from, unrewarding, and so on" (Glucksberg, Keysar, and McGlone, 1992, p. 578).

A superordinate category may be established on the basis of qualities ordinarily associated with the vehicle in a straightforward and unproblematic way. '*Willow-waisted*' establishes a category of THINGS THAT ARE THIN AND SUPPLE*. 'Cigarettes are *time bombs*' establishes a category of THINGS THAT CAUSE DEATH AT AN UNPREDICTABLE TIME*. Often, however, a superordinate category can only be established on the basis of highly abstract qualities.

In Tony Blair's phrase, "*steady hard slog* of decision-making," the topic entails sitting at a desk in a clean, air-conditioned room, wearing a shirt and tie, reading and making decisions on the basis of briefing papers. The vehicle entails marching a long distance down a muddy road or through deep snow, physical weariness, and misery with little or no conscious mental activity. There is no immediately apparent basis on which the vehicle might define a superordinate category that would include the topic.

In 'Sally is *a block of ice*,' there is no apparent attribute that could be transferred from *a block of ice* to *Sally* (Chapter 2); there is no apparent basis on which a meaningful category could be established by *a block of ice* that would include a living, breathing mammal with soft flesh and a body temperature of 98 degrees Fahrenheit. Even *sharks* and *lawyers* (Keysar and Glucksberg, 1992) pose difficulties. Both are vertebrates, which is not very interesting. As with "men are *wolves*" (Chapter 2), it is not apparent that lawyers are necessarily *predators* (some lawyers hunt and eat birds and game animals, but some lawyers are vegetarians).

Glucksberg (2008) proposes a "dual reference" model to address these problems and explain how superordinate categories can be identified. In this model, '*shark*' refers both to a basic category (a certain species of fish) and to the more abstract category of PREDATORS*. *Predators* itself must be reinterpreted as referring both to CREATURES THAT SURVIVE BY KILLING AND EATING OTHER CREATURES, and to a more abstract category of CREATURES COMMONLY BELIEVED TO EXHIBIT VICIOUSNESS AND LACK OF MERCY. According to this argument, the metaphor, 'my lawyer is *a shark*' establishes a superordinate category, based on the associated qualities (viciousness, lack of mercy, etc.), rather than the primary quality. How the same words (i.e. *vicious* and *merciless*) came to be associated with both *sharks* and *lawyers* is not addressed by the theory.

In order to test the dual reference model, Glucksberg, McGlone, and Manfredi (1997) asked people to read a sentence that primed an irrelevant property of the topic (*some lawyers are married*), a sentence that primed an irrelevant property of the vehicle (*sharks swim in the ocean*), or a neutral control sentence (*some tables are made out of wood*). Then participants were asked to read metaphors such as 'my lawyer is *a shark.*' Participants took significantly longer to process the metaphor when it was preceded by the irrelevant property of the vehicle (*sharks swim*) than when it was preceded by either a neutral sentence or a sentence mentioning an irrelevant attribute of the topic. Apparently priming an attribute of the FISH category interferes with access to the superordinate PREDATOR* category.

In related research, Glucksberg, Newsome, and Goldvarg (2001) asked people first to read a metaphor ('my lawyer is *a shark*') and then to verify literal statements about the vehicle. They found that the metaphor priming actively inhibits access to information associated with the literal meaning of the vehicle (*sharks are good swimmers*). This leads to a significantly longer response time than when they are primed with a literal statement ('hammerhead is a species of shark').

In order to test whether a similar process can be applied to verb metaphors, Torreano, Cacciari, and Glucksberg (2005) selected a set of verb pairs such that each verb came from the same semantic domain (*fly* and *travel*), but one was more abstract than the other. They then combined each verb with three nouns, selected so that one noun would allow the verb to be interpreted at the basic level of abstraction ('the bird *flew*'), but the other two would require that the verb be interpreted at a higher level of abstraction ('the boy *flew* home on his bicycle'). Participants were asked to evaluate the resulting phrases for comprehensibility, degree to which it is metaphorical, and aptness. The results support the conclusions that verb metaphors are comprehended in much the same way as nominal metaphors, and that the degree of abstraction provides a cue for recognizing verb metaphors as well as nominal metaphors.

It should also be possible to extend category-assignment theory to adjectives and stories. In Blair's speech, the metaphorical phrase "*hard slog*" might place *performing the duties of Prime Minister* into a category that consists of ACTIVITIES THAT ARE BORING AND TAKE A LONG TIME*. Similarly, the phrase "Some of you *throw a bit of crockery*" might place *political disagreement* into a category of DISPUTES THAT INVOLVE COMIC ELEMENTS OF LOW-LEVEL VIOLENCE*, which would help to account for the ironic understatement (see Chapter 9).

As mentioned previously, applying the categorization approach to novel metaphors requires a concept of *ad hoc categories*, which are formed on the spot for a particular situation. Unlike conventional categories these metaphor-generated categories are situation-bound and do not possess a conventional label. In Gary Snyder's lines from "Rain in Alleghany" (1969, p. 60), "it's a skinny awkward land / like a workt-out miner's hand," "*workt-out miner's hand*" might establish a category of something like THINGS THAT ONCE HAD SUBSTANCE AND STRENGTH BUT NO LONGER DO, with *miner's hand* as a prototypical member, but it seems unlikely that the category thus established would ever be used again. It is also unlikely that such a category could capture the full meaning of the metaphor in the context of the poem (for further discussion see Chapter 10).

In another example, discussed by Chiappe and Kennedy (2001, p. 266), the metaphor, 'rumors are *weeds*,' based on a conventional category of UNDESIRABLE PLANTS, creates a new ad hoc category of THINGS THAT ARE UNDESIRABLE, SPREAD FAST, AND ARE DIFFICULT TO ELIMIN-ATE*, a category that includes plants as one subcategory and rumors as another. Because members of the familiar category WEEDS are good examples of such things, *weeds* can stimulate us to think of the category, hence provide a naming example of the new ad hoc category.

The ad hoc category created by a metaphor refers to some but not all of the properties associated with the conventional category. "For instance, we can use the expression 'rumors are *weeds*' to convey that rumors spread very quickly and uncontrollably and are hard to get rid of, without committing ourselves to the claim that rumors are plants (Chiappe and Kennedy, 2001, p. 251). Similarly, the category created by Sandburg's poem "Fog," that includes both *fog* and *cats* does not include attributes of cats such as *warm-blooded* and *kills and eats small animals and birds*. The opening line, "fog comes in on little cat feet," creates a superordinate category defined by a subset of properties such as *quiet* and *soft*, and allows the restrictions on the use of the category name (e.g. *cats*) to be relaxed, so that the category name can be extended to a new superordinate category that includes *fog*. According to Glucksberg and McGlone (1999, p. 1546), for a metaphor to be accepted, the vehicle must "epitomize or symbolize" the category to the hearers or readers. In Chiappe and Kennedy's example, *weeds* epitomize the idea of *spreading fast*; in "Fog," *cat feet* epitomize the qualities of *soft* and *quiet*.

However, even this qualification is challenged by the original metaphorical expressions that appear in poetry and, occasionally, in everyday speech. For example, consider again the opening lines of Stephen Spender's (1955) poem, "Seascape": "There are some days the happy ocean lies / Like an unfingered harp, below the land." Both "*happy ocean*" and "*unfingered harp*" establish metaphorical relationships that are not immediately obvious to the reader. "*Happy ocean*" may in some sense epitomize a certain quality of calmness that contrasts with the sense of somber reflection that the poem develops, but "*unfingered harp*" does not epitomize any obvious qualities until the poem itself develops those qualities (see Chapter 10).

"*Swimming in* money," discussed in Chapter 2, seems less problematic at first – if one has a great abundance of some liquid, as in the case of a high tide or a filled reservoir, one might be *swimming* in it. But money, even '*liquid funds*,' is either solid metal, solid paper, or wholly immaterial *information* – a pattern of magnetized molecules in a computer data bank. None of these qualities suggests an obvious basis for establishing a superordinate category. In Obama's speech, "*blood*" cannot be connected directly with *ancestors* but must first be connected with *biological descent* in a superordinate category, which can then be connected with *ancestors* in yet another superordinate category. The crucial basis for the metaphor is not the biological connections or similarities but rather the erroneous belief that offspring are infused with their parents' (especially their father's) blood. This same belief also provides the basis for other familiar metaphors such as '*bloodlines*' and '*blue blood.*'

Glucksberg and McGlone argue that "in each context, the properties of an attributive category are realized in a different way" (1999, p. 1556). On the surface, this would seem to provide a potential way to account for "*blood*," but it raises other problems. The implication is that a reader or hearer must form a new superordinate category for each context in which a metaphor is used and for each possible interpretation of an evocative metaphor, and that this is accomplished by considering certain properties of the vehicle. Chiappe and Kennedy (2001) argue that it is to a large extent irrelevant whether we classify the metaphor as part of a superordinate category, or merely transfer some property from vehicle to topic. Referring to Keysar and Gluckberg's example, '*Jobs are jails*,' Chiappe and Kennedy claim that the interpretative realization "is not what the ad hoc category is ... Rather, the work of comprehension is done by determining properties that make up the ad hoc category ... people would likely infer that the relevant properties include the predicates, 'constraining,' 'confining,' and 'where people are held against their will.'" In brief, if the reader or hearer must form a new category in a unique way for each metaphor, based on properties of the vehicle, it is difficult to see what categorization theory adds to simple property attribution models. However, the comparison approach to property attribution is challenged by research on the comprehension process itself, as reviewed in the next section.

COMPARISON ASSIGNMENT VERSUS CATEGORY ASSIGNMENT

According to the standard model of language comprehension underlying the comparison models, nominal metaphors, such as 'my lawyer is *a shark*,' are literally false. Because they are false, they are defective. According to Glucksberg (2008) the comparison model implies three stages in metaphor comprehension. First, the literal meaning of a metaphor must be derived (my lawyer is a predatory fish with a cartilaginous skeleton). Then the literal meaning is evaluated to see if it makes sense. If the literal meaning does not make sense (my lawyer is clearly a mammal, not a fish), the interpreter must search for a non-literal meaning that does make sense. This requirement for sequential cognitive activity implies three assumptions that can be tested: literal meanings are always processed first, comparisons are always easy to understand, and metaphors are readily exchanged with similes, so that 'my lawyer is *a shark*' is equivalent to 'my lawyer is like a shark.'

The first implication is contradicted by evidence showing that novel metaphors are processed as rapidly as literal equivalents whenever the metaphors are apt (Blasko and Connine, 1993). Further evidence comes from brain-imaging studies of metaphor comprehension using functional Magnetic Resonance Imaging (fMRI), a technique for discerning which areas in the brain are most actively engaged at a given time. These experiments have found little difference in the brain areas activated while processing metaphorical and literal language.

The second implication has also been contradicted, by evidence that people are not able to ignore metaphorical meanings of language. Glucksberg, Gildea, and Bookin (1982) asked participants to read sentences of three types: obviously true ('some birds are robins'); obviously false ('some birds are tables'); and metaphorically true but literally false ('some birds are *flutes*'). Asked to indicate whether each sentence was literally true or false, participants took significantly longer to respond correctly ("false") to the metaphorically true sentences than to respond correctly to either of the other types of sentence. Contrary to the assumption that people are able to ignore metaphorical meanings of language, participants required extra processing time to consider and reject the metaphorical meaning.

Career of metaphor theory

The third assumption, that metaphors and similes are interchangeable, has been tested by Gentner and Bowdle (2001). Gentner and Bowdle combine comparison- and category-assignment approaches in the '*career of metaphor*' theory, an extension of the structure-mapping theory discussed in Chapter 2. They argue that familiar metaphors like 'my lawyer is *a shark*' began as novel metaphors that compared topics to vehicles according to certain attributes, in this example something like *ruthless* and *lacking scruples*. As the metaphor was re-used and applied to other topics (such as professional card players and pawnbrokers), the metaphor became lexicalized. In this example, *unscrupulous and ruthless person* eventually became a lexicalized subordinate meaning of *shark*. Thus, metaphoric categories begin as a by-product of the comparison process. As a metaphor vehicle is repeatedly encountered in ways that create similar interpretations, the metaphor category becomes more stable and the vehicle term becomes polysemous – the word *shark* ends up with a primary meaning of *a predatory fish* and a secondary meaning of *any unscrupulous and ruthless person*.

In order to test the implications of this theory, Bowdle and Gentner (2005) produced a list of conventional and novel metaphors and converted them to similes by adding *like*. 'My lawyer is *a shark*' would be converted to 'my lawyer is like *a shark*.' They measured how long it took research participants to comprehend each statement, and asked research participants to assess the quality of the statements. Participants preferred the novel metaphors when presented in simile form and understood them more quickly when presented in simile form, but with conventional metaphors, participants preferred them and understood them more quickly when they were presented in metaphor form (without *like*).

However, Glucksberg (2008) argues that many of Bowdle and Gentner's examples, such as 'a fisherman is (like) *a spider*,' were not good metaphors in the first place. In order to test this, Haught and Glucksberg (2004, described in Glucksberg, 2008) developed a set of metaphors by modifying conventional metaphors in a way that they would still be comprehensible, and would seem apt. For example, 'my lawyer was *a shark*' was transformed into 'my lawyer was *a well-paid shark*,' and the simile form, 'my lawyer was *like a well-paid shark*.' They then had one group of research participants rate the aptness of the transformed metaphors and similes and another group evaluate the ease of comprehension. The transformed metaphors proved to be as easily understood as the originals, and were rated as no less apt, but the transformed similes were more difficult to understand and rated as less apt than either the transformed metaphors or the original similes. However, these findings may be partly owing to the way the similes were transformed – "well-paid" applies literally to lawyers but not to sharks, and would be difficult even to apply metaphorically to sharks (Glucksberg, 2008).

In an extension of this research, Glucksberg and Haught (2006) created another set of metaphor/simile pairs, transformed by adding a modifier that would give the literal and metaphorical vehicle very different properties; for example, 'my lawyer was/was like *an old shark*.' Here, the metaphor version implies experience, but the simile version implies decrepitude and weakness. They asked participants to provide interpretations of one or the other version, and found that the metaphor and simile versions of the phrase generated consistently different interpretations.

Reversibility

An implication of earlier versions of categorization theory is that metaphors work in only one direction. If 'that lawyer is *a shark*' is reversed, the result, 'that shark is *a lawyer*' does not appear to be interpretable (Glucksberg, McGlone, and Manfredi, 1997). Even if the result can be interpreted, the relevant qualities would seem likely to differ radically. An example discussed by Keysar and Glucksberg (1992; see also Ritchie, 2003a), 'This encyclopedia is *a jungle*' can be reversed to get 'This jungle is *an encyclopedia*.' The first version is grounded in qualities such as difficult and complex; the second version is grounded in qualities such as interesting and informative. The reversed version is an entirely different metaphor. On the other hand, if the statement attributed to von Clausewitz that "War is *the continuation of diplomacy by other means*" is reversed, producing 'diplomacy is *the continuation of war by other means*,' the two versions of the metaphor would appear to draw on the same ground and would lead to very similar interpretations. More generally, there is an entire field of CONFLICT metaphors in which topics and vehicles are readily exchangeable (Ritchie, 2003b), for example BUSINESS IS WAR ('*invade* the competition's territory') and WAR IS BUSINESS ('an *unprofitable* campaign').

Campbell and Katz (2006) argue that the findings reported by Glucksberg, McGlone, and Manfredi, 1997) in support of their contention are in large part an artifact of the use of invented metaphor with no discursive context. To test this claim they prepared a set of twenty-four passages in which metaphors used by the Glucksberg group were presented either in the canonical order or in reversed order. In one condition these were presented with no context (similar to the Glucksberg group) and in another condition they were presented within a context that encouraged use of the same ground for interpretation. For example in one story a police chief reflected on his failed attempt to stop repeat offenders and concluded that "*Chronic crime is a disease*" (canonical version). In the reversed version, the police chief thought about his losing battle against lung cancer and concluded that '*The disease is chronic crime.*'

In one experiment Campbell and Katz (2006) asked participants to rate how understandable the target (metaphorical) sentence is, then write down their own interpretation. In another experiment Campbell and Katz measured participants' comprehension time. Although participants rated the canonical metaphors as somewhat more comprehensible, when Campbell and Katz presented the metaphor within a context reading times were significantly reduced and comprehensibility was significantly increased for both canonical and reversed metaphors. Campbell and Katz conclude that topic and vehicle can be reversed to yield interpretable metaphors and, if the metaphors are presented in an appropriate context, the reversed metaphor is likely to be interpreted according to the same ground as the canonical metaphor.

Summing up: the quality-of-metaphor hypothesis

Glucksberg (2008) sums up the accumulating evidence by rejecting some claims of both categorization and comparison approaches, as well as the career of metaphor theory. He rejects career of metaphor theory because "apt metaphors are not privileged in simile form over metaphor form" and because changing a metaphor to a simile often leads to a radically different interpretation (p. 80). Glucksberg suggests an alternative hypothesis, the "quality-of-metaphor hypothesis." The choice of comparison versus category-assignment is based not on whether the form is simile or metaphor, or whether it is novel or familiar. Rather, "Comparison and categorization are complementary strategies for understanding metaphors, with the choice of strategy dependent on the quality and aptness of the metaphor. Comparisons are resorted to when a categorization doesn't make much sense;

categorizations are used when a metaphor is apt, even when it is a novel metaphor" (2008, p. 80).

An alternative version of category-assignment theory has been proposed in recent work based on relevance theory (Sperber and Wilson, [1986] 1995; Wilson and Sperber, 2004). Although Wilson and Sperber's approach resembles Glucksberg's approach in several ways, it is based on quite different underlying assumptions. In the next section I will begin with an overview of relevance theory, and then discuss Wilson and Sperber's approach to metaphor.

RELEVANCE THEORY

> **Sara to room-mate:** 'Want to go out for a beer?'
> **Room-mate:** points to a stack of books next to her computer.

How is it that a simple gesture of this sort will not only be accepted as an answer to the invitation, but will also often be accepted as a *polite* answer? Sperber and Wilson ([1986] 1995; 2008) argue that the answer lies in Sara's ability to draw inferences, based on the assumption that her room-mate offers the gesture with the *intention* that it will provide all the evidence Sara needs to infer the meaning. Moreover, they argue, *all* intentional communication is accomplished through much the same processes of inference. "Whether or not it involves the use of a language or some other code, human communication is inferential communication. The communicator provides some evidence of her meaning, and the addressee infers this meaning on the basis of this evidence and the context. The evidence may or may not be coded, and if it is coded, it may or may not be linguistic, but in each case, it provides input to an inferential process whose goal is to interpret the communicator's meaning." (Sperber and Wilson, 2008, p. 87).

The explanation begins with what Sperber and Wilson call the "Cognitive principle of relevance: *Human cognition tends to be geared to the maximization of relevance*" (2008, p. 89, emphasis in original). In order to understand the implications of this principle for communication, it is useful to step back a bit and consider the broader function of perception in maintaining one's representation of the physical and social environment. For example, while I am hiking in the woods, if I see small hoof-prints on the trail, my representation of my environment is changed to include the recent presence of deer. If I see clouds growing rapidly above a nearby ridge, my representation of my environment is changed to include the increased probability of a thunderstorm.

A core insight of relevance theory is that communication, like perception, is accomplished by altering the reader's or hearer's representation of the world, including both the physical and the social environment, in a particular way. To extend the example of hiking in the woods, if I hear my companion say 'that looks like a thunderhead building up over the ridge,' the utterance will change my representation of the environment in much the same way that seeing the thunderhead for myself would. The utterance, like the direct perception, will add *thunderheads* to my representation of the local atmospheric conditions and increase my expectation of a storm. By extension, if my companion points to the sky above the ridge, I conclude that his most likely motive for the gesture is to draw my attention to the clouds that are beginning to pile up in that direction, and conclude that he intends me to understand that he expects a thunderstorm.

Relevance theory assumes that each person's representation of the world is organized in *cognitive contexts*. *Cognitive contexts* include current knowledge about the environment, including the physical and social environment, the nature of the conversation, and previous utterances. Thus, in the hiking example, my *cognitive context* includes my perception-based awareness of the atmospheric conditions, wind, air temperature, relevant characteristics of my companion, and the risks associated with being caught in the open during a thunderstorm. *Cognitive contexts* also include stored knowledge about the world, for example my understanding of how thunderheads arise and produce lightning and rain, and how the lightning sometimes starts fires, and knowledge about other participants in the interaction, including in this example what they know about weather as well as what they are likely to believe I know.

The *mutual cognitive environment* consists of those cognitive contexts – currently perceivable information plus stored knowledge – that participants believe to be known and readily accessible to all participants in the conversation. When two experienced hikers see small pointed hoof-prints, both participants are likely to assume that they share some knowledge of local animals and their prints. When they discuss the atmospheric conditions, both participants are likely to assume that they share extensive knowledge about thunderstorms, but if they lack information about each other's level of experience, they might not make that assumption. In the conversation about communicating science to non-scientists, participants could reasonably assume that they are mutually aware of how scientific research is funded. They could also reasonably assume that they were mutually aware of the common meaning of words and phrases like "*ivory tower*" and "*swimming in* money."

Sperber and Wilson argue that all intentional communication, including literal language as well as hyperbole, metaphor, and gesture, is accomplished through inferences based on assumptions of relevance. An input is defined as *relevant* "when processing it in the context of previously available information yields new cognitive effects" (Sperber and Wilson, 2008, p. 88). Relevance is understood in terms of cognitive effects, changes to the mutual cognitive environment, and the effort required to achieve those effects. "Other things being equal, the greater the cognitive effects, and the smaller the mental effort required to derive them (by representing the input, accessing a context and deriving any contextual implications), the greater the relevance of the input to the individual at that time" (Wilson and Carston, 2006, p. 407). Sperber and Wilson give the example of a caterer inquiring about the invited guests: "In general, it is more informative to learn that someone is a Buddhist than to learn that he is a vegetarian, but if the context is such that only his food preferences are consequential, then the less informative input is more relevant" because it requires less processing effort (Sperber and Wilson, 2008, p. 80).

In the example of a brief conversation between two room-mates, the academic routine of writing term papers and studying for exams is part of the mutual cognitive context. Sara's room-mate may reasonably assume that pointing toward the stack of books will provide the information Sara needs to infer the answer to her invitation and at the same time infer a reason for the refusal. Thus, the gesture may be more informative than giving the encoded reply, "no thanks," which would not by itself provide an explanation for the refusal.

Decoding language

Sperber and Wilson (2008) argue that human languages cannot be understood as purely code-like: "The sentences of a natural language are typically multiply ambiguous; they contain referential expressions whose values cannot be assigned by decoding alone … and there are still other ways in which the encoded meaning of a sentence falls short of determining what it may be used to communicate" (p. 85). As an example, 'Holland is flat' would ordinarily be understood in a way that incorporates the curvature of the earth, and allows for the ordinary slight unevenness of terrain. A literal statement that is more technically accurate seems quite odd: 'If Holland were flat, water would flow from the borders toward the center.'

This example illustrates that even a relatively precise word such as *flat* requires inference with respect to the context. To understand 'Holland is flat,' we must broaden the usual meaning of *flat* to include expanses of land that conform to the curvature of the earth, and that are crossed by elevated roadbeds and dikes, dotted with ponds, and so on. To use another example from Sperber and Wilson, if Mary says 'I have a temperature,' the ordinary meaning of *temperature* (every physical object has a temperature) is narrowed to include only temperatures that are higher than the normal human body temperature. This broadening and narrowing is done automatically, as needed to achieve relevance in the present context.

In Sperber and Wilson's view, comprehension must always involve *narrowing* (excluding properties that are irrelevant in the present context), *broadening* (extending the ordinary range of associated properties), or both. Wilson and Carston (2006) provide additional examples of both processes. In 'all politicians *drink*,' the ordinary reference of *drink* is narrowed to include only consumption of alcoholic beverages. In 'buying a house is easy if you've got *money*,' *money* is broadened to include ready credit and narrowed to include only large sums. In 'it's *boiling hot* today,' *boiling* is broadened to include any exceptionally high temperature, and narrowed to exclude temperatures that would actually boil water. In 'be sure to recycle your *empty bottles*,' *empty* is broadened to include bottles that may have a few drops of liquid remaining in the bottom and narrowed to exclude the requirement that the bottle contain a perfect vacuum.

Relevance and metaphor

Sperber and Wilson (2008) insist that metaphor does not require any special treatment. All forms of language use, including metaphor, rely on the same basic processes of inference, employing both broadening and narrowing in the search for optimal relevance. "We see metaphors as simply a range of cases at one end of a continuum that includes literal, loose, and hyperbolic interpretations. In our view, metaphorical interpretations are arrived at in exactly the same way as these other interpretations. There is no mechanism specific to metaphor, no interesting generalization that applies only to them" (Sperber and Wilson, 2008, p. 84).

Wilson and Carston offer as an example 'Caroline is *a princess*,' spoken in reply to a question, 'Will Caroline help with the packing?' According to Wilson and Carston, here '*princess*' is broadened to form an ad hoc concept, PRINCESS*, that includes "spoiled, indulged, and self-centered" (and narrowed to exclude "person born to a royal family"). Another example provided by Wilson and Carston, 'Robert is *a bulldozer*,' when spoken about an overbearing boss, is broadened to form an ad hoc concept, BULLDOZER*, that includes "disrespectful," "obstinate," "undermines people's feelings," "runs over people," and so on. The ad hoc concept is also narrowed to exclude "a type of heavy construction equipment."

Applying Wilson and Carston's account to the previously discussed example from Keysar and Glucksberg (1992), 'jobs are *jails*,' '*jail*' is broadened to form an ad hoc concept, JAIL*, that includes "frustrating, confining, and unpleasant," and narrowed to exclude barred windows and locked doors. Blair's "*throwing crockery*" story can similarly be broadened to form an ad hoc concept, MARITAL SPAT*, to include "any dispute between people who are engaged in an ongoing relationship." "*Hard, steady slog*" can be broadened to form an ad hoc concept, HARD SLOG*, that includes "any tedious activity."

Relevance theory assumes that human cognition has evolved to maximize relevance and accordingly that every utterance or gesture carries two presumptions. (1) It is sufficiently relevant to justify the effort required to make sense of it. (2) It is the most relevant communicative action that the communicator is able and willing to produce in the current situation. These assumptions lead to a comprehension procedure in which the audience follows a path of least effort that includes both broadening and narrowing the stimulus until either the resulting interpretation meets expectations of relevance or the attempt to accomplish relevance is abandoned.

In the scientists' conversation, when Jim says "I've never really *seen the ivory tower*," his comment might seem irrelevant in two respects. *Ivory tower* identifies a kind of structure that is at best improbable, and it has no apparent relation to the current topic of conversation, the difficulty of securing funding for research. But if the phrase is broadened to include situations that are in some sense similar to working in an ivory tower, then it can be understood as applying to a situation in which one need not be concerned with such practicalities. Thus, it has the potential to affect listeners' representations of the status of science. However, thus broadened, *ivory tower* no longer refers to an actual physical structure that can be *seen*, so *ivory tower* must be narrowed to exclude actual physical structures. According to relevance theory, the listeners will undertake the cognitive effort required to accomplish this broadening and narrowing of meanings only if the expected cognitive effects are sufficient to justify the effort. Additionally, according to the "Communicative principle of relevance," there is an expectation that the speaker could not have accomplished these effects in any way that would require less effort: "*Every act of inferential communication conveys a presumption of its own optimal relevance*" (Sperber and Wilson, 2008, p. 89).

The following example appears at the beginning of the scientists' conversation about communicating science with members of the general public (Ritchie and Schell, 2009). The facilitators of the event assigned the name "professional group" to the group that included six scientists plus one science lab administrator.

> FACILITATOR: I guess, we're calling ourselves "the professional group."
> We're all scientists. Ya right.
> JAN: That's right.
> FACILITATOR: Or "*thereabouts*"
> JAN: "*Thereabouts*"
> JIM: "*Pretty much.*"
> LARRY: Can we, can we change our names if we want?
> FACILITATOR: Sure
> LARRY: As first order of business, nerds and geeks
> JAN: Ya
> FACILITATOR: So. We're changing our names to what?
> LARRY: Geeks and nerds.
> JIM: I've been *called a lot of things* but never *professional*. (laughter all around).

Nerds and *Geeks*, the labels evidently preferred over *professionals* by the scientists in the group, ordinarily refer to adolescents who have a low level of social skills and who are preoccupied with activities such as playing computer games. The use of these ordinarily insulting terms in preference to the ordinarily complimentary term, *professional*, is itself ostensive and requires a search for contexts in which it will be non-contradictory and relevant. The terms, *Nerds* and *Geeks*, are often broadened to include anyone who is strongly interested in science and technology, regardless of their level of social skill; the knowledge of this broader usage provides part of the context in which the apparently contradictory usage of these terms can be relevant. On the other hand, *professional* is often broadened to include anyone who *applies* knowledge and narrowed to exclude those who *generate new* knowledge; hence it can be used to distinguish *applied* scientific research from *basic* research, which is far more prestigious within academic and scientific circles. This knowledge supplies the context in which both the preference for *nerds and geeks* over *profes-*

sionals and the subsequent comment, "I've been *called a lot of things,* but never *professional*," are relevant (Ritchie and Schell, 2009).

In all these examples, the broadening and narrowing are driven by the search for relevance. Thus, the search for relevance involves not only selecting or activating cognitive contexts in which the utterance will be relevant; it also involves modifying the schemas activated by an utterance as needed to accomplish relevance.

Carston (2002, p. 328) gives several examples of how broadening can explain the interpretation of metaphorical phrases. In one (apparently invented) example the speaker remarks, 'Here's my new *flatmate*,' referring to a newly acquired cat. Although ordinarily understood as a human being (who usually contributes to rent and other expenses), *flatmate (roommate* in the United States) is also ordinarily understood as providing companionship, which a pet cat is also expected to do. *Human being* is

> **Implicatures:** An implicature is an idea or concept that can be inferred from or is implied by a word or phrase. Implicatures may range from quite weak to very strong. A *weak* implicature of '*flatmate*' is that the cat demands the sort of consideration that a human flatmate would demand, including claims to private space, and so on. *Strong* implicatures of '*rubbish dump*' are that Jim's bedroom is disorganized and that it contains many objects that are of dubious worth.

a subcategory of *living animal*, which includes *cats*, along with other non-human animals that are known to provide companionship. Thus, broadening FLATMATE* to include other members of the inclusive category, LIVING ANIMAL, seems at most odd rather than contradictory.

A second example, 'Jim's bedroom is a *rubbish dump*,' affords a similar analysis. Although *rubbish dump* includes attributes (large trucks backing up and emptying their contents) that do not apply to a *bedroom*, it also includes qualities such as physical disorder, unsightliness, and uncleanness that *can* literally apply to a *bedroom*, and thus provide a straightforward basis for broadening RUBBISH DUMP* to include other members of the inclusive category, DISORDERLY, UNSIGHTLY, AND UNCLEAN SPACES.

In each of these cases, the broadening process that renders the phrase relevant in its context invites multiple weak implicatures, including those based on the incongruity of the ad hoc category (Raskin, 1985; Raskin and Attardo, 1994). These implicatures often, as in this example, provide a basis for humor. The potential for extensive implicatures justifies the use of the metaphorical phrase instead of a more literal alternative (e.g. *companion* or *unsightly mess*, respectively). However, the metaphorical versions do not necessarily require more processing efforts than a literal equivalent, and the contextual effects achieved are not necessarily proportional to the processing effort (Gibbs and Tendahl, 2006). On the other hand, Ritchie and Dyhouse (2008) argue that the humor and playfulness of metaphorical language may supply some of the cognitive effects, independently of any changes to the hearer's understanding of the topic.

Wilson and Carston (2006) discuss two other examples that pose slightly more difficulty. 'Caroline is *a princess*' is spoken in reply to a question, 'Will Caroline help with the packing?' According to Wilson and Carston, here *princess* is broadened to form an ad hoc concept, PRINCESS*, that includes "spoiled, indulged, and self-centered" (and narrowed to exclude "person born to a royal family"). But this metaphor is ambiguous: '*princess*' is also widely used as an endearment, suggesting qualities like "person who behaves nobly; person who is adored." (The masculine equivalent, *prince*, is virtually never used in a negative sense.) In order to disambiguate these alternative ad hoc concepts, the hearer may need to rely on extralinguistic cues including vocal inflections as well as background knowledge about Caroline and her relationship with the speaker.

The PRINCESS* example also illustrates the possibility that the cognitive effects from processing a phrase may include not only effects on the topic (packing for a move) but may also include changes to the hearer's understanding about the social and relational context. In this example, processing the '*princess*' remark may affect the hearer's ideas about Caroline's personality and the speaker's feelings about Caroline. The humorous remarks identifying a new pet as a '*flatmate*' and Jim's bedroom as a '*rubbish dump*' also seem likely to achieve cognitive effects on relational and social contexts as well as on the mental representations of the new pet and the physical environment of Jim's bedroom, respectively. In many instances, the effects on the hearer's understanding of the relational and social context may be more important than the effects on the hearer's ideas about the conversational topic itself.

Comparing the two theories

Although the two theories differ in some important respects, there are many similarities between relevance theory and Glucksberg's approach. Both versions emphasize the creation of ad hoc categories. Glucksberg emphasizes abstraction; relevance theory emphasizes broadening and narrowing of categories. Relevance theory connects ad hoc categories to a general theory of inferential interpretation that applies to all intentional communication, not just to metaphors.

Relevance theory incorporates both the proximate context of the utterance and the broader context of the interaction and surrounding events, and thereby provides a more solid basis for applying the theory to metaphor usage in actual conversation. Relevance theory presents metaphor comprehension as simply one form of language comprehension, dispensing with the difficult problem of classifying language as metaphorical or literal. (For a detailed discussion of the similarities and differences, see Wilson and Carston 2006, pp. 414–415.)

However, like the other theories discussed in Chapters 2 and 3, relevance theory is incomplete. Relevance theory does not provide an adequate solution to what I have previously called the "*circularity*" problem. In order to transfer any relevant quality from '*a block of ice*' to *Sally*, or to construct a useful ad hoc category that includes both topic and vehicle, either "*ice*" or some of the qualities associated with ice (notably, "*cold*") must already have been given a metaphorical interpretation. If Sally is physically *cold*, she needs a warmer sweater, and 'Sally is *a block of ice*' is simply hyperbole. 'Sally is *a block of ice*' can be said to characterize Sally as *emotionally unresponsive* only on the basis of an underlying metaphor, '*emotions are warm*' and by implication '*lack of emotions is cold.*' Before an ad hoc category can be formed that includes both *ice* and *unemotional*, the underlying metaphor, '*lack of emotions is cold*,' must already have been interpreted.

By the same token, in order to transfer any meaningful quality from "*ivory tower*" to *a well-funded research laboratory*, or to construct a meaningful category that includes both "*ivory tower*" and *a well-funded research laboratory*, "*ivory tower*" must already have been given a metaphorical interpretation. Thus, categorization and attribute transfer theories can help to explain some of what we do with metaphors, but they do not provide a satisfactory explanation of how metaphors are interpreted (Ritchie, 2003a).

The mechanisms of broadening and narrowing proposed by relevance theory go part of the way toward resolving the circularity problem, but only for certain kinds of metaphors. These mechanisms appear to be adequate for metaphors in which vehicle and topic perform similar sorts of actions or otherwise have similar sorts of qualities, such as *slenderness* in '*beanpole*' or *presenting a fictionalized or exaggerated character* in "*all the world's a stage.*" But they do not by themselves seem capable of explaining examples in which vehicle and topic are of radically different sorts, as in 'Robert is *a bulldozer*,' '*incendiary language*' or 'Sally is *a princess.*'

The problem of circularity ▬▬▬▬▬▬▬▬▬▬▬▬▬▬▬▬▬▬

(This section is based on arguments developed in detail in Ritchie, 2003a and 2009.)

Wilson and Carston acknowledge what they call the "metaphor within a metaphor" problem and I have called the "*circularity*" problem. How is it that the category, BULLDOZER, a heavy piece of construction equipment, can come to include qualities associated with thinking, emotional, social entities? In effect, in order to construct an ad hoc category, BULLDOZER*, that includes social behavior and emotional responses, either BULLDOZER or other concepts associated with it (such as PUSH AROUND or RUN OVER) must already have been given a metaphorical interpretation. Categorization theory cannot fully explain metaphorical interpretation because the explanation assumes that some degree of metaphorical interpretation has already happened.

A closer examination of the theories discussed in Chapters 2 and 3 suggests that *all* these accounts are fundamentally circular, at least in the sense that the attributes that are transferred and on which categories are based, must in many cases be interpreted *before* the stipulated cognitive processing can occur. The explanation for the metaphors make sense only if one begins by assuming a metaphorical mapping of the vehicle that is to be explained ('*ice*' or '*bulldozer*'; '*cold*' or '*push around*'). Cigarettes and time bombs share the literal quality of leading eventually to death, but *fog* and *cats* do not share any interesting literal qualities. Frequently fog does not even *arrive*, rather it *forms* as the temperature of supersaturated air drops. "*Slogging through the mud*" has little in common with *making decisions*. Slogging is a physical activity that requires no mental concentration, and soldiers have been known to sleep while slogging. Making decisions is a mental activity that does require mental alertness, but requires no physical exertion beyond moving a pen over paper or moving one's fingers over a keyboard. A *lawyer* or *loan officer* may be a vegan and animal rights advocate and still practice law in a way that could be metaphorically described as '*predatory.*' If so, this metaphorical mapping would be required *before* they could be included in an ad hoc category of PREDATORS*.

To return to the previously discussed example from Glucksberg (2008), *jobs* and *jails* both entail presence, often in an indoor space, but there ends the sharing of qualities. What makes a jail a jail is the locked doors, enforced periods of complete idleness, unappetizing food, and Spartan accommodation, such as a toilet consisting of a hole in the floor. In contrast, salaried workers are ordinarily neither

physically confined nor idle, receive two weeks or more of paid holi-
day, and may have rather luxurious bathrooms and break rooms. A
person who whines, 'this job is a jail' is not complaining about any of
the actual qualities that define jails. Rather, the complaint is about
some aspect of the experience that is associated with an imagined
experience of being in jail. For many of the most interesting metaphors, both superordinate categories and common properties rely on qualities that pertain literally to the vehicle but only metaphorically to
the topic. These qualities cannot be considered either common or
category-defining until after the work of metaphor interpretation has
already been accomplished.

What certain jobs have in common with being in jail is not the fact of
physical confinement, but an emotional response to the necessities
of the job that resembles what the speaker imagines it would feel
like to be in jail. In both cases, the metaphorical interpretation has
to be accomplished before any attribute transfer or metaphorical mapping can be considered. Even in a metaphor like 'willow-waisted,' the
metaphor may evoke a response that goes beyond the mere perceptual association of slenderness with willows; that is certainly the case
with 'cigarettes are time bombs.' And when Blair tells the British people
they can choose to "go off with Mr. Kennedy" he does not imply anything like an entire nation marching off across the Yorkshire moors
behind a new Prime Minister. What is transferred from "go off with" to
vote for in an election is a set of emotional and cognitive responses that
can only be uncovered by a prior act of metaphor interpretation. The
entire phrase, of course, belittled the opposition by activating entailments that trivialized their concerns.

The same argument applies to Gentner and Bowdle's (2001)
example, "men are wolves." 'Men prey on women,' makes sense only
after the phrase 'prey on' has been metaphorically interpreted. For the
most part, men do not 'prey on' women in any sense that bears any
resemblance to the relationship of wolves and deer. Wolves stalk, kill,
and eat deer; men seduce, have sexual intercourse with, impregnate,
and abandon women. The latter sequence of events constitutes 'preying on' only in a sense that is already metaphorical, and the structure
mapping cannot proceed until this basic metaphor has been interpreted. Men do, of course, prey on deer, as well as on elk, moose, and
other ungulates – and, like wolves, they usually eat the deer, elk, or
other prey (Ritchie, 2003a).

'That man is a wolf' is a particularly interesting example, because
the qualities that the metaphor invokes – unbridled lust and insati-
able carnal appetites – are not associated with the biological species,

lupus. The qualities of viciousness and remorseless pursuit are associated with wolves in folklore only, not in biology (and usually not on *The Nature Channel*). The work of metaphorical reinterpretation is often accomplished at both ends of the metaphor, and may reshape the way we understand the vehicle as well as the topic (Campbell and Katz, 2006).

Men seducing and abandoning women is metaphorically mapped onto wolves killing and eating deer because the wolf's success as a predator arouses feelings (visceral and emotional) that are easily associated with some women's feelings of helplessness and objectification in the face of unwanted sexual attentions. These feelings are already '*mapped onto*' our culturally transmitted image of a soft-eyed deer or lamb, helpless and objectified while attempting to hide from the wolf pack's single-minded and relentless stalking. These pre-existing linkages may create the respective categories of feeling helpless or objectified in the face of single-minded and relentless sexual seduction, and feeling oppressed by a commitment to an unpleasant situation, to which new experiences can readily be assigned ('a singles bar is a *meat market*,' 'That guy is a real *woman chaser*'). Similarly, an unrewarding job can be compared to jail because the emotional and social meaning associated with an unpleasant situation is already mapped onto our cultural ideas about jails and prisons. I will give an account of how this might happen in Chapters 4 and 5.

According to Sperber and Wilson, in Sandburg's poem, "fog comes in *on little cat feet*," the vehicle, ON-LITTLE-CAT-FEET* has as its "explicit content" "the concept of a property that is difficult or impossible to define." The specific ad hoc category is arrived at "by taking the poet to be attributing to the coming of the fog that property which contextually implies the very ideas suggested by the phrase 'little cat feet'" (2008, p. 102). This passage itself seems circular, and highlights the problem. How is it that "*little cat feet*" can express something about the experience of *fog* that seems elegant and true? What is that "property that is difficult or impossible to define" and how does "*little cat feet*" manage to suggest it?

Relevance theory: two (incomplete) solutions

Wilson and Carston suggest two possible solutions to the "*circularity*" or "metaphor within metaphor" problem (2006, p. 426), neither of which really solves the problem. One possible solution is that "these metaphorically extended senses have arisen through broadening of the basic physical senses ... to create superordinate concepts ... which are not purely psychological but have both physical and psychological instances." How this can be accomplished, and how a single superordinate concept can apply to both physical and psychological experience, are left unexplained. The second solution is that words and phrases like *hard* and *cold*, *push around*, and *remove obstacles* are polysemous, having distinct and independent physical and psychological meanings. Wilson and Carston acknowledge that these senses "might have arisen, in the history of the language or the individual, via narrowing of such broader superordinate senses," but they do not provide any mechanism by which such an extension might have come about in the first place. Both explanations push the question down a level (or back in history) without really explaining anything.

As noted in an earlier section, the proposed mechanisms of broadening and narrowing might be adequate for metaphors in which vehicle and topic perform similar sorts of actions or otherwise have similar sorts of qualities. To continue with the *'bulldozer'* example, if Robert happens to be an offensive lineman (in American Football) who is especially good at clearing a path for the ball-carrier, or a celebrity's body-guard who is good at clearing a path through a crowded street, then extending the concept of *obstacles* to embrace *opposing tacklers* or *other pedestrians* might be accomplished through a kind of 'broadening' of semantic reference; *'obstacles'* might easily be broadened to include people who impede movement (of the ball-carrier or of the celebrity). By the same token, *bulldozer* is easily broadened to include a person who is especially effective at physically removing these obstacles, and the opposing tacklers or obstructing pedestrians, like boulders on a construction site, are literally *pushed around* and may even be literally *run over*.

However, as the *'bulldozer'* example is presented by Wilson and Carston (2006; see also Vega Moreno, 2007), Robert is the speaker's boss (or colleague) who *'pushes* his own ideas *energetically'* and *'runs over'* other people's objections (thereby conveying a sense of disrespect and obstinacy and *'hurting'* listeners' feelings). But an objection to a proposed plan of action that someone raises in a staff meeting is an *'obstacle,'* and insisting on a particular idea is *'pushing'* that idea only *after* a metaphorical mapping has already been accomplished, and preventing further discussion of the objection constitutes *'removing'* it only in a sense that is also already metaphorical. Neither version of categorization theory provides an adequate explanation of how this prior metaphorical mapping might be accomplished (or, in the *polysemy* account, might have been accomplished in some linguistic pre-history). Both versions also fail to explain how the process of broadening and narrowing might be limited, so that bulldozers can be broadened and narrowed to express these meanings but *other* potential metaphor vehicles cannot.

Context

A shortcoming of all these approaches to metaphor is their reliance on artificial examples, invented to demonstrate a particular point, and in general on metaphors removed from any actual discursive context (Campbell and Katz, 2006; Edwards, 1997). In spite of the central emphasis in relevance theory on context, Wilson and Sperber and their colleagues also rely almost exclusively on examples that are either invented or abstracted from any actual conversational context. This shortcoming may be part of the reason they have not thus far managed to move the discussion beyond an implicit information-transfer model to incorporate the richer emotional and relational dimensions of language use (e.g. see Edwards, 1997). It is disappointing to see *context*, which in principle involves everything mutually known to the participants in a conversation, *including their relationship*, defined so narrowly. Wilson and Carston acknowledge the potential importance of aspects of the communicative interaction such as vocal inflection and gesture, but they do not incorporate any of this into their theory of metaphor. They entirely disregard the relational context, both as a resource in understanding utterances and as part of what may be changed by the effects of processing.

Consider the '*princess*' example from Wilson and Carston (2006). 'Will Caroline help with the packing?' Reply: 'Caroline is *a princess*.' This could, as Wilson and Carston suggest, lead to implicatures that Caroline is spoiled, self-indulgent, and so on, consequently that she cannot be expected to do her share. But it might also lead to the opposite conclusion, based on an entirely different set of implicatures. Which way it goes might depend on the accompanying vocal tone and gestures (rising vs. falling inflection, smile vs. grimace, etc.). It might also hinge on the hearer's assumptions about the speaker's relationship with Caroline. *Princess* is a complex concept, both in its literal usage and in its common figurative usage. It is unrealistic and simplistic to offer a single interpretation for a metaphorical use of '*princess*' without a much more detailed consideration of these broader contextual factors.

'*Bulldozer*' is also a complex concept. As with the '*princess*' example, 'Robert is a *bulldozer*' is easily used in praise ("Will Robert get the contract for our company?" "Do you think the meeting will end by the scheduled time?" "Who should we appoint as our chief negotiator?") Also like the '*princess*' example, 'Robert is a *bulldozer*' is easily used in blame ("Did Robert consider your objections to the proposal?"

"How did Robert convince you to attend this pointless meeting?"). Relevance theory, with its emphasis on contextual effects, provides a basis for explaining how listeners might select from among the available positive, negative, and neutral ideas associated with the vehicle to achieve optimal relevance, and relevance theory is easily extended to include relational and emotional effects. But these potentialities have thus far been underexploited by relevance theorists. More to the point, it is difficult to see how relevance theory, by itself, could possibly explain how these apparently unrelated ideas come to be associated with the vehicle in the first place (see Ritchie, 2003a and 2009a for a more extensive and detailed development of these arguments).

Wilson and Carston claim that no really good solution to this problem has been offered. The next few chapters will present approaches that help solve the circularity problem and, in doing so, extend our kit of tools for analyzing and understanding metaphors.

SUMMARY

As discussed in Chapter 2, comparison and attribution theories seem to provide a good explanation for the most simple metaphors, and the structure-mapping approach provides a useful way of analyzing extended metaphors such as "All the world's *a stage*" and Tony Blair's metaphorical story about "*throwing crockery*." However, the research described in detail by Glucksberg (2008) and summarized earlier in this chapter raises serious doubts about whether any of these approaches on their own can be developed into a comprehensive account of metaphor use and understanding. The categorization approach introduced by Glucksberg and the category broadening and narrowing approach advocated by Wilson and Sperber are promising, and both explain certain simple metaphors quite well, conventional metaphors in particular. However, these approaches have difficulty with abstract metaphors, for which some previous act of metaphor interpretation is required prior to the formation of an ad hoc category that could explain how the metaphor is interpreted. Chapters 4–6 will present some theories that help fill this gap.

DISCUSSION

The research initially reported by Glucksberg in support of category assignment and dual reference is all based on nominal metaphors.

More recently Torreano, Cacciari, and Glucksberg (2005) extended the research to verb metaphors. How might replications be designed for other metaphor forms such as metaphorical stories and phrases in which the metaphor vehicle is not explicit?

How many metaphor vehicles have the capacity to be interpreted in more than one way? Can the categorization models be modified so as to deal more effectively with these?

Students have informed me that '*wolf*' is no longer used as a metaphor for a sexually exploitative male. Can you think of a basis for this change in metaphor usage in broader cultural and political contexts?

SUGGESTED READINGS

- Gibbs, R. W., Jr., and Tendahl, M. (2006). Cognitive effort and effects in metaphor comprehension: Relevance theory and psycholinguistics. *Mind and Language, 21*, 379–403. In this essay Gibbs and Tendahl summarize and critique the relevance theory account of categorization theory, and show how it can be merged with conceptual metaphor theory (which I will discuss in Chapter 5).
- Glucksberg, S. (2008). How metaphors create categories – quickly. In Gibbs, R.W., Jr. (ed.), *The Cambridge handbook of metaphor and thought*. Cambridge University Press, pp. 67–83. In this chapter, Glucksberg provides a thorough review of recent research relevant to the debate between comparison and category-assignment theories, embedded in a clear and logical argument.
- Ritchie, D. (2003a). Categories and similarities: A note on circularity. *Metaphor and Symbol, 18*, 49–53. Ritchie, L. D. (2009). Relevance and simulation in metaphor. *Metaphor and Symbol, 24*, 249–262. Much of the last part of this chapter is based on these two essays, in which I provide a more detailed critique of the circularity issue as it appears in both comparison and categorization theories.
- Wilson, D., and Carston, R. (2006). Metaphor, relevance and the 'emergent property' issue. *Mind and Language, 21*, 404–433. In this essay, Wilson and Carston set forth the relevance approach to metaphor in very clear terms.

4 Conceptual metaphors

> While he was *in* school he *fell in* love, but the relationship didn't *go anywhere* and it quickly *cooled off* – it was a complete *dead-end*.

In 1980 George Lakoff and Mark Johnson proposed an approach to metaphor radically different from those described in Chapters 2 and 3. Lakoff and Johnson argue that metaphorical expressions in language express underlying *conceptual metaphors*, in which the metaphor topic is *experienced as* the vehicle. "Our ordinary conceptual system, in terms of which we both think and act, is fundamentally metaphorical in nature" (Lakoff and Johnson, 1980, p. 3). According to Lakoff and Johnson, '*fell* in love' expresses the conceptual metaphors LOVE IS A CONTAINER and CONTROL IS UP / LOSS OF CONTROL IS DOWN. "The essence of metaphor is understanding and experiencing one kind of thing in terms of another" (Lakoff and Johnson, 1980, p. 5).

When we use these metaphors we experience *love* as *a container* that *encloses* the lover. We experience the onset of love, in which lovers are no longer in control of their emotions, as *falling through physical space*. When we speak or hear of a relationship that '*didn't go anywhere*' and was '*a dead-end,*' we understand the relationship in terms of the conceptual metaphor LOVE IS A JOURNEY, and experience the failure as *a cessation of motion through physical space* that is caused by being '*on a street that is blocked.*' I will begin this chapter with a summary of conceptual metaphor theory, and then discuss several examples of conceptual metaphors.

CONCEPTUAL METAPHOR THEORY (CMT)

Metaphor theorists and researchers have typically regarded metaphors as a matter of how language is used. In a traditional approach to metaphor, a sentence links one word or phrase to another word or phrase from a different domain, and the problem is to explain how these interconnected words are comprehended and how they create meaning. 'Sally is *a block of ice*' connects *Sally* with *a block of ice*, and the problem is to explain how that connection is able to express something about Sally that hearers will accept as meaningful and at least potentially true. Lakoff and Johnson (1980) reversed this order, arguing that metaphors connect underlying concepts, and that the metaphorical words and phrases encountered in language are but surface expressions of these underlying conceptual relationships.

According to Lakoff and Johnson (1980), 'Sally is *a block of ice*' expresses an underlying relationship between the concepts of *emotion* and *physical temperature* that can be summarized as EMOTION IS WARMTH or PASSION IS HEAT. Since *ice* is characterized by a relative lack of warmth or heat, the metaphor 'Sally is *a block of ice*' leads the hearer to experience Sally as *lacking emotional expression or passion*. These conceptual metaphors also provide the basis for many other familiar metaphorical phrases, such as 'a *hot* affair,' 'a *chilly* reception,' 'a *warm* relationship,' and '*hot under the collar*,' as well as Reverend Wright's "*incendiary* language," as described in Obama's speech. It is important to remember that the phrase EMOTION IS WARMTH is intended to designate an underlying relationship between the two concepts, *emotion* and *warmth*, and is not intended to be read as a relationship between the words that express these concepts.

Lakoff and Johnson (1980) claim that these conceptual metaphors are "embodied," by which they mean that conceptual metaphors originate when an abstract concept (*emotion* or *passion*) is repeatedly experienced in conjunction with a physical sensation (*warmth* or *heat*). To continue with the same example, beginning in infancy we experience *affection* in conjunction with the physical presence of the mother or other caregiver, including direct physical contact, and come to associate *affection* with *physical proximity* and *physical warmth*. In later life, passions such as *anger* and *sexual desire* are often associated with the flow of blood to the skin and an increase in body temperature. As the child comes to understand abstract concepts such as *affection* and *passion*, these concepts are already linked in experience with physical feelings of *proximity* and *warmth*. These associations supply a conceptual basis or '*grounding*' for the language we use to talk about these abstract concepts, and the underlying conceptual metaphor is reinforced through cultural experience as the child hears others use related metaphorical phrases. It feels so natural to think and speak in terms of 'a *warm*' relationship, 'a *hot* love affair,' or '*burning up* with anger' that people often find it difficult to think of these phrases as metaphorical.

Because the concept of *affection* is partially understood in terms of the conceptual metaphors AFFECTION IS PROXIMITY and EMOTION IS WARMTH, the same neural circuits activated by the physical experience of *closeness* and *warmth* become partially or weakly activated by the emotional experience of *affection*. Conversely, the neural circuits activated by the physical experience of *distance* or *cold* become partially activated by the emotional experience of a *lack of affection*. As a result, we actually experience *affection* as *proximity* and *warmth*, and *lack of affection* as *distance* and *coldness*. 'A *close* relationship' and 'a *warm* greeting' express the experience of *affection* as *physical proximity* and *warmth*, respectively. Conversely, 'a *block of ice*' and other metaphorical expressions such as '*icy* greeting' and '*frosty* glance' exaggerate and emphasize the underlying experience of a lack of emotion as an extreme 'lack of *warmth*,' that is, as '*being very cold*.'

According to CMT, relatively few concepts are based on direct physical experience. These would include *hunger, temperature, pain, physical orientation*, and so on. Most of our abstract concepts are based on conceptual metaphors that originate in experienced correlations with these direct physical experiences and the "embodied" concepts associated with them. The most basic embodied concepts begin in early infancy; these include *heat* and *cold*, *absence* and *presence* of the mother or other caregiver, *hunger* and *thirst*, *pain* and *pleasure*, *eating* and *drinking*, *light* and *sound*, *physical orientation* (*up/down, front/back*), and *manipulating objects*. These sensory experiences provide the basis for conceptual metaphors that express more abstract concepts like *love, caring*, and *need* or *desire* in terms of fundamental physiological experiences including physical needs and their satisfaction. In addition to LOVE IS PHYSICAL PROXIMITY (and WARMTH), there is also NEED or DESIRE IS HUNGER, as in '*starved for* attention' and '*hungry* for affection.'

As the child interacts with objects in the world, other primary concepts are developed and generalized as metaphors for associated abstract concepts. From playing with blocks and observing other stacks of objects the child acquires conceptual metaphors like MORE IS UP, the basis for expressions like '*a high temperature*,' '*rising prices*,' and '*lowered expectations*.' From the experience of getting sick and lying down, then recovering and arising from the sickbed, we have HEALTHY IS UP / UNHEALTHY IS DOWN, the basis for linguistic expressions like '*high spirits*' and '*feeling low*.' Many experiences at this stage contribute to an association of *importance* and *power* with *size* and *height*, and provide the basis for conceptual metaphors like POWERFUL IS HIGH,

POWERFUL IS BIG, and IMPORTANT IS BIG. These conceptual metaphors in turn provide the basis for linguistic expressions like '*higher* authorities,' 'the *big* boss,' '*a big* problem,' and '*a big* fuss.' Experiences with objects and textures also give us UNYIELDING IS HARD ('*hard-hearted*' and 'a *hard* problem' – and the opposite, 'a *soft* job,' 'a *soft* heart').

Experiences with food give us UNPLEASANT IS BITTER or SOUR ('*bitter* memories,' '*bitter* about his divorce,' 'a *sour* mood'), PLEASANT IS SWEET ('a *sweet* disposition,' '*sweet* dreams'). Food also gives us EXCITING IS SPICY ('a *spicy* novel,' 'a *bland* disposition'). Association between high temperature and the pain caused by capsicum on lips and tongue gives us PEPPERY IS HOT ('*hot* chili sauce'). Other expressions using HOT as a vehicle may be experienced as physical temperature, spiciness, or both: 'a *hot* romance,' 'a *spicy* novel.' Both senses are combined in the lyrics from the country-western song *Jackson* (Lieber and Wheeler, 1963), "We got married *in a fever, hotter than a pepper sprout.*"

As we mature and begin to interact with machinery, weapons and tools, these embodied physical and social interactions provide the basis of more complex conceptual metaphors. We may describe someone as having a '*sharp* tongue' (EMOTIONAL DISTRESS IS PHYSICAL PAIN; HUMILIATION IS A WOUND) or '*sharp* cheese' (INTENSE TASTE IS INTENSE TACTILE EXPERIENCE). We may worry that a relationship is '*on a shaky foundation*' (A RELATIONSHIP IS A BUILDING). Drawing on social and cultural institutions and customs, we routinely discuss business and political relationships in terms of family relationships: a corporate acquisition may be 'a *forced marriage*' or 'a *marriage of convenience*' and if a venture is unprofitable or bosses' egos conflict, it may '*lead to* a *divorce.*'

The primary importance of social interaction in our lives leads to many *personification* metaphors, in which an abstract concept or process is represented as a person. Thus we complain that 'inflation is *killing us*' and we might consider 'a *seductive* opportunity.' Emily Dickinson's "Because I could not stop for Death / He *kindly stopped for me*" expresses DEATH IS A PERSON, which also gives us phrases like 'the *grim reaper*' (in combination with DEATH IS HARVEST). The association of motion with various social and intellectual processes provides the basis for many metaphors that take the form X IS A JOURNEY. Thus we have 'this relationship is *going nowhere*' and its opposite, 'a *whirlwind* romance'; a '*dead-end job*' and its opposite, 'the *fast track to* success.' 'A *whirlwind* romance' also draws on one of many conceptual metaphors based on our experience with weather, that is, FAST AND UNPREDICTABLE IS A WINDSTORM.

A FEW COMMON CONCEPTUAL METAPHORS

In this section I will list just a few of the conceptual metaphors that have been identified and discussed by Lakoff and Johnson (1980), and by other researchers who have been influenced by their theory. PASSION IS HEAT and DESTRUCTIVE VIOLENCE IS FIRE

> **Notation:** As a matter of notational convenience, Lakoff and Johnson use the most specific metaphorical concept to characterize the entire system, for example TIME IS MONEY, rather than a more general phrase such as TIME IS VALUE (1980; p. 9). This should not be interpreted as asserting that we experience time specifically in terms of money to the exclusion of other stores of value.

> 'hot under the collar,' 'steaming mad,' "incendiary language," (from Obama's speech) "fire-storm" (of criticism) (from Obama's speech), 'a hot affair,' 'a chilly reception,' 'burning desire,' but also, 'icy stare,' 'makes my blood run cold.'

MORE IS UP and IMPORTANCE IS SIZE

> 'the Dow rose 39 points,' 'a high fever,' 'a big problem,' 'earn big money,' 'the big boss,' 'rising expectations,' 'climb the ladder of success,' 'fall from grace,' and the idiomatic saying, 'the bigger they come, the harder they fall.'

TIME IS MONEY

> 'spend time,' 'save time,' 'give me a moment,' 'invest the time,' 'not worth the time.'

MATURATION IS MOVEMENT THROUGH SPACE and THE FUTURE IS IN FRONT

> 'My brother was two years ahead of me in school,' 'get ahead in your career,' 'medical advances,' 'falling behind the rest of the class,' and 'that's all behind us now.'

IDEAS ARE OBJECTS, THINKING IS MAKING OBJECTS

> 'put your thoughts into words,' 'give me your thoughts,' 'that's a weighty idea,' 'I had no idea,' 'empty rhetoric,' and 'he piled one fact on top of another,' also "decision-making" (from Blair's speech), 'fabricate a lie,' 'making up a story.'

EMBODIED METAPHORS AND THE "CIRCULARITY" PROBLEM

In Chapter 3, I discussed the problem of *circularity* or *metaphor within metaphor*. For example, we might explain 'Sally is a block of ice' or 'my boss is a *bulldozer*' by saying that the first transfers the quality of *cold* and the second the qualities of *pushy* and *insensitive* from vehicle to topic, but that leaves us with other metaphors ('*cold*,' '*pushy*,' and '*insensitive*') to explain. Categorization theory presents much the same problem: if we claim that these metaphors create categories based on selected qualities of the vehicle, we still have to explain how a single category could include '*cold*' and *lacking affection* or '*pushy*' and *domineering*. CMT solves the circularity problem by tracing the metaphorical mappings between emotional and physical concepts to correlations in physical experience.

As discussed in a previous section, according to Lakoff and Johnson (1980), *love* (and affection generally) is originally experienced in terms of the caregiver's proximity and bodily warmth, providing the basis for LOVE IS WARMTH and LOVE IS PHYSICAL PROXIMITY, and their opposites, LACK OF AFFECTION IS COLDNESS and LACK OF AFFECTION IS DISTANCE. To review, according to Lakoff and Johnson, correlations in experience between *affection* and *warmth* create neural connections between parts of the brain associated with these separate experiences. The social experience of the absence of a caregiver and the consequent emotional feeling of abandonment comes to be associated with the physical feeling of lower temperature. This association provides a basis for experiencing *a lack of emotional responsiveness* as *a drop in physical temperature*. In turn this provides a basis for expanding the category COLD to include *a lack of emotional responsiveness* and for attributing *a lack of emotional responsiveness* to Sally when she is described as '*a block of ice*.'

Ice is extremely cold, an exaggeration of the sensation of physical coldness that has come to be experientially associated with physical separation from the caregiver or social rejection from a group. Consequently *ice* comes to be associated with *emotional detachment* and associated emotions such as *anxiety* and *sadness*. This experiential association provides the basis for the conceptual metaphor EMOTIONALLY UNRESPONSIVE IS COLD. Hearing that 'Sally is *a block of ice*,' we experience social interactions with Sally as *interacting with ice* – an extreme lack of physical warmth, entailing an extreme lack of emotional responsiveness.

A closely related metaphor, ACCEPTANCE IS WARMTH, leads to 'his proposal got a *warm* reception.' As noted before, extreme passions such as anger and sexual arousal often lead to a more extreme sensation of warmth; this association is strengthened by observing the destructiveness of fire. From these associations we have PASSION IS HEAT ("we got married *in a fever*") and EXTREME ANGER IS FIRE ("*incendiary* language" and "*firestorm*" from Obama's speech, "A More Perfect Union").

Thus, Lakoff and Johnson (1980) claim that CMT provides an essentially neurological solution to the circularity problem discussed in the last chapter. They claim that expressions like 'a *heated* argument,' 'a *warm* relationship,' '*hot under the collar*,' 'an *icy* stare,' and 'a *chilly* reception' seem natural and come readily to mind because when we experience social acceptance, affection, and passion, the neural circuits associated with warmth are activated so that we experience a sensation of physical warmth as part of the emotional experience. Conversely, we experience *social rejection* or *the lack of emotional response* as a sensation of *coldness*. The schemas, embodied in neurological circuits that are activated when we experience physical *warmth* or physical *chill*, are also activated when we experience *love* or *rejection*. Hearing or reading these expressions induces the listener or reader to experience a physical *warmth* in association with *affection* or *acceptance* and a physical *chill* in association with *lack of affection* or *social rejection*.

The structuring of a concept through metaphorical entailments can never be complete, since only limited aspects of the vehicle will be relevant to the topic. However, metaphors for abstract concepts often generate entire families of metaphorical expressions. Thus, TIME IS MONEY produces '*spend time*,' '*save time*,' '*give some time*,' and even '*invest the time*.' IDEAS ARE OBJECTS yields '*put your thoughts into* words,' '*give me* your thoughts,' 'that's a *weighty* idea,' 'I *had no* idea,' '*empty* rhetoric,' and '*pile* one fact *on top of* another.'

Because MOVEMENT THROUGH SPACE is associated with many ordinary activities, *motion or stillness*, *journey*, and *path* or *road* provide the basis for many conceptual metaphors. Lakoff and Johnson discuss LIFE IS A JOURNEY and LOVE IS A JOURNEY, with expressions like '*dead-end* relationship' or '*dead-end* job,' '*reached a crossroads*' or '*turning point*,' '*stuck in a rut*,' '*a new start*,' and so on. Lakoff and Johnson (1980) claim that many of the phrases we use to discuss verbal arguments are based on ARGUMENT IS WAR. Thus we have '*win*' or '*lose*' an argument, '*attack* an opponent's *position*,' '*undermine*' an opponent's *arguments*,' and so on.

Metaphors are widely shared both because of the commonalities of embodied experience (larger objects pose greater challenges than smaller ones for everyone, and the proximity and bodily warmth of caregivers are associated with gratification of needs for all infants) and because culturally prominent metaphors are reinforced in everyday conversation. Children are primed by their prelinguistic experience to understand MORE IS UP and AFFECTION IS WARMTH, and these conceptual metaphors are reinforced in the language they hear throughout life. Because primary metaphorical concepts are based on common physical experiences, those based on experiences linked to the physical conditions of life are likely to occur across many cultures, as subsequent research has confirmed (Lakoff and Johnson, 1999; Kövecses, 2002; 2005).

COMPOSITE METAPHORS

Grady (1997; Grady, Taub, and Morgan, 1996) has shown how more complex metaphors can be constructed as *compound* metaphors by connecting simpler, more direct metaphors. Grady built much of his analysis on the conceptual metaphor THEORIES ARE BUILDINGS, which Lakoff and Johnson (1980) infer from common phrases such as '*foundation for a theory*,' '*build*' or '*demolish*' a theory. An oft-quoted example of this metaphor is Sherlock Holmes' exclamation: "'Data! Data!' he cried impatiently. 'I cannot *make bricks without clay*'" (Conan Doyle, 1984, p. 214). Grady claims that it is unlikely that the metaphor THEORIES ARE BUILDINGS could have arisen directly through experiences with buildings, and that it is formed of a compound of two more basic conceptual metaphors, ORGANIZATION IS PHYSICAL STRUCTURE and PERSISTING IS REMAINING ERECT.

This particular example is not entirely convincing. Both the process of construction and the finished buildings are familiar to most people, so it seems reasonable to suppose that they could become directly associated with various concepts, including theories, marriages, and so on. These and other abstract concepts can be on a more or less '*firm foundation*,' can '*provide shelter*,' and so on (Ritchie, 2006). Nonetheless, Grady's fundamental insight about the possibility of combining metaphors to form more complex compound metaphors seems valid, and it provides a useful tool for metaphor analysis.

Wilson and Sperber's (2004) invented example, 'Fred is *a bulldozer*,' may provide a better example of a composite metaphor. Beginning in childhood we encounter an association between objects that impede physical motion and a feeling of frustrated desires. Sometimes the "obstacle" is another person, as when two people are chatting in front of a drinking fountain and thus blocking access to it, or when a group of people are blocking a busy sidewalk. This provides the basis for a conceptual metaphor IMPEDING ANOTHER PERSON'S ACTIONS OR DESIRES IS BEING AN OBSTACLE. Beginning in early childhood, we frequently experience situations in which a dominant person physically pushes other persons while demanding that they comply with the aggressor's wishes, leading to a conceptual metaphor that might be labeled INSISTING IS PUSH-ING or BOSSINESS IS PUSHING. Thus when an acquaintance describes her mother-in-law as '*pushy*,' we may experience the topic person as physically pushing her daughter-in-law. When she describes her boss as a '*bulldozer*' we may experience our friend and her cowork-ers as '*obstacles*' to the boss's plans, and her boss as a *powerful and irresistible machine, pushing* his employees *aside*. This application of conceptual metaphor theory thus provides an experiential ground-ing for the broadening and narrowing of concepts hypothesized by Wilson and Sperber (2004).

HEARTBREAK: an international metaphor

A familiar example in which primary metaphors are combined to form a more complex metaphor is '*heartbreak*' or '*broken heart*.' Strong emotion causes the heart to beat noticeably faster, which in itself provides the basis for an association between *love* and *heart*. This asso-ciation is probably strengthened by the heart's location near the cen-ter of the body, and by its crucial role in the circulation of blood. It is also strengthened by cultural beliefs in which the heart and other central organs (especially stomach and liver) are associated with emo-tions and even with reasoning. This association gives rise to a family of conceptual metaphors that includes COURAGE IS HEART, HOPE IS HEART, and, germane to the present discussion, LOVE IS HEART, which is commonly expressed visually in the stylized heart symbol, as in "I ♥ New York."

A different set of experiences links failure and disappointment with physical damage and breakage, giving rise to a conceptual meta-phor, FAILING or BEING DISAPPOINTED IS BEING BROKEN or SPOILED, expressed in metaphors like '*broken dreams*,' 'a *broken* marriage,' '*spoiled* chances,' and '*a ruined* career.' Combine these two metaphors, and the result is a composite conceptual metaphor DISAPPOINTED LOVE IS HEARTBREAK. According to conceptual metaphor theory, the experiences that give rise to these primary conceptual metaphors are derived from human physiology and experience common to many if not most cultures, and it would be somewhat surprising if related expressions did not occur in many languages.

Journalist Meghan Laslocky has inquired about '*heartbreak*' on the Cognitive Linguistics listserv (www.cognitivelinguistics.org/list-servs.shtml. Last accessed April 2011) and the responses over several days included many examples that illustrate both the conceptual commonalities across languages and the language-specific differences in the way similar underlying conceptual metaphors are expressed. In the next few paragraphs I will summarize some of the ensuing discussion. From Italian comes *crepacuore*, from *crepa*, "suddenly die," and *cuore*, heart. A common idiom is *morire di crepacuore*, 'to *die of heartbreak*' (Federico Gobbo, Cognitive Linguistics listserv, April 2011). In Hungarian a slightly different construction is used: *szívszaggató* as an adjective, as 'something is *heart tearing*,' and *valakinek megszakad a szíve* 'somebody's *heart is tearing/breaking*'. Sometimes *összetört/megtört szív*, '*broken heart*' may be used poetically (Katalin Fenyvesi, Cognitive Linguistics listserv, April 2011). '*Broken heart*' appears in Chinese as "心碎," combining "心," *heart*, with "碎," *break* (Ling Ma, personal communication, April 15, 2011).

Japanese also has phrases that can be translated to '*hurt heart*' or '*torn heart*,' but not '*broken heart*' (Masami Nishishiba, personal communication, April 14, 2011). In English, a slightly less severe form of '*heartbreak*' is '*heartache*' – similar to the Japanese '*hurt heart*.' '*Torn heart*' corresponds to English '*heart-rending*,' also used as an adjective, but less commonly for disappointed love than for something that elicits acute sympathy, as in 'the *heart-rending* photographs of wounded children.' However, in "Bird on a Wire" (*Songs from a Room*) Leonard Cohen developed the '*torn*' metaphor in reference to a lover's regret for his unfeeling actions, in an evocative contrast with the literal meaning:

> Like a *baby, stillborn,*
> Like a *beast with his horn*
> I have *torn* everyone who *reached out for me*
> (Cohen, 1969)

In German, *jemandem das Herz brechen*, 'to *break someone's heart*,' and *es bricht mir das Herz*, 'it *breaks my heart*' are typically used in connection with unhappy love affairs, but they may also be used in response to something that causes emotional pain more generally. "It can be (semi-) literalised when someone is said to *die of a broken heart, an gebrochenem Herzen sterben*" (Veronika Koller, Cognitive Linguistics listserv April, 2011). In Croation, *slomiti srce*, 'to break one's heart' and *slomljeno srce*, 'broken heart' are used in relation to disappointed love; *prepuklo srce*, 'broken heart' is acquired from the literary heritage and is now used only with respect to pain following a loved one's death, usually a mother grieving for a child (Mima Dedaic, Cognitive Linguistics listserv, April 2011). From Persian comes *del-shekasteh*, 'heart-broken,' *del-shekastan*, 'heart-to-break,' but *del* can refer to the abdomen generally, not just the heart (Farzad Sharifian, Cognitive Linguistics listserv, April, 2011).

Danish does not have an exact equivalent of 'heartbreak,' but it does offer *at være knust*, 'to be broken/shattered,' roughly equivalent to 'heartbroken,' although it can be applied more broadly. One might say *han er helt knust*, 'he is completely *shattered*' about someone abandoned by a lover, but also of someone whose dog has died or a professor who did not get tenure (Peter Werth, Cognitive Linguistics listserv, April 2011). 'Shattered' can be used in American English with a similar range of meanings, either alone ('I was *shattered* when she left me for another man') or in combination with a noun, often itself metaphorical ('my *world was shattered* by the death of my father'). Anders Hougaard notes that Danish also has *hårdt hjerte*, 'hard heart,' to describe someone who is cynical or unfeeling, and *hjerteknuser*, 'heart breaker,' often referring to someone who is very attractive and who may not return the affection lavished upon them (Anders Hougaard, Cognitive Linguistics listserv, April 2011). English has almost identical expressions, 'hard-hearted' and its opposite, 'soft-hearted,' and 'heart-breaker' (who may also be a 'home-wrecker').

These examples are all consistent with a common set of conceptual mappings, EMOTION IS THE HEART and THE HEART IS A FRAGILE OBJECT. It is easy enough to see how this conceptual mapping might arise from the physiological reactions to disappointment and grief, which can include acute physical pain caused by constriction of abdominal muscles. Cultural associations of emotions with internal organs (the heart in European cultures, the gall bladder in Chinese culture) may also contribute to the conceptual underpinnings of these 'heartbreak' metaphors.

Culture-specific metaphors

Many primary metaphorical concepts are based on culture-specific experiences. TIME IS MONEY, TIME IS A RESOURCE, and TIME IS A VALUABLE COMMODITY ('save time,' 'spend time') are grounded in our experience of a wage-based economy. Other primary metaphors based on culture-specific experiences include gardening ('spread like weeds,' 'plant the seeds of a new idea') or mechanics ('social breakdown,' 'the wheels are turning,' 'repair the relationship'). The internet has yielded a raft of culturally based metaphors, although given the worldwide adoption of computer technology these are likely to be quite widespread.

Maalej (2004) provides several examples from Tunisian Arabic to show that "embodiment" of conceptual metaphors is itself often influenced by cultural beliefs and practices. He begins with the standard account that ANGER IS HEAT originates with feeling physically hot as a result of blood rushing to the surface of the skin (Kövecses, 1990; Lakoff and Kövecses, 1987). He then discusses several Tunisian Arabic expressions for anger that are based on culture-specific beliefs about physiology. These include "He caused *my brain to burn*," "My heart is *sloshing with anger*," and "He made my *nerves swell*." Then he discusses several other metaphors that apply culture-specific culinary practices (butchering and preparing meat) to anger. These include "He *broke my bones into small bits*" and "He *caused my stomach to burst*." As Maalej notes, it is important to include cultural practices in any account of conceptual metaphors.

METHOD

Like previous theorists, Lakoff and Johnson developed their original arguments almost entirely through examples they invented, based on their own language experience and linguistic intuitions. However, in subsequent research, Lakoff and his colleagues have used CMT to investigate metaphors drawn from

> **A thought experiment** On a piece of scrap paper, fill in the blank letters in the following, then write down your interpretation of the metaphor. Ask some of your friends to do the same. I will discuss it later in this chapter.
> 'In order to do well in this class, you really need to t_ _ the line.'

literature (Lakoff and Turner, 1989), mathematics (Lakoff and Nunez, 2000) and other fields of discourse. Metaphors are identified in much the same way as discussed in Chapter 1: if a word or phrase is used in a way that is markedly different from its primary or customary meaning, it is counted as metaphorical, even if the metaphorical meaning has come to be accepted as an alternative meaning of the word or phrase. Thus, in 'I *see* what you mean,' even though *understand* has come to be accepted as an alternative meaning of *see*, CMT treats *see* as a metaphor vehicle.

In order to identify the underlying conceptual metaphor, the CMT analyst identifies the most general abstract concept as the topic, and the most basic embodied experience as the vehicle. In 'I *see* what you mean,' the most general abstract concept is *understanding* and the most basic embodied experience is *seeing*, so the conceptual metaphor is identified as UNDERSTANDING IS SEEING. (The more general UNDERSTANDING IS PERCEIVING would also be acceptable.) The '*bulldozer*' example is more complex. To make sense of this metaphor we first need to analyze the traits and actions of an actual bulldozer (e.g. *push* objects, *run over* objects, and *remove* obstacles). Then we need to look for potential underlying conceptual metaphors (NON-COMPLIANT HUMANS ARE OBSTACLES, INSISTING ON ONE'S OWN WAY IS PUSHING, and OVERCOMING NON-COMPLIANCE IS REMOVING OBSTACLES). Finally we need to identify the potential metaphorical mappings that seem most relevant.

In many cases, the topic, vehicle, or both topic and vehicle could reasonably be identified with several different words that are synonyms or near synonyms. The exact word choice is not important, and Lakoff and Johnson warn against treating the label (*seeing* in UNDERSTANDING IS SEEING) as the concept. However, it is best to maintain consistent labels throughout a discussion. (This may require going back to change the conceptual metaphor label used earlier in an analysis.) In some cases, like 'I *see* what you mean,' the vehicle and topic in the underlying conceptual metaphor may be more or less identical with the vehicle and topic in the linguistic metaphor. In other cases, like 'My boss is a *bulldozer*,' it will make more sense to identify a more basic topic and/or vehicle, in this case the topic is something like *stubborn* and *domineering*; the vehicle is something like PUSHY and IMPOSSIBLE TO RESIST. None of these words appear in the actual observed metaphor. It is important to notice here that analysis of the metaphor must begin with analysis of the meaning of the metaphorical phrase in the context in which it appears.

In the years since Lakoff and Johnson's initial (1980) publication, a number of researchers have applied more objective research methods to testing some of the basic claims of CMT. In a recent study, Katz and Taylor (2008) used a set of recall procedures adapted from memory research to test some implications of the conceptual metaphor LIFE IS A JOURNEY, discussed by Lakoff and Johnson (1980) and several others since. In the first experiment they asked students to list life events that would be expected to have happened to a typical 70-year-old man or woman. Most of the events produced were transitional content or events, and for the events identified by several participants, there was a high degree of agreement about the age at which it would be likely to occur. Moreover, the order in which events were named was strongly correlated with the age at which they were expected to occur. These results are consistent with the claim that participants use the metaphor LIFE IS A JOURNEY to organize their knowledge about life events. (These results are also consistent with the more general LIFE IS A SEQUENCE OF EVENTS, which is not necessarily metaphorical.)

In another study Katz and Taylor (2008) asked a separate group of participants to sort phrases representing forty of the life events identified in the first study into groups that go together. Katz and Taylor produced a similarity matrix from the resulting sorts and used cluster analysis to identify thematically related groups. Re-examining the output data from the first study, they discovered that events within each thematic group were recalled in the order in which they would be expected to occur, which is also consistent with the JOURNEY metaphor. These results also support the claim that a higher-level JOURNEY metaphor is transferred to lower-level conceptual domains, producing metaphors like LOVE IS A JOURNEY, A CAREER IS A JOURNEY, and PARENTING IS A JOURNEY, although the results are also consistent with other SEQUENCE metaphors and with a general concept of SEQUENCE.

Conceptual metaphors in actual discourse

Many examples of conceptual metaphors are also evident in the other discourse samples described in earlier chapters. In her online essay about the grieving process, grief counselor Pat Obst (2003) describes *grief* as a JOURNEY; the participants in a discussion of homelessness also described homelessness, life, and a conversation as a JOURNEY (Ritchie, 2011b). Obst also uses metaphors such as GRIEF IS A WOUND (*"recovering from our wounds"*) and a STRUCTURE metaphor for accomplishing our objectives (*"support* from others"). In Tony Blair's 2005 speech we encounter ACCOMPLISHMENT IS MOTION and BETTER IS IN FRONT (*"back* with the Tories" from the Labour Party slogan) and at least one variation on ARGUMENT IS WAR, in the *"marital spat"* metaphor for Blair's disagreements with Labour Party regulars and some members of the voting public.

Early in Obama's speech we encounter "The document they *produced … was stained by … slavery, a question that divided the colonies and brought the convention to a stalemate.*" "*Produced*" (along with "*decision-making*") is based on INTELLECTUAL WORK IS MANUFACTURE; "*stained by*" is based on IMMORALITY IS DIRT. "*Divided the colonies*" is based on AGREEMENT IS BEING ONE ENTITY; "*brought the convention to a stalemate*" is based on ACCOMPLISHMENT IS A JOURNEY and ARGUMENT IS A GAME OF CHESS, which is also related to ARGUMENT IS WAR (Ritchie 2003b; Vervaeke and Kennedy, 1996).

CRITICISMS OF CMT

Conceptual metaphor theory has been criticized on several grounds. One objection is based on Lakoff and Johnson's assumption that conceptual metaphors represent unitary and consistent mappings between concepts and direct experiences. Contrary to this claim, the underlying mappings often seem to be ambiguous, and may be interpreted differently by different people, based on their own unique experiences. The underlying mappings may also change over time, as familiar metaphors are reinterpreted in the light of new cultural experiences.

I have frequently asked groups, including students in various classes, to write down, then explain, the metaphor introduced in the *thought experiment* box a few pages back. Consistently, roughly half spell it 'toe the line,' and half spell it 'tow the line.' Of those who spell it 'toe the line,' somewhat more than half understand it in terms of a military or other disciplined unit lining up in formation, as for an inspection (with their toes touching an imaginary line on the drill field), and somewhat fewer understand it in terms of athletes preparing for a foot-race (with their toes behind the starting line). Either way, people who 'toe the line' can be said to *comply with the rules*. Those who spell it 'tow the line' are divided about evenly between a *tugboat* (or other vehicular) explanation and a game of 'tug-o-war'; either way people who 'tow the line' can be said to *do their share*. It seems reasonable to conclude that, on any occasion when this familiar idiom is used, speakers and listeners are likely to understand it in terms of very different conceptual metaphors. The entailments are similar, although 'toe' implies *passive* compliance and 'tow' implies *active* compliance. When we encounter this expression in conversation it is usually impossible to know how others actually understand it, although this ambiguity probably does not seriously impair our ability to understand one another.

Vervaeke and Kennedy (1996) make a similar point in their critique of Lakoff and Johnson's extended discussion of ARGUMENT IS WAR. Vervaeke and Kennedy point out that many of the verbal metaphors produced by Lakoff and Johnson to support their case ('*win* or *lose* an argument,' '*defend* a *position*,' '*attack* the *opponent*') can equally well be understood in terms of an unbounded set of alternative vehicles, such as ARGUMENT IS FOOTBALL or ARGUMENT IS BRIDGE. A related difficulty arises with respect to the claim that conceptual metaphors connect topic with vehicle in a unique conceptual metaphor, so that LIFE IS A JOURNEY and LOVE IS A JOURNEY are independent conceptual metaphors.

The idea of conceptual metaphors might usefully be recast in terms of *generic metaphors* (Tourangeau and Rips, 1991; see Chapter 2), connected in multi-dimensioned '*fields of meaning*' (Ritchie, 2003b). To continue with the WAR example, many forms of conflict, competition, and disagreement are used as metaphor vehicles. ARGUMENT IS WAR generalizes to X IS WAR, and links with X IS A GAME, X IS ATHLETIC COMPETITION, X IS A DEBATE, and so on in a field of meaning related to disagreement and conflict. Within this general field of meaning we can have, for example, BUSINESS IS WAR (*'bidding war,' 'invade a competitor's markets'*) but also WAR IS BUSINESS (*'an unprofitable attack'*; see Ritchie, 2003b; 2006). We also have ARGUMENT IS SPORTS '*score one* for you,' BUSINESS IS WAR (*'invade* a competitor's *territory'*), WAR IS BUSINESS, BUSINESS IS SPORTS, and so on. Each of these vehicles can be applied to many topics, for example to *love*, as in '*laid siege* to her heart,' '*win* her hand,' '*sexual conquest*' and 'didn't *get to first base*'.

The JOURNEY vehicle also serves as a generic metaphor. Experiences of purposive movement through space, including extended journeys, are very common, and they are linked together by many common elements, which collectively form the basis for a generic metaphor, X IS A JOURNEY. X IS A JOURNEY can be applied to *any* topic that shares some of these elements, thus producing, for example, SOLVING A PROBLEM IN GEOMETRY IS A JOURNEY (*'a turning point in the proof'*) or GRIEF IS A JOURNEY (Obst, 2003). These generic metaphors are in turn linked with each other, so in addition to X IS A JOURNEY we have X IS A PATH ('I don't *see where this is leading us*') and X IS A VEHICLE ('that argument doesn't *carry much weight*' or 'won't *get you very far*'), all drawing on an interconnected set of commonplace experiences, and each capable of expressing a different nuance of experience.

Yet another difficulty with CMT arises from Lakoff and Johnson's claim that conceptual metaphors are acquired either directly through correlations in experience, or by combining directly acquired metaphors. Landauer and Dumais (1997) point out that, at least in literate societies, the majority of any individual's vocabulary is learned through reading. Landauer and Dumais further show that many aspects of language comprehension can be at least partially accounted for by relationships among words, independent of word definitions. Kintsch (2008) has shown that at least some metaphors can be reliably interpreted by analyzing their semantic connections alone.

Metaphors based on vehicles that either exist only in myth or are impossible to experience directly would, in particular, seem to be based on relationships among words rather than on direct experience. Examples of metaphors based on myth include 'she's a *dragon*,' 'a *ghost* of a chance,' and 'a *snowball's chance in Hell.*' Metaphor vehicles that cannot possibly be directly experienced include 'I'll love you *until the end of time*' and 'my desk is *a black hole.*'

It also seems likely that many metaphor vehicles that may eventually be personally experienced are *first* encountered through secondary sources such as literature or mass media. At least in the United States and Europe, most children first learn about war through accounts in stories, movies, and history lessons, and very likely understand metaphors based on WAR through the semantic connections acquired through these indirect sources (Ritchie, 2003b; 2006; Howe, 2008). "*Ivory tower*" refers to a non-existent object, and it is almost certainly acquired initially through semantic connections. However, like '*bulldozer*' and '*dragon*,' "*ivory tower*" may nonetheless activate very powerful perceptual images.

Several critics have objected to Lakoff and Johnson's discussion of conceptual metaphors, ARGUMENT IS WAR in particular, on the grounds that they actually identify metonyms rather than metaphor (e.g. Vervaeke and Kennedy, 1996; Howe, 2008). Although it is not clear from their discussion, it seems fair to infer that Lakoff and Johnson intend WAR as a catch-all category for all levels of physical conflict. Lakoff and Johnson concede that interactions we call *arguments* range from abstract intellectual debates to angry exchanges that threaten at any time to end in a fist-fight or even use of weapons (and sometimes do, especially if alcohol is involved). At least in the United States, *argument* is probably used more frequently in reference to *conflict* than to *intellectual debate*. Indeed, I often have difficulty getting students to understand what I mean when I instruct them that their papers should "develop an argument."

Conversely, on more than one occasion an intellectual or political debate at an academic conference – or in a legislative chamber – has led to violence or near violence. At the extreme, in the United States the "argument" about slavery provoked physical brawls on the floor of the Senate and eventually ended in a very long and bloody civil war. Sometimes argument *is* war. Thus, as Lakoff and Johnson themselves pointed out (1980), in many instances ARGUMENT IS WAR can reasonably be classified as a metonym. Even if ARGUMENT IS WAR did not originate in an embodied experience of actual war (Howe, 2008; Ritchie, 2003b), it may have its origins in childhood experiences of disagreements that include physical violence.

Lakoff and Johnson's (1980) explanation for the origins of the most common basic level metaphors in embodied experience also suggests that metaphors like BEING UPRIGHT IS BEING WELL, MORE IS UP, PHYSICAL PROXIMITY IS AFFECTION, and WARMTH IS AFFECTION begin as metonyms. Students in my metaphor classes have also pointed out that SOCIAL REJECTION IS COLD/SOCIAL ACCEPTANCE IS WARM are at least sometimes metonymic, since the emotions associated with these experiences often involve physiological changes that may lead to changes in experienced physical temperature.

Conceptual metaphor theory is often criticized on logical grounds. From their discussion it appears that Lakoff and Johnson begin with the observations that metaphors are often found in thematically related groups, and from this they deduce the existence of underlying general metaphors. Common metaphors related to love include '*dead-end* relationship,' 'this relationship *isn't getting me anywhere*,' '*turning point*,' '*cross-roads*,' '*moving too fast*,' providing evidence for an underlying metaphor, LOVE IS A JOURNEY. Similar groups of metaphors are easily found for many other general topics, providing evidence for the claim that conceptual thought is based on metaphors. According to this line of criticism, if this is a literal claim, it appears to contradict itself (I am indebted for this insight to an anonymous reviewer).

Defenders of CMT may point out that the appearance of contradiction is based on a misunderstanding of CMT. Lakoff and Johnson (1980) do not claim that *linguistic* metaphors such as '*dead-end* relationship' or the underlying generalized metaphors such as LOVE IS A JOURNEY are the basis for thought. Rather, they claim that abstract concepts are formed from associations in perceptual experience, and these abstract concepts provide the basis both for abstract thought and for linguistic metaphors. Thus, linguistic metaphors like '*dead-end* relationship' provide evidence for the underlying conceptual metaphor, LOVE IS A JOURNEY, and groups of thematically related linguistic metaphors can be used as a tool to detect underlying conceptual metaphors, but the underlying conceptual metaphors are not based on the linguistic metaphors. The confusion probably derives from Lakoff and Johnson's decision to use *metaphor*, a term commonly understood as denoting a relationship between words or phrases, to designate a *conceptual* relationship between abstract concepts and perceptual and motor experiences.

A more fundamental objection to CMT is that it is built entirely on what may be little more than coincidences in language use, with no evidence to test or confirm that people actually experience the stipulated connections between experiences and concepts. However, in the thirty years since publication of *Metaphors We Live By*, researchers have built up evidence using several experimental designs that supports many of the claims of CMT. In Chapter 5 I will describe a theory of cognition, perceptual simulation theory, that provides a more detailed explanation of how conceptual metaphors might be processed in the brain, and then review experimental evidence that tests and seems to support many of the claims of conceptual metaphor theory and perceptual simulation theory.

DISCUSSION

To what extent are people's responses influenced by conceptual metaphors? Does this influence depend on whether or not they are aware that a phrase is metaphorical?

When multiple conceptual metaphors are potentially relevant (as in '*tow the line*' vs. '*toe the line*'), what determines which are activated? How does ambiguity affect the common ground among participants in a communicative event? Does it matter if one person thinks '*tow*' and the other thinks '*toe*'?

Lakoff and Johnson's approach – CMT – implies that many prepositions are fundamentally metaphorical. Do people experience *love* as a container when they speak of '*being in love*'? Does thinking of LOVE IS A CONTAINER add anything to our understanding of the experience?

How does '*falling in love*' fit with other metaphors based on UP/DOWN, such as UP IS GOOD and UP IS HEALTHY?

How do the many variations on '*heartbreak*' fit with CMT? Can these metaphors be explained as well by other metaphor theories we have discussed as by CMT?

SUGGESTED READINGS

- Lakoff, G., and Johnson, M. (1980). *Metaphors we live by*. University of Chicago Press. This deceptively simple book has been very influential in metaphor theory. Lakoff and Johnson's thinking has progressed and CMT has become somewhat more complex, but this book is still a recommended starting place – and it is very easy to read.
- Sharifian, F., Dirven, R., Yu, N., and Neiemier, S. (eds.) (2008). *Culture, body, and language: Conceptualizations of internal body organs across cultures and languages*. New York: Mouton De Gruyter. This is one of many recent volumes exploring the conceptual underpinnings of emotion metaphors.

Critiques of CMT

- Howe, J. (2008). Argument is argument: An essay on conceptual metaphor and verbal dispute. *Metaphor and Symbol, 23*, 1–23.
- Müller, C. (2008). *Metaphors dead and alive, sleeping and waking: A dynamic view.* University of Chicago Press.
- Ritchie, L. D. (2003b). "ARGUMENT IS WAR" – Or is it a game of chess? Multiple meanings in the analysis of implicit metaphors. *Metaphor and Symbol, 18*, 125–146.
- Vervaeke, J., and Kennedy, J. M. (1996). Metaphors in language and thought: Falsification and multiple meanings. *Metaphor and Symbolic Activity, 11*(4), 273–284.

5   Perceptual simulation

Romney's vulture capitalist problem.
(*Forbes* online headline, January 12, 2012)

Lakoff and Johnson (1980; 1999) claim that most concepts are fundamentally metaphorical, and that most verbal metaphors are expressions of underlying conceptual metaphors. According to CMT, '*rising* prices' expresses the underlying conceptual metaphor MORE IS UP and '*high* status' expresses the underlying metaphor IMPORTANT IS UP. Based on these assertions, Lakoff and Johnson claim that speaker and hearer actually experience both the price of a more expensive item and the position of a more prestigious person as *physically higher* in relation to a less expensive item or less prestigious person. Similarly, they claim that 'a *dead-end* relationship' expresses the underlying conceptual metaphor LOVE IS A JOURNEY, and speaker and hearer will experience the current state of the relationship in terms of *impeded physical motion*. According to CMT, basic conceptual metaphors are often combined to form compound metaphors. Thus, "*vulture* capitalism" is based on a combination of underlying metaphors that might be characterized as something like AN ENTERPRISE IS A LIVING ORGANISM, FAILURE IS DYING, and PROFITING FROM THE FAILURE OF OTHERS IS FEEDING ON CARRION.

A frequent criticism of CMT is that it remains unclear exactly what it means to experience an abstract concept as a physical entity; for example to experience *an enterprise* as *an organism* or to experience *price*, *social status*, or *an unsatisfying relationship* as physical states or motion in physical space. In this chapter I will discuss another theoretical approach, perceptual simulation theory, that helps to explain how we might experience an abstract concept (a metaphor topic) as a physical sensation related to a metaphor vehicle. I will also discuss some of the experimental evidence that supports both conceptual metaphor theory and perceptual simulation theory. At the end of the chapter I will propose an account of metaphor processing and understanding that integrates these ideas with several ideas from previous chapters.

PERCEPTUAL SIMULATION

Gibbs (2006) argues that language interpretation involves embodied simulation, the active "construction of a simulation whereby we imagine performing the bodily actions referred to in the language" (p. 434). Thus, when a friend describes a recent basketball game, we understand the story by partial activation of the neuron groups that would become activated if we were either to witness or perform the described actions. We may also experience partial activation of the neuron groups that would become activated while actually experiencing the thoughts and emotions of the players, the disappointment of a missed basket or the elation of a completed basket. Applied to metaphors, this proposal helps to fill in and extend the basic insights of CMT, by defining what it means to experience the topic *as* the vehicle, to experience *love* as a *journey* or to experience *affection* as *proximity* or *warmth*. According to the simulation account, each of these metaphors activates partial simulations of the perceptions associated with the vehicle, which then become part of the meaning of the topic.

Barsalou (1999; 2008) provides a more detailed explanation of how perceptual simulation contributes to cognition generally, and to language processing in particular. He begins with the perceptual neural system, which includes all of the "five senses" (sight, hearing, smell, taste, and touch) as well as *interoception* (awareness of one's own body states, such as hunger or tiredness) and *introspection* (awareness of one's own thought processes, such as disagreeing with something, trying to recall something, or questioning an assertion). He argues that a *conceptual* neural system parallels and interacts with the perceptual neural system. In the conceptual neural system, concepts are represented by the partial simulation of associated perception. Barsalou claims that conceptual thought is accomplished by means of these partial simulations. In this section I will begin with a brief overview of the perceptual neural system, then discuss how the conceptual neural system interacts with the perceptual neural system, and finally discuss how the perceptual simulation process might help to explain how we understand metaphors.

To begin with the example of visual perception, the retina is made up of a dense layer of photoreceptor cells. When a cat crosses one's field of vision, photons of light reflecting off the cat are transmitted through the lens of the eye and projected onto the retina, where they strike the layer of photoreceptor cells, which vary in sensitivity to wavelength and to intensity. When a sufficient number of photons of a certain wavelength strike a particular photoreceptor cell, the cell "*fires*"; that is, it emits an electrochemical pulse that is transmitted to neurons behind the retina. Each of these neurons receives and reacts to pulses from thousands of retinal cells, aggregating and transmitting information about the pattern of light and dark to other sets of neurons, which further aggregate and transfer the information, and so on. Information from the retinal cells is processed and transmitted in parallel through separate channels that detect features such as edges (the outline of the cat), masses (its size), colors, textures (its fur and eyes), and motion. These patterns of shape, motion, color, and so on are aggregated and eventually recombined as representations of objects in action (the lowest level at which we are aware of them).

There are still higher levels of processing and aggregation as the image is identified by comparing it with elements of schemas from our long-term memory (a general set of shapes, colors, textures, and motions we have learned to associate with *cat*). We may be somewhat aware of this process of comparison and identification, but it mostly happens automatically and below the threshold of conscious attention. I may be conscious of trying to recognize a familiar face in a crowd, but if it is a close friend the recognition will be instant and automatic. If I see an unfamiliar animal, I may be aware of comparing its features with various animal schemas, but if the object is a cat or other familiar animal I am likely to recognize it unconsciously and instantaneously.

Each sense functions in the same way: the activation or "*firing*" of individual sensory neurons is aggregated at ever higher levels of abstraction to produce composite sensations such as a sound, which is experienced as a unity of loudness, duration, and tone, or a taste, which is experienced as a unity of salt, sweet, bitter, sour, and intense. These composite sensations are compared with schemas in memory and identified, a process that often includes activation of associated words.

According to Barsalou, the conceptual neural system parallels the perceptual system at least down to the level of shapes and colors (in vision) and loudness, duration, and tone (in sound). When one thinks of a concept, neural groups associated with perceptual features of the concept are partially activated, and experienced as a *simulation* of the objects and events associated with the concept. For example, the concept *cat* might be represented and experienced as a combination of shapes, movements, sounds, and tactile perceptions associated with cats. The concept *hammer* might be represented and experienced in terms of the shape of a typical hammer, the sound of a hammer striking metal, the heft of a hammer in one's hand, and so on.

Because of memory constraints, activation of perceptual simulations is never complete. Thinking about *zebra* is likely to activate a simulation of black and white stripes, but not in sufficient detail that we could count the stripes. Moreover, the simulations that are activated are likely to be influenced by the context in which the concept is encountered. During the preceding discussion, it is unlikely that the reader has experienced a perceptual simulation of a cat stalking a bird or flexing its claws, even though these actions are part of most people's *cat* schema, and were readily activated by processing this sentence.

The conceptual neural system also embraces and parallels neural systems for motor control, interoception (perception of internal bodily states), and introspection (perception of thoughts and thought processes). To continue with the example of *hammer*, depending on the context one might experience a simulation or partial activation of the muscle movements required to grasp and use a hammer, the interoceptive awareness of the effect of holding and using a hammer on the sense of balance, and introspective awareness of thought processes such as lining up boards that are to be hammered. In the case of *cat*, in addition to the typical shape, sounds, and tactile perceptions associated with cats one might experience a partial simulation of the weight of a cat on one's lap or of concern about a friend who is allergic to cat hair. Barsalou suggests that the *conceptual* neural system parallels the *perceptual* neural system at every level, and that thinking, including language processing, is primarily accomplished by way of the simulations generated by this conceptual neural system.

The interaction of the perceptual neural system with the conceptual neural system is illustrated for visual perceptions in Figure 5.1. Perceptions are filtered, combined, and abstracted into objects, actions, and events at ever higher levels of processing in the perceptual neural system, ultimately activating schemas and associated language. Conversely, in the conceptual neural system, words and phrases activate conceptual schemas and the conceptual schemas activate neuron groups (*simulators*) that partially simulate the perceptual features associated with the concept. These simulations are compared with perceptual features in the perceptual neural system during the identification of objects, and subsequently may fill in vague or ambiguous features.

The interaction of the conceptual and perceptual neural systems is why, when we are faced with an ambiguous stimulus such as a poorly heard sound or a poorly seen object, it may seem indistinct until we have identified it, then will often seem to "come into focus." Once we have identified it, the features seem to become more distinct and

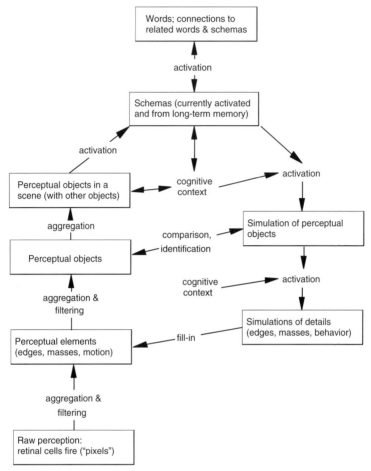

Figure 5.1 Perceptual neural system and conceptual neural system (vision)

definite because they are being filled in by simulations from the conceptual neural system.

According to Barsalou (1999), the conceptual neural system parallels and interacts with the perceptual neural system at every level. The perceptual neural system includes interoception and introspection, and the conceptual neural system also includes parallel neuron groups that simulate or partially activate interoception and introspection. Conceptual thought is accomplished by way of these perceptual simulations, partial activation of neuron groups that are associated with and simulate the actual perceptions of sensory information, thoughts, emotions, and bodily states.

The conceptual neural system is capable of producing a wide range of simulations associated with any concept, but in any particular situation, because of limitations in our active working memory, only a limited subset of potential simulations will actually be experienced. A simulation can be thought of as a kind of fragmentary imagining, and simulation plays a role in imagination. When thinking about *cat*, one might experience no more than an abstract simulation of shape or, depending on the context, one might experience the texture and color of the animal's fur, its motion, or the feeling of a cat's weight and its claws flexing into one's thigh.

To consider another example, the concept of *cave* might in one context or situation produce a very limited partial simulation of the visual perception of darkness and the tactile perceptions of coolness and dampness, perhaps accompanied by emotional perceptions of claustrophobia. In a different context, *cave* might be experienced as a more complete simulation of a dark, cool, slightly damp place, with the associated simulations of subdued echoes and emotional responses related to mystery as well as claustrophobia. In yet another context *cave* might be experienced as an apparently quite detailed simulation of a large, open place dimly lighted by electric lamps, with stalactites, the sound of dripping water, muffled voices, and echoes, a musty smell, and the muscular movements involved in crawling through a small opening in the cave. The social category, *my wife*, might be experienced as a simulation of quiet conversation or a candle-lit dinner on one occasion, on another occasion might be experienced as a simulation of love-making, and on yet another occasion might be experienced as a simulation of holding hands while walking in the park (Niedenthal *et al.*, 2005), or merely as a simulation of her voice and some of her facial features.

Language constitutes a powerful system for activating simulations and, conversely, both direct perception and simulations can activate language. Once we have identified a familiar kind of object, it can be difficult to suppress its name. Simulations interact with perception at every level; as noted before, simulations may be compared with perceptual features as part of the process of recognition and identification, and simulations may fill in missing features of a perceived object. If a wild animal is partially seen in the woods and tentatively identified as a deer or elk, simulations may fill in details including body shape, antlers, and so on. Sometimes it can be very difficult to distinguish the information provided directly by our senses from the information filled in by perceptual simulation from our stored schemas. The processes of recognition and filling-in are far from reliable, as is attested by countless accidents every autumn. All too frequently, a hunter becomes convinced that an object is a deer, actually *sees* the object as a deer, and shoots at it – but it turns out to be another hunter, or a cow, or even a child waiting at a school-bus stop.

In Barsalou's earlier work (e.g. 1999), perceptual simulation theory was presented as an *alternative* to more conventional computation theories, which are based entirely on the manipulation of abstract symbols. In computational theories of language (see Chapter 1), words and phrases are translated into abstract mental symbols associated with other abstract mental symbols by a process analogous to looking words up in a kind of mental dictionary and the meanings of sentence are determined by computational processes on these abstract symbols.

In more recent work, Barsalou (2007) has developed a more comprehensive theory, Language and Situated Simulation (LASS), that combines perceptual simulations with more conventional computational theories. According to LASS, when language is encountered connections with other words and phrases are activated, along with propositional knowledge about the underlying concepts. At the same time, associated perceptual simulations may also be activated. For simpler tasks, the superficial processing by means of the propositional knowledge linked to words and phrases may be sufficient, and the deeper conceptual processing in which perceptual simulations become activated may not be required. This may help to explain findings, reported by researchers such as Kintsch (1998; 2008), that computer programs based on word–word association matrices perform at levels comparable to human agents on multiple-choice vocabulary tests, grading student essays, and many other cognitively superficial language tasks.

It is also likely that words vary in the degree to which they activate perceptual simulations. As Landauer and Dumais (1997) point out, many words are encountered first, and often only, in reading and may not be grounded at all in embodied experience. Abstract or rarely encountered words are unlikely to activate many perceptual simulations if they activate any at all. For most people, conceptual terms like *abstract* and *cognitive* are unlikely to activate perceptual simulations, and are understood primarily in terms of their connections with other words, including formal definitions and explanations. On the other hand, a mythical entity like *dragon* may come to be associated with real entities like *lizard*, so that perceptual simulations associated with actual *lizards* become attached to the mythical *dragon*. In general, cultural depictions (e.g. in drawings and movies) are likely to have provided the primary basis for the perceptual simulations associated with such commonplace mythical entities as dragons and fairies.

When a word or phrase activates other words that are closely associated in semantic memory, these may in turn activate perceptual simulations *in addition to* those activated by the initial word or phrase (Barsalou, 2007). For me, "*swimming in* money," from the scientists' conversation, activates simulations directly associated with swimming in water and with holding a handful of coins – along with a visual simulation, recalled from childhood comic books, of 'Unca' Scrooge' in his money bin. The link to Disney Comics also activates even more remote simulations drawn from childhood memories of reading Disney Comics on a hot Saturday afternoon.

In some circumstances, these secondary contextual memories may contribute to the cognitive effects (the relevance) of the original word or phrase. "*Swimming in* money" also activates links to other words and phrases such as *wealthy*, which in turn activate perceptual simulations of activities such as making purchases with a credit card. Depending on the requirements of the task and the cognitive resources available, the semantic connection and perceptual simulation systems may operate independently or may interact in complex ways.

Simulation and metaphors

Combining Gibbs' (2006) insights with Barsalou's (2008) more completely specified model of simulation, it seems likely that a metaphor may activate perceptual simulations along with semantically and experientially related words and phrases. When any word or phrase, including a metaphorical word or phrase, is encountered, the words and simulations that are not relevant in the present context (Sperber and Wilson, [1986] 1995), that cannot be readily connected with ideas already activated in working memory, may not be activated in the first place. If they are activated, they are likely to be reduced in activation and may be suppressed altogether. Those words and simulations that are relevant in the present context will become more highly activated (Gernsbacher *et al.*, 2001; Kintsch, 1998), and will produce context-relevant simulations that will attach to the topic as part of the meaning in this context, producing the changes to cognitive context described by Sperber and Wilson ([1986] 1995; see Chapter 3) as *relevance*.

Perceptual simulation theory, and the more current version, LASS, supplement conceptual metaphor theory in several ways. In the example of '*toe / tow the line*,' discussed in Chapter 4, speaker and

different hearers may experience quite different visual and interoceptive simulations. Some may experience a simulation of athletes or
soldiers lining up behind a line and others may experience a tugboat
towing a barge. However, these differences may not seriously interfere
with the communicative interchange if speaker and hearers experience similar *introspective* simulations of acquiescence and conformity.
The immediate simulation of a soldier or tugboat is secondary to the
introspective simulation of compliance. Consistent with Wilson and
Sperber (2004), it may not even be important to decide whether a word
or phrase is experienced as a metaphor. More important questions may
be whether and to what degree a hearer or reader experiences simulations in response to the word or phrase, what simulations are most
likely to become activated, and how they are relevant to the topic.

Along with CMT, perceptual simulation theory and its successor,
LASS, resolve the circularity issue by providing mechanisms to explain
how a conceptual category can be broadened sufficiently to include a
totally unrelated phenomenon. The broadening occurs, primarily or
entirely, within the associations, the "non-propositional effects" such
as the striking images and "qualitative states of mind" mentioned
by Carston (2002, p. 356). In fact, it may be precisely these "non-
propositional effects" that account for much of metaphor use and
understanding and provide the basis for the versatility and expressive
power of metaphors. On the other hand, conceptual metaphor theory
provides at least part of the explanation of how concepts in extremely
different domains of experience, such as love and body temperature
or physical proximity, come to be linked together by common "non-
propositional effects" that include introspective thoughts, emotional
responses, and subtle aspects of sensory perceptions.

EVIDENCE

Evidence in support of perceptual simulation theory has been accumulating for at least two decades, drawing on a variety of research
approaches. In this section I will review just a handful of recent studies. None of these on its own is conclusive, but in my view the accumulating weight of evidence is fairly convincing. (For a contrary view
see Shapiro, 2010.)

Interference and facilitation

Participants were asked to perform physical actions such as forming a
fist or moving a lever toward the body while evaluating sentences as

meaningful or not. When the sentences described unrelated actions, such as *aim a dart*, they took more time to verify the sentence than when the sentences described related actions (Klatsky *et al.*, 1989). When subjects were asked to rotate a knob in a clockwise direction, they were slower to verify as meaningful statements like *Eric turned down the volume*, which implies a counter-clockwise motion (Zwaan and Taylor, 2006).

Wilson and Gibbs (2007) asked people to perform either a relevant action (grasp an object) or an irrelevant action (kick an object) and then asked them to assess whether a phrase (either metaphorical or literal) was meaningful or not. Response time was significantly faster when a relevant action (grasp an object) preceded a metaphor ('*grasp the concept*') than when the metaphor was preceded by an irrelevant action (kick an object), or when it was preceded by no action at all. (A subsequent study ruled out the possibility that grasping the object primed the word in semantic memory.) A second study merely asked subjects to imagine performing the relevant or irrelevant action, and produced similar results. These experiments suggest that the literal meaning may facilitate understanding the metaphorical meaning by priming the simulation of the actions or perceptions associated with the vehicle (Gibbs, 2006; Gibbs and Matlock, 2008; see also Giora, 2003).

Consistent with the conceptual metaphors, SOCIAL STATUS IS UP and EQUALITY IS PHYSICAL PROXIMITY, Schubert, Waldzus, and Seibt (2008) describe several studies supporting the claim that people actually experience differences in social status and power as differences in height and elevation, and experience social affiliation as physical proximity. In one test, Schubert and Waldzus (unpublished data reported in Schubert, Waldzus, and Seibt, 2008) presented pairs of words such as teacher/student and boss/employee in different font sizes (42 point vs. 12 point). Half the participants were asked to identify which group had the most power and the other half were asked to identify which group had the least power. Participants made significantly more errors when the more powerful group label was printed in smaller font and the less powerful group label was printed in larger font.

Using a different manipulation, Schubert (2005, discussed in Schubert, Waldzus, and Seibt, 2008) presented the powerful or powerless group labels either at the top of a computer screen or at the bottom, and participants were asked to press a key to indicate whether the presented group was typically powerful or powerless. In one condition, groups were presented individually; in another condition, they were presented in pairs. In either condition, the powerful group was identified significantly more quickly if presented at the top of the screen and the powerless group was identified significantly more quickly if presented at the bottom of the screen.

Embodiment of metaphorical concepts

'Next Wednesday's meeting has been moved forward two days.' Will the meeting take place on Monday or on Friday? People who have recently experienced forward motion (standing near the front of a long line at a café, or near the end of a long train ride) were more likely than people who had experienced less forward motion (in the back half of the line or just beginning a journey) to say that the meeting had been rescheduled to Friday (Boroditsky and Ramscar, 2002). In a separate experiment by Boroditsky and Ramscar, participants were shown a drawing of a chair with a rope attached. Some participants were asked to imagine pulling the chair toward themselves with the rope; others were asked to imagine sitting in the chair and using the rope to pull themselves along. Participants who imagined pulling the chair toward themselves were more likely to answer that the meeting was rescheduled for Monday, consistent with the idea that time is a moving object. Participants who imagined pulling themselves with the rope were more likely to answer Friday, consistent with the idea that time is a stationary object toward which we move (Gibbs, 2006; Gibbs and Matlock, 2008).

In another series of studies, participants read one of four stories about a new relationship. Two stories included a single metaphorical sentence in the middle; for example 'your relationship was *moving along in a good direction.*' This was followed by four sentences describing the relationship as either improving or deteriorating. A matching pair of stories included no metaphorical sentences. In one experiment in this series, after reading the story each participant was shown a ball that was forty feet away, then blindfolded and asked to walk to the ball. In the metaphor conditions, participants who read about the successful relationship walked for significantly more time (15.7 seconds vs. 12.8 seconds) and covered more distance (2.4 feet beyond the ball vs. 2.3 feet short of the ball). In the non-metaphorical condition, the differences between successful and non-successful relationship stories were very small and not statistically significant. In a replication, participants were blindfolded, handed a stopwatch, and asked to imagine walking to the ball, then click the stopwatch when they reached the ball. The results were very similar to those when the participants were actually asked to walk to the ball. These results support the interpretation that people experience a simulation of physical movement when they process a movement metaphor (Gibbs, 2006; Gibbs and Matlock, 2008).

Zhong and Liljenquist (2006) note that people use terms related to physical cleanliness ('a *clean* record,' 'a *stain* on his reputation') to describe moral transgressions. After asking people to recall past misdeeds, they found that people experience a need to cleanse themselves physically.

Zhong and Leonardelli (2008) report on three experiments testing the relationship between emotional evaluations and responses and temperature. In one study, conducted by Williams and Bargh (2008), people were asked to hold a hot or cold beverage container temporarily, and then fill out a trait assessment questionnaire for a randomly chosen person. Those who held the hot beverage container rated the target person as being warmer and friendlier than those who held the cold beverage container.

Zhong and Leonardelli (2008) conducted two experiments to test whether being socially included or excluded would affect people's judgments about the ambient temperature. In the first study, participants were asked to recall a situation in which they felt either included or excluded by others. Afterwards, participants were asked to estimate the temperature in the lab, after being informed that the maintenance staff had requested this information. Participants who recalled exclusion estimated the temperature to be significantly lower than those who recalled social inclusion (mean temperature 21.4 vs. 24.0 degrees C).

In a second study, participants engaged in a computer game that involved tossing a virtual ball around with three other online participants. The game was actually controlled by a computer program that either included the participants randomly throughout the game or included the participants for two throws and then excluded them for the entire remainder of the game. Afterward, participants were invited to participate in a supposedly unrelated market survey and rate the desirability of five products on a scale from 1 = extremely undesirable to 7 = extremely desirable. One product was hot coffee, another hot soup, and the other three were neutral control products (apple, crackers, and cola). Participants who had been excluded during the game rated warm food and drinks significantly more highly than those in the inclusion condition (M = 5.17 vs. M = 4.33), but there was no significant difference between ratings of the neutral products. The results of these experiments suggest that people who either experience social exclusion or recall an experience of exclusion feel colder and compensate by seeking warmth.

PULLING THE THREADS TOGETHER: A COGNITIVE
ACCOUNT OF METAPHOR

Wilson and Sperber (2004) claim that all language, and by extension all communicative action, is processed in roughly the same way. (One implication of this claim is that it may not be very important to determine whether a given unit of language satisfies the definition of a metaphor.) When a unit of language is encountered (a word, phrase, or highly conventionalized gesture), the lexical or conventional meanings, including idiomatic meanings for conventional metaphors, are at least partially activated. These include semantic connections to related words and phrases, including those that would be considered part of the word's definition as well as "encyclopedic" knowledge related to the word or phrase. Depending on the situation and the amount of attention the hearer is investing, related schemas may be partially or fully activated and experienced as simulations of associated sensations, motor actions, emotions, and so on.

Given the limitations of human cognitive capacity, only a small subset of the potential array of semantic connections, encyclopedic knowledge, schemas, and perceptual simulations will become activated. This process is subject in part to relative salience, influenced for example by the priming effects of the cognitive context, including other words and ideas currently active in working memory. It is also largely subject to active processes of relevance seeking. The search for relevance begins with attempting to connect the schemas and semantic knowledge immediately activated by a phrase with the most salient cognitive context that is currently activated. If the fit is good and yields sufficient changes to the cognitive context, that may be the end of it. If not, the search for relevance continues both by searching for other, less salient cognitive contexts that might provide a better fit, and by adjusting the schemas activated by the phrase – broadening and narrowing – until either a good fit (relevance) is achieved or the effort comes to seem disproportionate to any expected effects.

In processing metaphors and other figurative language, such as wordplay and irony, the semantic links may be less relevant than the perceptual simulations activated by a word or phrase. In the extreme, the semantic links associated with the "literal" meaning of words and phrases may be uninterpretable and meaningless, and accordingly be suppressed, leaving only the more abstract schemas and simulations indirectly associated with the target. "*Swimming in* money" (from the scientists' conversation) provides an example in which the definitional semantic links do not connect either with the linguistic context of the overall utterance or with the expanded context of the conversation: only the schemas associated with conventional metaphorical phrases that take the form "*Swimming in X*" provide opportunities for relevance. The same applies to many of the stock examples in the metaphor theory literature, such as 'my lawyer is *a shark*' and 'Sally is *a block of ice*.' In some cases, as Carston (2002) notes with '*bulldozer*,' the semantic links and perceptual simulations associated with the literal or customary uses of the metaphor vehicle may remain activated, often because they are amusing.

When "*ivory tower*" (from the scientists' conversation) is encountered, both words, *ivory* and *tower*, may activate limited networks of semantic association, but these are not likely to be very detailed. *Ivory* may activate knowledge of the color and texture of the substance, of its rarity and market value, and perhaps of its symbolic association with *purity*, but knowledge about its origins (e.g. in elephant tusks) or about the criminal trade in poached ivory is unlikely to be activated. For those familiar with the idiom, the entire phrase, *ivory tower*, may be processed as a unit, and may activate additional semantic links, including links to words and phrases such as *impractical* and *academic* as well as links to emotional responses of various sorts. How many semantic links and perceptual simulations are activated will depend in part on the hearer's motivation to process the phrase. When one of the participants in the scientists' conversation started playing with and distorting the idiom, the number and range of active associations are likely to have expanded rapidly for all the participants.

I have already discussed the connection of relevance theory to Keysar and Glucksberg's (1992) work on ad hoc categories, which in my view is extended and filled in by relevance theory. It should also be apparent how the perceptual simulation theories discussed in this chapter extend and fill in the theories of comparison and attribute transfer, discussed in Chapter 2, by showing exactly what provides the basis for comparing vehicle to topic, and exactly what attributes are "*transferred*" from vehicle to topic. (Often it is the introspective simulations activated by the vehicle that are transferred and provide most of the meaning of the metaphor, as with metaphors like 'my job is *a jail*.') These earlier theories can largely be seen as limited and partial versions of the composite account I have proposed in this chapter.

Implications for metaphor production

To date, the bulk of metaphor research has focused on the comprehension rather than on the production of metaphors (Flor and Hadar,

2005). The account proposed in this chapter provides a potential avenue for explaining production as well as comprehension. Perceptual simulations can be activated by language and by language-based schemas, but they can also activate language-based schemas and related words and phrases. If words and phrases are selected for production based on the meanings (including perceptual simulations) they are expected to activate, then potential metaphor vehicles are likely to be activated along with other words and phrases.

Which word or phrase is actually selected for production will depend on the speaker's communicative intentions. Thus, when then-Senator Obama (and his speech writer) thought about the angry response to certain of Reverend Wright's statements, their own responses to these statements may have activated words like *heedless* and *controversial* along with feelings of *extreme heat*, which in turn activated schemas of large, destructive fires. These *destructive fire* schemas in turn activated words like *fire-storm* and *incendiary*. Because the metaphorical words expressed his own feelings and his understanding of others' feelings better than literal words (like *controversial*), Obama selected (or his speech writer selected and he retained) the metaphorical words.

When Prime Minister Blair thought about the quarrels within the Labour Party, his own response may have activated words like *self-defeating* and *petty*. His response may have included feelings of frustration, disaffection, and so on, which activated schemas of family quarrels and related scripts from television sitcoms. These schemas in turn activated a variety of stories with differing sets of perceptual simulations including emotional associations; the '*comedic quarrel between spouses*' activated the simulations that most closely approximated what he wished to express, and so was chosen.

This account should be easily adaptable to explain the selection of metaphors by poets, novelists, and even scientists on the one hand and by conversationalists on the other hand.

The extended context

Most metaphor research and theorizing to date has been based on metaphors presented either with no context at all or in a context that is limited to an immediate sentence (see also Campbell and Katz, 2006). Yet, as discussed with respect to the BULLDOZER and PRINCESS metaphor vehicles (Chapter 3), the context of a metaphor can strongly affect its interpretation. Context has a central place in relevance theory (Sperber and Wilson, [1986] 1995; Wilson and Sperber, 2004) since relevance is defined in terms of the effect of a communicative action on a context and the comprehension process is largely a search for a context in which a communicative action will have sufficient effects to justify the effort of processing it.

Although Sperber and Wilson ([1986] 1995) do not provide a detailed definition of context, it is evident from their discussion that context includes knowledge about the physical and social setting and what has already happened in the exchange (the traditional and most restrictive meanings of *context*) as well as general world knowledge, that is, historical and cultural knowledge. A specific *cognitive context* can be understood as an individual's representation of this general world knowledge, something like a *schema*, organized knowledge and thoughts about a topic or concept. A *mutual cognitive context* implies that speaker and hearer both recognize that they have similar schemas activated and accessible. The *mutual cognitive environment* consists of all the contexts which participants in a conversation or other communicative event believe to be accessible and salient to themselves and all other participants.

Sperber and Wilson ([1986] 1995) originally implied that the "search for relevance" stops as soon as one context is identified for which a communicative act has relevance. However, in their later work they acknowledge that the search for relevance may sometimes continue, so that a communicative act may have relevance to several contexts and lead to changes in several schemas at once. We have already seen several examples in which this seems likely to occur.

This account of *context* is in principle fairly open ended. *Context* can be understood at several levels, each represented cognitively as a *cognitive context* and each potentially present to the participants in a conversation or other discourse event as part of the *mutual cognitive environment*. A cognitive context is *mutual* if all participants believe that all participants are aware of it and regard it as part of their common ground, so that it can serve as a mutual resource for communication.

When Obama stated in his speech, "A More Perfect Union," that "my wife *carries the blood of slaves and slave-owners*," the context included the physical location in which he gave the speech as well as facts about the political campaign and his pastor's controversial remarks. The context also included historical facts about conditions on southern plantations, the sexual exploitation and rape of slave women by owners and overseers, and so on. These contexts were present to Obama and various listeners in the form of mental representations, political schemas relevant to the campaign and historical schemas relevant to the plantation system and slavery. They were part of the *mutual cognitive environment* to the extent that Obama and various listeners believed that all participants were aware of approximately the same facts and that approximately the same facts (as well as beliefs and attitudes) were salient to all participants. However, in this case as in many other similar cases it is likely that various members of the audience may have assumed quite divergent facts and ideas about this "shared history," with the result that Obama's stories and metaphors may have yielded quite different interpretations for different listeners.

Participants in a discourse event can never be certain what contexts are salient to others or how others process and react to a communicative action, and researchers may have even less certainty about what is going on. Participants and researchers alike make inferences about others' cognitive processes based on overt signs (other utterances and events in the same discourse event) and on their assumptions about the common ground among participants. Participants will frequently correct their assumptions to reflect new information as the discourse unfolds – and researchers must do likewise.

Potential effects of metaphors on extended context

It is also useful to look at the other side of the relevance equation – at the changes to cognitive context that stem from processing a particular metaphor. The context for Tony Blair's Gateshead speech included his troubled relationship with dissatisfied members of the Labour Party, and an immediate effect of his "*throwing crockery*" story was most likely to change, or perhaps strengthen, listeners' understanding of how he viewed that relationship. The emotional state of listeners was also part of the cognitive context, and here it is useful to consider again the probability that very different contexts were active for different listeners. Blair supporters probably entertained feelings of affection and sympathy; for these listeners, the humor in the story would strengthen their positive feelings, and probably enrich them with feelings of satisfaction. Blair critics probably entertained feelings of resentment and concern, and (if they felt that the story was directed toward them), the intended humor and the implicit dismissal and belittling of their legitimate concerns may have aggravated these negative feelings. (Depending on the questions asked by public opinion poll-takers at the time, it might be possible to test these speculations by comparing responses to the speech by various members of Blair's constituency.)

More broadly, as I have pointed out in earlier passages, the context of the speech also included the relationship between Blair and all of his constituents and his ideas about the nature of government in a democracy. The humorously metaphorical comparison of himself to an exasperated and intransigent husband and the voters to an angry and possibly hysterical wife is likely also to have affected *that* part of the cognitive context. And finally, as subsequent events suggest, the story may have had ramifications that echoed, and may continue to echo, throughout the much broader context, the British political system.

DISCUSSION

How compatible is Wilson and Sperber's approach to categorization (Chapter 3) with perceptual simulation theory?

What if any perceptual simulations do you think people experience when they speak of '*falling in love*'? What about '*broken heart*'?

SUGGESTED READINGS

- Barsalou, L. W. (2008). Grounding symbolic operations in the brain's modal systems. In Semin, G. R., and Smith, E. R. (eds.), *Embodied grounding: Social, cognitive, affective, and neuroscientific approaches.* Cambridge University Press, pp. 9–42. This is one of the clearest of Barsalou's expositions of his theories of perceptual simulation. It is not easy reading – his writing is dense and academic – but it is well worth the effort. Several other studies in Gün and Smith are also relevant to this chapter and well worth reading.
- Gibbs, R. W., Jr. (2006). Metaphor interpretation as embodied simulation. *Mind and Language, 21*, 434–458. This essay provides a nice introduction to perceptual simulation theory, accompanied by a good review of the experimental literature.

6 Metaphors and framing effects

[T]here you are, the British people, thinking: you're not listening and I think: you're not hearing me. And before you know it you raise your voice. I raise mine. Some of you throw a bit of crockery. And now you, the British people, have to sit down and decide whether you want the relationship to continue.

(Blair, 2005)

Researchers working in several traditions have adopted a common metaphor for various ways in which language can affect communication, referring to a particular way of thinking about a topic or a social interaction as a *'frame'* and the process of using words and phrases to establish a particular way of thinking about a topic or a social interaction as *'framing.'* Some writers use *frame* more or less as a synonym for *cognitive schema*, but more frequently *frame* refers to a pattern of language use.

In the passage quoted above, Tony Blair used a metaphorical story to frame the disagreements within the Labour Party as a *domestic* dispute, with the implication that these disagreements were not necessarily to be taken seriously. "Some of you throw a bit of crockery" frames the criticisms of his policies in terms of comic violence. The entire *"throwing crockery"* story frames the situation as one in which the decision about the future relationship rests entirely with "the British people" (the *'wife'* in the story) – and the *'husband,'* Tony Blair, has no responsibility to change his own behavior or adjust his policies.

In research on political communication, framing has most commonly been applied to the way news organizations present the news. Gamson (1992) argued that journalists present issues within certain *story frames* that reflect journalistic *news values* and influence both the reader's reading strategy and how the story is understood. Iyengar (1991) argued that news organizations tend to frame stories as *episodes,* for example by focusing on the stories of individuals who are unemployed, and de-emphasize *thematic* issues such as the social, political, and economic processes that affect unemployment. Both of these approaches can be readily adapted to Blair's Gateshead speech. Consistent with Gamson's approach to framing, Blair presented the intra-party dispute within a familiar *domestic quarrel* story frame. Consistent with Iyengar's approach, Blair's metaphorical story also emphasized the *episodic* nature of the quarrel ("you ... have to sit down and decide") and downplayed the *thematic* issues (discontent over his own alleged abandonment of traditional Labour issues and positions and over his participation in the Iraq war).

Price, Tewksbury, and Powers (1997) demonstrated that the wording used to frame a news story activates one or another of the readers' accessible cognitive schemas, which are then more likely to be employed in processing and generating responses to the story. These schemas may originate in personal experience but they are often influenced and shaped by media content. Accordingly, we might expect that Blair's language would have activated a *domestic quarrel* schema, familiar from television sitcoms and comic strips. Reg Smythe's comic strip character Andy Capp, for example, is frequently depicted as having dishes thrown at him by his wife. This schema would then be accessible to help in interpreting the rest of this passage from the speech, and by extension for interpreting the state of Mr. Blair's relationship with his party and with the British electorate generally. Notice that this account dovetails neatly with structure-mapping theory (Gentner, 1983), discussed in Chapter 2.

Tracy (1997) has taken the framing metaphor in a different direction, and applied it to the way people understand their social interactions, conversations, and social relationships. The language encountered by participants in a conversation can shape their understanding of what is expected of them in a social situation and how they can expect others to react. Tracy analyzed transcripts of emergency calls to a 911 calling center and showed that communication failures between emergency calling centers' call takers and callers can often be traced to contradictory frames. Tracy found that, when a caller approaches the interaction from a *customer service* frame and call takers from a *public service* frame, the result is contradictory expectations about their respective roles and how the call will proceed. These contradictory expectations then lead to conflict and occasionally to a total failure to achieve either person's objectives. The call takers' role (outlined in procedures manuals) requires them to obtain detailed information about the nature of the emergency, the name of the caller, and the caller's exact address, along with other information that the first responder may need. The call takers' *public service* frame takes the need for this information for granted, as a result of which the reasons for the questions they ask are not always explained clearly. On the other end of the line, the callers' *customer service* frame does not include apparently irrelevant information and is focused on prompt provision of needed services, often leading the callers to interpret the call takers' questions as irrelevant and even intrusive. The result is frustration and sometimes premature termination of the call.

Gamson's and Iyengar's approach to framing in news accounts can be summarized as "What kind of story is this? What background knowledge is relevant to understanding the story, and how does it relate to on-going concerns?" Tracy's approach to framing in interpersonal conversations can be summarized as "What kind of conversation is this? What is the nature of each participant's role?" Framing may be accomplished by language choices, including metaphors and stories, but in principle can also be accomplished by other elements such as gestures, facial expression, clothing choices, and so on.

Schön (1993) suggested a definition of metaphor in terms of framing, and applied this idea to discourse about social policies. Writing in the same volume, Reddy (1993) extended Schön's concept of metaphorical framing to "meta-language," the words and phrases we use to talk and write about communication itself. I will review these seminal ideas, discuss some other examples of metaphorical framing, then discuss another approach that extends the logic of frame analysis, conceptual integration or conceptual-blending theory (Fauconnier and Turner, 2002).

TOPIC FRAMING

Generative metaphor: urban slums

Schön proposed that metaphor can be understood as "a way of looking at things" and "a process by which new perspectives on the world come into existence" (1993, p. 137). More specifically, he proposed *generative metaphor* as a term for the process by which frames or perspectives are transferred from one domain of experience (the vehicle) to another (the topic). Applying this idea to discussion of social policy as problem-solving, he proposed that "problem-setting" is more basic, since how we frame a problem establishes the limits and the nature of solutions we find. He argued that "framing of problems often depends upon metaphors underlying the stories" we tell about social issues (1993, p. 138), and thus it is important in policy debates to pay close attention to the stories and their underlying metaphors.

As an example, Schön analyzed the debate, in the 1950s, over what to do about slums, areas of dense residential and small-scale commercial development, in which many of the buildings are poorly maintained, and rates of crime are often high. Schön described how a community in Washington, DC was described as once having been '*healthy*,' but having become '*blighted*' and '*diseased*.' The city planners determined that the community could be '*cured*' only by tearing down, redesigning, and rebuilding the entire area – otherwise it would "revert again to a … slum area, as though possessed of a *congenital disease*." Schön (1993, p. 145) cites a competing metaphor, of "the slum as a *natural community*, with a complex social organization and social relationships that are important in the lives of its inhabitants."

Each of these metaphors implies a story, both a story about how the community came to be that way and a story of its future. Each metaphor, with the stories it implies, provides a *frame* that '*highlights*' certain aspects of a situation or concept and '*hides*' others, calls attention to some features and suppresses or diverts attention away from other features, so that one set of responses comes to seem natural and correct and alternatives come to seem wrong and irresponsible. If the slum is a '*blighted*' or '*diseased*' area, we know that blight must be removed and diseased tissue must be either treated or cut out. The consequence of this kind of metaphor was 'slum clearance,' the destruction of whole tracts of residential neighborhoods and their replacement with new and quite different residential buildings. On the other hand, if the slum is a '*natural community*,' then we should avoid exactly the kind of wholesale destruction and replacement called for by the '*blight*' metaphor, and instead investigate ways to identify and shore up the '*strength*' and '*vitality*' of the community.

Schön points out that, when participants in a policy debate understand issues in terms of conflicting or contradictory frames, generated by different metaphors, facts will not resolve the differences; rather "we need to understand the metaphors, and generate a new, all-encompassing metaphor that incorporates elements of both, transforms both into a new generative metaphor" (1993, p. 139).

The conduit metaphor: framing our understanding of communication

Reddy (1993) argued that the language we have at our disposal for discussing communication is strongly biased toward what he called the CONDUIT metaphor. This metaphor frames communication in a way that conflicts with the nature of communication and makes it very difficult to think clearly about communication generally or about specific communicative interactions, including failures of communication. As examples of the CONDUIT metaphor Reddy cites phrases like '*get* your thoughts *across*,' '*give* me an idea,' '*put* your thoughts *into* words,' '*force* meanings into the wrong *words*,' 'a sentence *filled with* emotion,' 'your words are *hollow*,' '*impenetrable* prose,' 'write more *clearly*,' 'read meaning *into* a poem,' '*get* the meaning *out of* the poem,' and so on. Reddy argues that the CONDUIT metaphor frames communication in a way that favors a particular set of solutions for communication difficulties: the speaker may fail to '*put enough* meanings *into* words,' or '*put* meanings *in the wrong place*' or '*in the wrong words*.' Alternatively, the listener may not be sufficiently skilled to '*find* the meaning' or '*get the meaning out of* a passage,' or the listener may even '*get the wrong meaning out of* a passage.'

Reddy argues that the CONDUIT metaphor has a framework that includes at least four propositions: (1) thoughts are '*objects*,' language consists of '*containers*,' and thoughts are '*transferred*' in words by language between persons; (2) thoughts and feelings must be '*inserted*' into words; (3) words '*contain*' thoughts and feelings, which they '*transfer*' to others, and (4) the hearers or readers must '*take*' the thoughts and feelings '*out of*' the words. The idea that thoughts are '*objects*' implies that they are somehow '*solid*,' '*immutable*,' and independent of the thinker. The idea that language consists of '*containers*' suggests that thoughts are also independent of the words and phrases that merely '*contain*' them. This metaphorical frame is at odds with the fundamental ambiguity of language, and all too often leads to an impasse when one person is convinced that he has spoken clearly, the other person that she has listened attentively, but they still cannot agree on what was said.

Metaphorical framing of crime: experimental evidence of framing

Thibodeau and Boroditsky (2011) demonstrated, in an ingenious series of experiments, that the metaphors used to describe crime as a social problem can have strong effects on how people think about the problem, the solutions they favor, and their strategies for searching out additional information about crime. They created a brief paragraph describing a crime wave in the fictitious city of Addison, then asked participants to propose solutions to the problem, and finally asked participants to identify the passage in the story that most influenced their thinking about a solution. In the first experiment, the crime was described in terms of one of two metaphors, 'a *beast preying on* Addison' or 'a *virus infecting* Addison'; these metaphors were introduced early in the report and reinforced through use of thematically related metaphors. When crime was described as a '*virus*,' participants recommended investigating the causes and '*inoculating*' the community through various social reforms. When crime was described as a '*beast*,' participants recommended catching and imprisoning criminals through more vigorous law enforcement.

In a follow-up experiment, Thibodeau and Boroditsky (2011) eliminated all of the supportive metaphors, retaining only the initial appearance of either 'a *beast preying on* Addison' or 'a *virus infecting* Addison' in the initial sentence. The results were virtually identical to those using the initial format, demonstrating that reinforcement is not needed if the framing metaphor is introduced early. In order to test whether the responses might simply be a result of the priming effect in which the metaphor vehicles primed associated thoughts, Thibodeau and Boroditsky removed the metaphors from the stimulus material, but preceded the *crime* task with an ostensibly unrelated task. Participants were presented with one or the other vehicle, 'beast' or 'virus,' and asked to name a synonym. In this experiment, no differences were observed between the two conditions, ruling out the "priming effect" explanation.

In a fourth experiment, after reading one or the other of the two metaphorically primed paragraphs participants were given the opportunity to search for additional relevant information. Those in the '*virus*' condition searched for more information relevant to finding and ameliorating the root causes of crime, and those in the '*beast*' condition searched for more information relevant to increasing enforcement activities. In a fifth experiment, Thibodeau and Boroditsky (2011) tested whether the effect resulted from simply thinking about the vehicle term by shifting the priming sentence from the beginning to the end of the paragraph. When the metaphorical frame was introduced at the end, no differences in information search was observed between the two conditions, supporting the conclusion that early presentation of the metaphorical frame led participants to structure subsequent information in ways consistent with the frame.

When participants were asked to identify the passages that influenced their recommendations, most participants identified the statistics (which were identical in the two conditions); only 3 percent of the participants identified the framing metaphor. (When the responses from these participants were removed, the overall results were unchanged.) Although self-identified Democrats and Independents were more strongly influenced by the metaphorical frames, self-identified Republicans were also influenced by them, consistent with the conclusion that the framing effect operates independently of prior ideological views. Thibodeau and Boroditsky (2011) point out that the results of this series of experiments are consistent with structure-mapping theory (Gentner and Bowdle, 2001); they are also consistent with conceptual metaphor theory (Lakoff and Johnson, 1980).

Framing police use of violence

In a conversation about public safety and police–community relations, among a group of White, politically liberal urban homeowners, the topic of alleged ethnic profiling and excessive use of force by police officers was discussed (Ritchie, 2011a). One of the participants, Todd, referred to an explanation that is often given when a police officer shoots an unarmed civilian:

> whenever I hear a an officer say ... it seems like the *magic words* ... like the *get-out-of-jail-free card* ... is ... 'I felt ... that ... my life was in ... that I was being threatened or ... ' like these *magical phrases* that police officers it's like ... they're trained that's the word like if anything bad ever *goes down* say ... 'I felt you know I felt that my life was in jeopardy.'

The implication is that the officers who investigate a shooting incident, and the police officers involved in the incident, initially frame the incident in terms of self-defense.

Magic words and *get-out-of-jail-free card* are both likely to activate schemas of childhood fantasy and play, and thus reframe the incident. *Magic words* reframes the incident, and the explanation given, in terms of a "*magic*" schema, in which utterance of a particular word or phrase will cause something unpleasant or threatening to disappear, or will change the situation in some other favorable way. *Get-out-of-jail-free card* refers to the popular game, Monopoly™, and is widely used in the United States as a metaphor for any situation in which people are able to avoid being held accountable for adverse effects of their actions by producing evidence of some irrelevant or minimally relevant fact. Used here, both metaphors reframe the phrase "my life was in danger" as a move in a childish game – hence as not to be taken seriously (see Figure 6.1).

In this passage, Todd referred to a frame conflict that appeared in many of the conversations in this series. This frame conflict reflects a more general struggle over allegations of ethnic profiling and excessive use of force by police officers that has continued for the past several decades in Portland, Oregon, where these conversations were held. (Similar allegations have been made in many other major cities in the United States.) The ironic metaphors Todd used in this brief passage also appeared in several other conversations in the series.

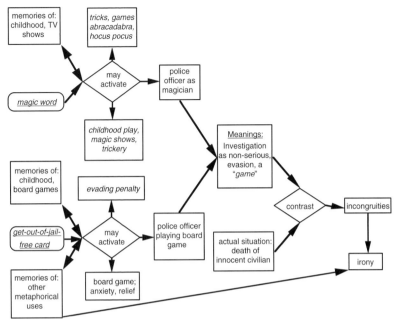

Figure 6.1 Get-out-of-jail-free card
Source: This figure first appeared in Ritchie, 2010b; 2011a

Issue framing: some other examples

A well-known example of metaphorical frame conflict comes from the abortion rights debate. "Framing the issue as 'pro-life' … forces the oppositional label 'anti-life.'" This activated schemas that are advantageous to the anti-abortion group, an advantage only partially overcome when the abortion rights groups began to frame their position as 'pro-choice.' Both of these metaphors direct attention toward certain features of the controversy and away from other aspects that might have provided a basis for reframing the issue in ways that could lead to constructive engagement and compromise (Schneider, 2008).

In a study of the debate over direct-to-consumer (DTC) advertising of prescription drugs, Coleman and Ritchie (2011) discuss several metaphors used to frame both the DTC debate and other controversial issues in public policy debates. One widely used set of framing metaphors is created by attaching the first two syllables of *Frankenstein*, Shelley's (1969) monster-creating "mad scientist," to any suspect product of technology, such as '*frankenfood*' and '*frankenfish*.' This metaphor is likely to activate fearsome images from one or more of the movies that have been based on the novel, along with semantic connections and ideas associated with both the "uncontrollable monster" schema and the "irresponsible science" schema. Thus it serves to reframe the debate in a way that hides potential benefits of scientific advances and highlights potential harms. Yet another framing metaphor discussed by Coleman and Ritchie is "*death taxes*," which directs attention away from the fact that inheritance taxes are paid by the heirs, who are very much alive.

In a study of newspaper editorials, political speeches, and other documents from the early nineteenth century, O'Brien (2003) identifies several metaphors that were used in the debate about immigration policy to denigrate and dehumanize immigrants. Metaphors based on ORGANISM and DISEASE correspond to the more general a NATION IS A BODY metaphor. ORGANIC metaphors refer to the need to "*digest*" or "*absorb*" new immigrants (Roberts, 1924). DISEASE metaphors compare immigrants to a "*poison* against which we have no *antidote*" (Cannon, 1923) and a reference to fear of immigrants as "not only the *germ of bodily disease*, but the *germ of anarchy*" (McLaughlin, 1903). NATURAL CATASTROPHE metaphors refer to an "*incoming tide*" of immigrants that "*threatens to overwhelm us*" (Darlington, 1906). Other metaphors identified by O'Brien are based on conceptualizing immigrants as '*objects*,' '*animals*,' and '*invading armies*.' Many of these metaphors still appear, in modified form, in contemporary debates about immigration and other social issues (Biria, 2012).

O'Brien (2003) emphasizes the potential of metaphors of this sort to justify regressive social policies. As O'Brien points out, if members of any group are understood as having qualities associated with disease, natural catastrophe, or invading armies (attribute transfer) or belonging to those categories, then they may well seem legitimate targets of violence and discrimination. Conceptual metaphor theory and perceptual simulation theory go somewhat further, suggesting that these metaphors will induce hearers and readers to experience the immigrant (or member of other target groups) *as* a disease, flood, invader, or other threat and connect related perceptions and emotions with members of the target group. Thus, as O'Brien suggests, analysis of the metaphors used in debate about social policy can help to elucidate the possible effects of these metaphors not merely on public opinion but also on subsequent actions.

Strengths and weaknesses

A primary criticism is that framing is not really a coherent theory. Various researchers have defined framing in many different ways, which makes it difficult to compare results of framing research. The relationships of framing to other media practices such as gatekeeping and agenda setting on the one hand, and to other cognitive concepts such as schemas on the other hand, is ambiguous. However, it is apparent from results reported by Price *et al.* (1997), Thibodeau and Boroditsky (2011), and other researchers that the underlying cognitive processes are real and potentially powerful, and that they can be achieved by either literal language (Price *et al.*) or metaphorical language (Thibodeau and Boroditsky).

CONCEPTUAL INTEGRATION THEORY

In Chapter 4 I discussed Grady's (1997) claim that simple metaphors are combined somehow to form composite metaphors (Grady, 1997). Fauconnier and Turner (1998; 2002) have proposed a model of how this might be accomplished, through what they call "conceptual *blending*" or "conceptual *integration*." Fauconnier and Turner explain conceptual integration theory (CIT) in terms of "mental *spaces* … small conceptual *packets*" that are connected both to specific situational knowledge and to frames, which they describe as "long-term schematic knowledge" (2002, pp. 39ff.). The "*mental spaces*" are often graphically illustrated by circles, with relevant attributes listed or iconically displayed inside (see Figure 6.2).

The model posits a minimum of four "*mental spaces*" (representing concepts): two "*input spaces*," a "*generic space*" that contains attributes common to the two inputs, and a "*blended space*" that contains contextually relevant elements from each "*input space*." Additional elements may be added to the "*blended space*" as "*emergent structure*." "*Emergent structure*" may include information from long-term memory as well as the result of comparing or elaborating on attributes common to the "*input spaces*" in a way analogous to a computer program ("*running* the *blend*").

According to Fauconnier and Turner (2002), these "*mental spaces*" (or concepts) exist in the brain as "neural assemblages," and integration or "*blending*" involves altering existing synaptic connections among these neural assemblages or creating entirely new connections. The "*generic space*" provides one possible basis for initiating new synaptic connections. The conceptual integration approach is illustrated in Figure 6.2, using Tony Blair's "*throw a bit of crockery*" metaphorical story as an example.

The *generic space* in Figure 6.2 is a general *dispute* schema, which includes elements such as *insulting and accusing*, *physical violence*, and

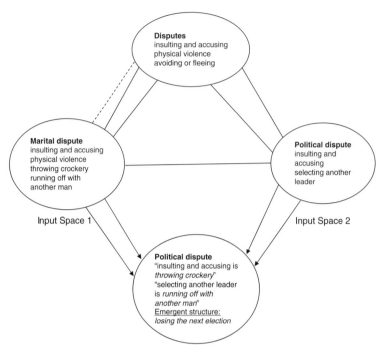

Figure 6.2 Conceptual integration theory applied to "*throw a bit of crockery*"

avoiding or fleeing. These general elements map onto different particular elements in the two input spaces. *Insulting and accusing* is part of the *marital dispute* space and it is the implicit topic in the *political dispute* space, but it is not mentioned in Blair's speech. *Physical violence* maps onto the *marital dispute* space as *throwing crockery*, but it is not part of the *political dispute* space. *Avoiding or fleeing* maps onto *running off with another man* in the *marital dispute* space and onto *choosing another leader* in the *political dispute* space. These separate elements combine into implicit metaphors in the *blended* space as shown in Figure 6.2.

Strengths of conceptual integration theory

The explanation of the "*throwing crockery*" metaphor illustrates some of the primary strengths of Fauconnier and Turner's approach. It provides a convenient notational format for diagramming the kind of conceptual integration or "*blending*" that seems necessary for explaining how the "*throwing crockery*" metaphor works in the context of Blair's speech. As other examples in Fauconnier and Turner illustrate, it can also be applied to help explain irony and various kinds of intellectual puzzles. Fauconnier and Turner's discussion of cognitive processes involved in conceptual integration (2002, pp. 93–101) and their exploration of different kinds of integration network (pp. 120–131) are evocative, and have the potential to provide a bridge between abstract formal logic approaches to language and neurological and cognitive approaches (Fauconnier, 1994; Lakoff and Sweetser, 1994).

Metaphorical terminology

Fauconnier and Turner's metaphorical terminology is grounded in early cognitive science approaches to language (Ritchie, 2004; 2006). "*Mental space*" was used as early as the 1950s to describe implicit conceptual schemas associated with graphic representation of similarities and differences among words, images, or other perceptual elements in research using techniques such as multidimensional scaling (Kruskal and Wish, 1981), and is still often used in discussing the results of this kind of research (Maeda and Ritchie, 2004; Nishishiba and Ritchie, 2000). "*Conceptual packets*" expresses the container or conduit metaphor for language and cognition (Reddy, 1993). "*Emergent structure*" expresses a more general construction metaphor for mental activity, and "*input space*" combines a computer metaphor for the brain with the "*mental space*" metaphor.

Weaknesses of conceptual integration theory

Gibbs objected that CIT does not provide a coherent unified theory, although it does provide "a broad framework that suggests a variety of localized hypotheses, each of which may be experimentally examined under different empirical conditions" (2000, p. 349). Gibbs further objected that CIT has not been specified in a way that supports empirical testing. Fauconnier and Turner (2002, pp. 54–56) dismissed the call for falsifiability by comparing CIT to "sciences like evolutionary biology" that "are not about making falsifiable predictions regarding future events." However, this claim is based on a false premise since evolutionary biologists have in fact been able to develop and test a number of claims, particularly in the past few decades (Ritchie, 2004; 2006). Moreover, many of the examples developed by Fauconnier and Turner can be readily explained by other extant theories (Ritchie, 2004; 2006).

Overall assessment

Conceptual integration theory is based at least in part on an elaborate system of meta-metaphors (i.e. metaphors used to discuss or explain how metaphors are used and understood, such as "mental *spaces*"), and does not appear to constitute a coherent testable theory, but it provides a useful set of analytical tools. As illustrated by the "*throwing crockery*" example, it appears to be compatible with other approaches, and Lakoff and Johnson (1999) have explicitly incorporated CIT into their account of conceptual metaphor theory. At the very least, CIT provides a useful structure for analyzing composite metaphors and the emergent entailments of these metaphors.

CONCLUSION

Schön (1993) defined metaphor as a form of framing, and showed how this approach can illuminate debate over public policies such as urban renewal. Theorists and researchers interested in conversation have defined framing as a way of influencing participants' understanding of the type of discourse they are engaged in and consequently the nature of appropriate contributions (Tracy, 1997). Theorists and researchers interested in political communication have defined framing as a way of influencing audience members' expectations about the topic of a news article or other piece of discourse and thus influencing the nature of their thoughts and responses (e.g. see Iyengar, 1991; Pan and Kosicki, 1997; Price, Tewksbury, and Powers, 1997). These framing effects can be achieved in many ways, including speaking or writing style and the context in which communication occurs, but as we have shown metaphors often have framing effects and often appear to be selected at least in part for their framing effects. Metaphors may also appear as part of a struggle over how to frame an event or topic, as illustrated by the contrast between '*virus*' and '*beast*' as metaphors for crime.

In some cases, as in O'Brien's discussion of metaphor use in the early twentieth-century immigration debate, at a basic level it may not be important how people actually process the metaphors – analyzing these metaphors in terms of any of the theories we have discussed will support very similar conclusions about the potential effects of framing in terms of hiding certain features of the topic, highlighting others, and imputing still other attributes that are wholly imaginary. However, even in the case of immigration debate metaphors, analysis in terms of conceptual metaphor theory and perceptual simulation theory suggests that the effects of these metaphors may be more penetrating and more enduring than an attribute transfer approach would suggest. If the metaphors are processed deeply rather than at a surface level, they may alter audience members' underlying cognitive structures and change the way readers or hearers react to future messages.

Conceptual integration theory (CIT) extends and modifies the "*framing*" metaphor in a way that provides a useful tool for analyzing both metaphors and other forms of figurative language. CIT can also be combined with framing analysis, and both CIT and framing analysis can readily be combined with conceptual metaphor theory and perceptual simulation theory as well as structure-mapping theory (Gentner, 1983).

DISCUSSION

Thibodeau and Boroditsky's (2011) research demonstrated that metaphors can powerfully influence how people interpret and respond to stories about crime, including how they search for additional information about the topic. How well would their findings apply to metaphors in other contexts such as politics and healthcare, and how might this influence information seeking, problem defining, and problem solving? Could similar methods be applied to metaphorical framing of a communication event itself, for example of a conversation (Tracy, 1997)?

How do the playful metaphors in sports headlines discussed in Chapter 8 frame the games described? How does the use of this kind of metaphor frame professional athletics?

How do metaphors used in discussion of war and other public policy issues frame these issues?

Do euphemisms like "*pass away*" frame the way we think about life and death?

SUGGESTED READINGS

- Pan, Z., and Kosicki, G. M. (1997). Priming and media impact on the evaluations of the president's performance. *Communication Research, 24*, 3–30. Price, V., Tewksbury, D., and Powers, E. (1997). Switching trains of thought: The impact of news frames on reader's cognitive responses. *Communication Research 24*, 481. These two articles discuss framing in political discourse.

- Thibodeau, P. H., and Boroditsky, L. (2011). Metaphors we think with: The role of metaphor in reasoning. *PLoS ONE, 6*(2): e16782. doi:10.1371/journal. www-psych.stanford.edu/~lera/papers/crime-metaphors.pdf Last accessed May 3, 2011. This article summarizes recent experiments that demonstrate strong effects of metaphors in framing the way people think about, discuss, and solve problems.
- Tracy, K. (1997). Interactional trouble in emergency service requests: A problem of frames. *Research on Language and Social Interaction, 30,* 315–343. This article discusses framing in interpersonal communication.

7 Language play: metaphors, stories, and humor

Although metaphors are often used with very serious intent, as in Obama's phrases, "*carries the blood of slaves and slave-owners*" and "*incendiary* language," they are also used in a playful way, as when the scientists in the discussion of communicating science to the public extended and developed the metaphor "*ivory tower*" (Ritchie and Schell, 2009). The scientists' play with "*ivory tower*," including the teasing that began the passage, also illustrates how metaphors can be developed into stories, and how the playful use of metaphors can contribute to humor. A similar blend of metaphors, storytelling, and humor appears in the "*throwing crockery*" passage from Tony Blair's Gateshead speech, and several other examples will appear in the next few chapters. Research on the use and understanding of metaphorical language in actual discourse must often consider language play, humor, and storytelling as well. In this chapter I will review theories and research related to language play and humor, and show how they can contribute to understanding metaphors that appear in actual discourse.

PLAY

From the infant's earliest babbling, play is part of communication (Kerr and Apter, 1991). As soon as they master them, children distort linguistic forms, semantic meanings, and pragmatic uses – and adults continue this language play, usually but not always in more sophisticated forms. Metaphor invention and use often seems to be a form of language play, for example in the "*ivory tower*" conversation and Blair's "*throwing crockery*" story. In the example from Blair, the playfulness also serves a serious purpose, but sometimes playfulness is indulged purely for its own sake. Even when the tone is serious, speakers and writers often "play" with language and with idiomatic metaphors, as is illustrated by Willard's transformation of '*we're all in the same boat'* into a brief hypothetical story about a person *"knocking a hole in the boat"* to *"get me some water"* in a conversation about police–community relations among a group of four middle-class Black men (Ritchie, 2010a).

Play is complex and serves many functions, including social organizing and facilitation as well as the probably more basic biological functions of skill rehearsal and sexual display. Play is intrinsically rewarding, and among laboratory animals, the opportunity to play can be as effective as food in conditioning experiments (Fagen, 1995). Among humans, smiling and laughing as well as vigorous physical activity release opioids, and both joking and wordplay are probably important to the social-facilitative talk that Dunbar (1996) calls "grooming."

Grooming

Robin Dunbar has proposed that language developed as a response to the pressures of life in large socially complex groups, at least in part as an extension of primate social grooming. Among primates such as chimpanzees, members of a troop may spend hours grooming each other – the grooming animal picks lice, twigs, burrs, and so on from the other animal's hair while the groomed animal sits placidly in an apparently euphoric state. Research has shown that grooming leads to the release of pleasurable endorphins in the animal being groomed, and serves to build and maintain coalitions. Grooming also alleviates social tensions associated with the constant struggle for status in the social hierarchy of the troop, as when the victor in a fight grooms the defeated animal. Dunbar points out that physical grooming is limited to one-on-one, but among humans language allows an individual to groom three or four people at once, and thereby facilitates the emergence of larger and more complex social structures. Consistent with this theory, Dunbar reports that primary group size among most human cultures is around 150, compared to about fifty among chimpanzees and other social primates. Finally, Dunbar reports from his own conversational data that about 65 percent of adult conversation is devoted to social functions that can be characterized as *"grooming"* (making others feel good) and *"gossip"* (exchanging information about others' relationships, social behavior, and social status).

For humans, language play, storytelling, and humor are intrinsically enjoyable: among other benefits, these activities have been shown to reduce stress and contribute to a sense of wellbeing. These uses of language provide a ready vehicle for shared pleasure, which can support social bonding in the same way that physical grooming does among other primates. Humor, storytelling, and language play can also contribute to social solidarity by emphasizing common group membership and cultural knowledge. The ability to use language in a skillful way that contributes to the pleasure of others and to group solidarity then becomes a valued trait, which enhances the social status and, hence, the reproductive fitness of those who possess it. This, in turn, can lead to competitive display of language skill as a direct means to achieve and maintain social status.

Language play

Research on language play has emphasized goal-directed functions including the development and rehearsal of language and cognitive skills (Cook, 2000). Discussions of adult play have tended to emphasize the competitive and social status elements in play (Huizinga, 1955; Stephenson, 1967) at the expense of activities done "just for fun." Studies of language play have emphasized competitive rhyming or insulting matches at the expense of cooperative activities in which participants build on rather than undermine or attempt to outdo each other's productions. However, play also includes fantasy, solving puzzles, and playing with objects. Fantasy and object play as well as puzzle-solving may involve elaborate simulations, with external props often serving as markers or tokens (Clark, 1997). Children and adults alike often engage in wordplay, which may include playing with interesting sounds, rhyming, alliteration, and other ways of distorting words and meanings.

Both adults and children exploit and distort every feature of language, including sounds, word order, and meaning (Cook, 2000). Rhyme, rhythm, alliteration, and overtly meaningless combinations of sounds, words, and phrases are heard in nonsense verses, wordplay, and jokes. In poetry words are chosen for sound as well as meaning, and incidental or secondary meanings may be given primacy over usual or "literal" meanings. Puns and humorous quips often depend on purely random coincidences of sound and meaning.

In his analysis of the Owl and the Pussy-cat, Cook points out that the entire story line is developed according to the requirement of the rhyme scheme rather than any objective sense of narrative possibility. "The fiction thus created ... seems to incorporate a wild and random element, to be controlled by language itself rather than by reality or the will of the writer" (2000, p. 49). Even in serious verse forms such as the sonnet, the adoption of a rhyme scheme, metric scheme, or other formal "rules" has the effect of inverting the usual relationship of language to reality and thus subverts the task-accomplishment functions of language. In more playful and comic forms, the relationship of language to reality may be transformed in a way that deliberately violates our knowledge about the world, as in *The Owl and the Pussy-cat*, or it may be abandoned altogether, as in Lewis Carroll's (1872) *Jabberwocky*.

Cook argues that the possibilities of language become increasingly constrained as we gain increased mastery over the formal rules of language. In a somewhat dreary view of adulthood, Cook describes adulthood as a time when the "magic" of childhood is lost. But adulthood can also be seen as a time when our ability to invent

> The Owl and the Pussy-cat went to sea
>
> In a beautiful pea green boat,
>
> They took some honey, and plenty of money,
>
> Wrapped up in a five pound note.
>
> (From *The Owl and the Pussy-cat*, Lear, 1871)

and follow ever more complex rules for the subversion of ordinary meaning and sense permits us to enhance rather than suppress the "magical," to use playful subversion of reality to create forms of language play that far exceed the delights of childhood nonsense rhymes (Ritchie, 2005; Ritchie and Dyhouse, 2008) – as Lewis Carroll's work and the extended skat singing of jazz artists like Ella Fitzgerald and Carmen MacRae illustrate.

Play seems to be an important part of creativity (Kerr and Apter, 1991). When members of a research seminar talk about "*playing*" with an idea they are not speaking metaphorically. The juxtaposition of abstract ideas, often on the basis

> 'Twas brillig, and the slithy toves
>
> Did gyre and gimble in the wabe:
>
> All mimsy were the borogoves,
>
> And the mome raths outgrabe.
>
> (From *Jabberwocky*, Carroll, 1872)

of apparent coincidence, can activate elaborate introspective simulations that are sometimes merely amusing, but may lead to models and theories that are worth formalizing and testing. Watson and Crick's physical play with their models of protein molecules as well as their playful conversations in the local pubs appear to have contributed substantially to their discovery of the structure of DNA (Watson, 1968; Ritchie, 2008). The playful subversion of ordinary reality and creation of new realities are evident in many forms of "intellectual play" beyond language – in the fine and performing arts as well as in mathematics and theoretical physics.

Expressive language, including wordplay and humor as well as metaphors, may activate a multitude of emotional and introspective simulations, which contribute to interpreting utterances (Ritchie,

2008). It is likely that, beginning in early childhood, humans develop a "language play" schema that is activated by obviously playful language (and may differ from one culture to the next). If this is the case, we would predict that nonsense verse, skat singing, or other wordplay would increase the likelihood that a hearer would recognize subsequent playful language use and that a subsequent speaker would extend the language play. This would explain "chaining," in which a single pun or double entendre is followed by a series of puns and quips (Cook, 2000).

Playful metaphors

Although metaphors are often used with serious intent, other metaphors are created and used in a spirit of wordplay. Ritchie and Dyhouse (2008) provide several examples, including this charming exchange of greetings:

> "Howdy, John, how doin'?"
> "*Fine as frog's hair*, Skeeter. You?"
> "*Fit as a fiddle.*"

Although both phrases (as well as the nickname, "Skeeter") take the form of apparent metaphors, both are difficult or impossible to interpret through a straightforward metaphorical mapping. Attempts to devise a metaphorical mapping leads to humorous incongruities, which appear to accomplish two communicative objectives at once. By sharing the pleasure of an exchange of humorously nonsensical greetings, the two men affirm and reinforce their social solidarity. At the same time, the ability and willingness to engage in light-hearted wordplay provides evidence of a general state of wellbeing, hence is indirectly relevant to the initiating question, "How doin'?" The very use of these expressions, which sound like metaphors but cannot be readily interpreted, provides part of the meaning. As a response to a polite inquiry into one's health, "*fit as a fiddle*" implies that there is nothing of note to report, and "*no news is good news.*" It also signals a readiness to engage in playful banter and thus a positive disposition toward everyone present.

Many metaphors share this quality of wordplay, including some that can be given a reasonable interpretation. A '*gully-washer*' is a heavy rainstorm and, especially in areas where the top-soil has been disturbed, if it persists for long it will create ('*wash out*') some gullies. But the phrase is ordinarily used for its amusing sound, and is not intended to predict impending soil erosion. '*Raining buckets*' is, like '*gully-washer*,' probably best characterized as hyperbolic metonym rather than as metaphor: the phrase implies that it is raining hard enough to fill a bucket, or raining drops as large as a bucket. On the other hand, *'raining cats and dogs,'* like *"fine as frog's hair,"* can be interpreted only in terms of the associated semantic links and perceptual simulations. Similarly, *'a snowball's chance in Hell,'* combines extreme exaggeration with interesting rhythm (a *snowball's chance in Hell*) and amusingly incongruous perceptual simulations.

'Cute as a bug's ear' and *'cute as a tick,'* like *"fine as frog's hair"* turn on a metaphorical connection, *'cute is small'* – but for most people there is nothing cute about a tick, and bugs do not have ears in the ordinary sense. Again, the "meaning" is in the amusing combination of perceptual simulations activated by these idiomatic metaphors. Similarly, *"in a gnat's eye"* turns on a hyperbolic exaggeration – a gnat is very small, so a gnat's eye is an even smaller place to locate something (just as an *eye of a needle* is a very small opening for a *camel*); the probability of the referenced state of affairs being true is thus metaphorically expressed in terms of a very small physical location. The grating sound of *gnat* reinforces the apparent aggressiveness of the retort but it is softened by the interesting and humorous simulations activated.

Carter (2004) and Kövecses (2005) provide many examples of playful puns, metaphors, and similes. Carter mentions an Irish petrol company called *Emerald Oil* and a hair salon named *'A Cut Above.'* In the United States there are many taverns with names like *'The Dew Drop Inn'* and (for singles bars) *'The Meet Market.'* *'A Cut Above'* and *'The Meet Market'* are more interesting than the others because these puns also serve as topically relevant metaphors. *'A Cut Above'* activates the conceptual metaphor GOOD IS UP while referring to the activity that takes place in the establishment (cutting hair). *'Meat market'* is a common derogatory metaphor for a situation in which people seek interpersonal encounters (*meet* other people) for purely sexual purposes (*"meat"*).

Kövecses reports playfully metaphorical sports headlines, including "Clemson *cooks* Rice" and "Cowboys *corral* Buffaloes." To *'cook'* something requires that one *'turn the heat up'*; the metaphor builds on the rice/Rice pun, and also seems to invoke the idiomatic metaphor, *'cook one's goose.'* To find a superordinate category that includes both *cook* and *defeat* requires somewhat more inventiveness. The metaphor seems likely to activate interesting perceptual simulations, but in a way that implies a blending of images: rice (the food) in a pot on a hot stove must be somehow blended with Rice (the university football team) being outplayed by another team.

"Cowboys *corral* Buffaloes" is easier to fit to categorization theory. *Corral* is part of a general category of actions that includes *control* and *dominate*; fitting the action of a victorious team toward a defeated team seems somewhat easier with this example.

"Cowboys *corral* Buffaloes" is also more interesting and more likely to activate detailed perceptual simulations because buffaloes are large and powerful animals, *corral* implies restraint, and the reader can draw on a store of images from old Western movies in which cowboys herd cattle into corrals. As with "Clemson *cooks* Rice," the simulations that are activated seem to require blending, and may produce an image something like a group of athletes on horses herding another group of athletes milling around in a cloud of dust into a fenced enclosure. Simple attribution transfer or categorization theory may explain the linguistic processes but they do not seem adequate to explain the pleasure provided by these humorous headlines. An interesting variation of the "*herding*" metaphor appears in the idiom 'like *herding cats*,' which depends on the storied independence of house cats. An amusing visualization of '*herding cats*' was developed in a television commercial for an information management company (www.youtube.com/watch?v=Pk7yqlTMvp8; last accessed July 18, 2012).

Kövecses also quotes some of news anchor Dan Rather's famous similes: "hotter than *a Laredo parking lot*" and "*sweeping* the south like a *tornado through a trailer park*." Glucksberg provides several examples of wordplay that revive idiomatic '*dead*' metaphors: 'he didn't *spill a single bean*' and a financial page headline: "*Main Street Bulls take bears by the horns*." In a play on the title of a Browning sonnet, Glucksberg titles one of his sub-chapters "How Are Idioms Understood? Let Me Count the Ways" (2001, p. 23).

According to attribute transfer accounts, metaphors are selected for their ability to activate a quality that is more commonly associated with the metaphor vehicle and associate it with the topic. Categorization theory would argue that the metaphor vehicle is selected for its ability to create an ad hoc category defined by qualities that also apply to the topic. But these examples of playful metaphors suggest that metaphors may also be selected for the amusement and pleasure of the simulations they activate. If language represents an extension of primate grooming, a way to maintain social relationships (Dunbar, 1996), then the pleasure that playful language gives others is more than a happy coincidence. It also serves a primary social-bonding purpose of language.

HUMOR

Many of the metaphors discussed in the last section have a humorous quality that contributes to their pleasure, and humor can give pleasure and strengthen social bonds. Conversely, humor often includes metaphorical elements. In this section I will discuss a few of the major theories of humor, and then return to the relationship of humor to language play and metaphor.

Humor as sublimated aggression

Most extant theories of humor rely on one or more of three explanatory mechanisms: aggression, incongruity, and arousal-safety (Martin, 2007). Each of these approaches explains some aspects of humor, but none seems complete on its own.

Aggression-based theories (Gruner, 1997) assume that jokes constitute an attack by the joke teller upon the target of the joke, either individually or as a representative of a disfavored group. The aggression approach is supported by the persistent popularity of sexist, ethnic, and other jokes that play on stereotypes, usually targeted at lower-status and powerless groups. For example, jokes of the "light bulb" genre (Attardo, 2001) ask how many members of some group ("dumb blonds," Polacks, and so on) it takes to screw in a lightbulb, then give some response that demonstrates how stupid members of that group must be. (A typical punch line is "Five, one to hold the bulb and four to turn the chair.") Consequently jokes of this type represent a metaphorical attack on all members of that group. Most racial, ethnic, and gender-based jokes insult and disparage the targets, and they often serve both to exclude the target group and to enhance the social solidarity of the joke teller and audience (Attardo, 2001; Norrick, 2003). Zillmann and Cantor (1976) argue that appreciation of this type of joke is conditional on the hearer's disposition toward the targeted person or group: people who are favorably disposed toward the target are less likely to appreciate the joke, and those who are unfavorably disposed will enjoy it more.

Aggression and disparagement, moderated by the hearer's disposition toward the target group, clearly play a role in many examples of humor, but these processes are not easily applied to absurdist jokes such as those of the "elephant joke" genre (Martin, 2007). "How does an elephant hide in a strawberry patch? It paints its toenails red." The best an aggression approach can do with a joke of this sort is to argue that these jokes somehow constitute an "aggression" against the hearer. However, for this explanation to work the word "*aggression*" would have to be understood in a metaphorical sense – and the closest a typical hearer comes to reacting in accordance with the aggression explanation is to utter an exaggerated groan. Aggression theory is also difficult to apply to the following:

> A kangaroo walked into a tavern and ordered a beer. The bartender served him and said, "ten dollars, please." The kangaroo paid the money and sipped on his beer. The bartender kept glancing at the kangaroo out of the corner of his eye, then finally walked back over and commented,
> "You know, we don't get many kangaroos in here."
> The kangaroo replied,
> "Well at these prices it's no wonder."

It is not easy to identify a target of aggression in this joke – certainly not kangaroos, and probably not bartenders as a class. It is difficult to see how the joke qualifies as aggression unless the aggression is against inflation as an *institutional process* or Capitalism as an *institution*, taken as an "ideological target" (Attardo, 2001). But it is hard to interpret an action directed at an "ideological target" as '*aggression*' except in a metaphorical sense.

Norrick (1993) shows that apparently aggressive humor is prevalent in joking and teasing among friends and family members, and it is often not only accepted but actively enjoyed by the target. Norrick argues that the humor in these exchanges cannot be genuinely aggressive, or it would be protested. In support of this, he relates some instances in which a teasing remark '*goes too far*,' is protested, and is withdrawn or negated. In her analysis of joking and teasing in her own family, Everts (2003) makes a similar point.

In sum, it appears that aggression and superiority does play a role in some humor, but in many cases in which aggression appears to play a role it is playful (mock aggression rather than genuine aggression) in intention and reception. It is useful to separate apparently aggressive humor into instances that display genuine hostility and have the effect (and probably intention) of *excluding* the target of the joke, and instances in which the hostility is "pretend," the intention playful, and the effect is to *include* the target of the joke. The difference may be apparent from para-linguistic signals such as vocal tone or facial expression, or it may be apparent only from the context itself.

Incongruity, frame-shifting, and relevance approaches

An alternative approach emphasizes the "surprise" element in humor and the sudden flood of incongruity created by the punchline (Raskin, 1985; Perlmutter, 2002). There is certainly something incongruous about an elephant trying to hide in a strawberry patch and about a kangaroo walking into a bar, but the incongruity in these cases precedes the punchline. As Perlmutter points out, jokes of this sort require a fine balance between suspending everyday reality with its assumed logical relationships, and applying precisely those logical relationships that are required by the punchline. The incongruity itself contributes to the humorous enjoyment, but only when it has been resolved in an even more incongruous fashion ("by painting its toenails red").

Not all jokes and quips are necessarily incongruous, at least not in the sense of a mismatch between two or more central elements of the utterance. Consider a quip from the sociable conversation among a group of male firefighters that followed one of Gamson's (1992) focus groups.

> KEN: "I didn't *pull any punches.*"
> JOE: "You didn't *throw any*, either."

The teasing put-down is not incongruous in any obvious sense, although it does provide a nice example of playing with a common metaphorical idiom, based on boxing. (In a practice sparring match, the superior boxer will often '*pull*' his punches to soften the blow and avoid injuring an outmatched sparring partner.) The second speaker's quip is, on the surface, aggressive toward the first speaker, but like the examples Norrick (1993) provides, it is apparently offered and taken in good humor, between two men who work together on a daily basis and are on good terms with each other. Moreover, not all incongruities are humorous or even amusing (Ritchie, 2005). Raskin, Attardo, and other incongruity theorists acknowledge these difficulties, but their attempts to resolve them are not convincing (Brône and Feyaerts, 2004). As with aggression, it may be useful to distinguish between a deep level of incongruity (walking into a pub and ordering a beer is profoundly incongruous with what we know about kangaroos) and a purely linguistic incongruity, as between the commonplace metaphor, "*pull your punches*" and the less common extension, "*throw a punch.*"

A related approach emphasizes the shift from the frame established by the beginning of the joke to an alternative frame (Coulson, 2001). The kangaroo joke requires both a frame shift and the kind of suspension of normal logic described by Perlmutter. The hearer focuses on the incongruity of the kangaroo ordering and drinking a beer, and then the punchline forces a shift to a completely different frame, an economic frame involving inflated prices. In this alternative economic frame, the initially salient fact that the drinker is a kangaroo is irrelevant. Here the enjoyment of the joke is greatly enhanced by the perceptual simulations, both those activated by the initial frame and the introspective simulations activated by the substitute frame of the punchline.

Another example of a frame shift comes in a joke about hunting:

> Two hunters are out in the woods when one of them collapses. He doesn't seem to be breathing and his eyes are glazed. The other guy whips out his phone and calls the emergency services. He gasps, "My friend is dead! What can I do?"
> The operator says "Calm down. I can help. First, let's make sure he's dead."
> There is a silence, and then a shot is heard. Back on the phone, the hunter says "OK, now what?"

The 911 operator introduces an ambiguity that is not noticed until the punchline. Initially "*make sure* he's dead" is idiomatically understood as "check to see if he is really dead," and activates a frame in which one is expected to check for heartbeat and breathing. The punchline activates a very different frame associated with the phrase (if he isn't dead, kill him). One could interpret this in terms of aggression theory only with a considerable stretch, but neither does incongruity theory seem entirely adequate. As with the kangaroo joke, the perceptual simulations activated by the narrative seem crucial to the comprehension and enjoyment of the joke.

According to Giora (2003) we access the most salient meaning of a phrase such as "make sure he's dead" first. Humor exploits this tendency by providing an initial account consistent with a highly salient interpretation; the punch line forces us to revisit initially activated, but contextually suppressed schemas. A crucial feature of Giora's account is the prediction that jokes involve not merely a surprise ending, but active suppression of the original interpretation: "Whereas understanding irony and metaphor involves retention of salient, though contextually incompatible meanings … joke interpretation does not" (2003, p. 175).

Vaid *et al.* (2003) support Giora's claims with two semantic priming experiments, showing that the sense initially primed by a joke remained activated only at a low level during the final, resolution phase. On the other hand, in the "elephant" joke it is the contrast between the logical and "expected" schema-driven answer and the substitute schema activated by the punchline that renders the joke humorously absurd. Yus makes a similar point with respect to puns; for example: "Why did the cookie cry? Because its mother had been a wafer so long." As Yus points out, "Having decided that the text is intended as a joke, the hearer concludes that the two senses are supposed to co-exist humorously" (2003, p. 1299). Yus suggests that at least part of the humor derives from the pleasure of discovering the congruous elements, "a hypothesis which underlies so-called *arousal-safety theories*: the tension involved in searching for a solution may be released when the 'meaning' of a joke is discovered" (2003, p. 1314).

Sperber and Wilson (1986) initially argued that the search for a relevant context ceases with the *first* interpretation relevant in the currently active context. The punchline of a joke invalidates this initial interpretation by introducing totally irrelevant elements, and activates a new search for relevance, leading to a new interpretation based on an entirely different context, often a context that was initially rejected. The humorous effect results from a kind of "flood of relevance." This account also supports the importance of *cleverness* in the way ambiguity is resolved and the shift in frame accomplished. In the best jokes, the resolution unexpectedly *fits*. If the fit requires too great a '*stretch* of the imagination,' the joke or pun is likely to elicit a loud groan rather than the expected laughter.

The more dimensions of ambiguity the punchline is able to resolve, the better the joke. A good punchline will activate a context that is relevant in more than one way, thus leading to an unexpected increase in cognitive effects and an unexpected boost in relevance. A really *good* joke expresses some deeper and at least partially suppressed social truth, so that the increase in relevance produces changes in social and cultural contexts as well as cognitive and emotional contexts. The kangaroo joke is funny in part because it expresses a suppressed feeling of outrage many of us have felt when faced with an unexpectedly large restaurant or bar tab. These multi-level contextual effects supply the *meaning* of a good joke (Ritchie, 2005).

A cognitive evolutionary account of humor

Hurley, Dennett, and Adams (2011) propose a theory, which they claim subsumes all of these theories. Drawing on ideas from evolutionary psychology, combined with elements of incongruity theory and Fauconnier's (1994) concept of "mental *spaces*," Hurley, Dennett, and Adams argue in effect that humor has evolved as a mechanism that rewards the brain for identifying and correcting false assumptions. In brief, according to their model, evolution has rewarded development of two contradictory skills in our brains. On the one hand, we need to develop anticipations of future events rapidly and in great variety, in support of our ability to benefit from opportunities and avoid calamities. On the other hand, this anticipation-development function repeatedly produces erroneous assumptions, beliefs and expectations. These erroneous assumptions, beliefs, and expectations undermine the integrity of our representation of reality and require a balancing "*custodial*" task of detecting and correcting errors. This "*custodial*" task requires significant expenditure of mental effort, which is rewarded by the pleasure associated with mirth when we discover contradictions within our representation of reality. What produces genuine mirth is not the incongruity itself, but rather the sudden and unexpected identification and correction of the contradictory assumptions embedded in the incongruity.

As a joke or a comic scene in a movie unfolds, we set up a mental space in which is represented the comic character's beliefs, assumptions, inferences, and intentions. We set up another mental space in which is represented what we know about the true state of affairs. Mirth is produced when these mental spaces are merged or blended, the contradictory assumptions identified, and the false assumptions are corrected. The enjoyment of humor is frequently enhanced by combining this basic mirth with other positive emotions, including sexual arousal in off-color jokes, appreciation for cleverness or skill in setting up and telling a joke, enjoyment of wordplay and distorted images.

Playful humor

Most humor is playful in at least some sense. Jokes and quips often play with the form, sound, and meanings of words and phrases. As in the kangaroo and elephant jokes, they also play with our sense of ordinary reality. The hunter joke plays with the ambiguity of the phrase "make sure," and probably activates memories of B movies in which one character directs another to "make sure he's dead," along with the frustration listeners have felt when receiving poorly worded instructions.

In the quip from Gamson, Ken uses a familiar metaphorical idiom for speaking frankly and without reservation, "I didn't *pull any punches*." Joe's retort distorts the idiom, activates the underlying metaphor, and uses it to undermine Ken's bit of puffery: "You didn't *throw* any, either." Here, as in Norrick's (1993) data, the playful element in the give and take between these two firefighters is obviously an expression of the teasing that is basic to their friendship, and not an expression of hostility or superiority. They can tease each other back and forth precisely because they trust each other not to mean it or take it seriously; the teasing thus asserts and reaffirms their friendship.

TAUTOLOGIES AND NONSENSE

An interesting form of language play is the apparent tautology; for example, 'boys *will be boys*.' Here the first *boys* refers literally to juvenile males, but the second needs to be analyzed either as a metonymic reference to certain properties or actions associated with boys or even as a metaphor for certain forms of childish behavior associated with boys. Similarly, 'enough is enough' uses *enough* in the second position to imply a normative limit to whatever action or discourse has immediately preceded the statement, referenced by *enough* in the first position.

Many favorite examples come from the colorful baseball personality, Yogi Berra (2001), including "The game ain't over 'til it's over." Here *over* in both positions is a metaphor for the completion of a ball game or other activity. In the first position *over* refers to a common habit of sports commentators and others to assign victory to an athlete or team prior to the completion of the season or game, on the basis of an apparent insurmountable lead. In the second position, *over* refers to the actual completion of regulation play. The juxtaposition of the two turns the first position into a double metaphor.

Another common tautology, 'when ya gotta go ya gotta go' is applied to many forms of departure; it is also frequently applied to '*go*' as a metonymic reference to '*go to the bathroom*,' and the necessary bodily functions associated with that space. In either usage, the second position assigns finality and/or urgency to the first position. The phrase is also frequently used, at least in the United States, to attribute a scatological explanation for apparently nervous behavior. For example, in the Louis Armstrong version of "Baby it's cold outside," his duet partner, explaining why she could not stay for one more drink, sings "my father will be pacin' the floor," and Armstrong replies with a spoken aside, "when ya gotta go ya gotta go," which invites a double interpretation, both as a reference to her insistence on returning home and as an explanation of her father's nervous pacing (Armstrong and Middleton, 1949).

A different form is exemplified by the quote (possibly apocryphal) attributed to John Paul Jones when, his ship in ruins and apparently sinking beneath him, he was asked by the opposing British Captain, "Are you prepared to strike your colors?" (i.e., surrender), and Jones is quoted as replying "I have not yet begun to fight" (Bowen-Hassel *et al.*, 2003). This is a reverse or negative tautology – it is obvious from the context that Jones had been fighting for some time. The use of *"begin"* here suggests that what has come before was not *actually* fighting, which would be exemplified by what was to come.

Many tautologies are idiomatic, but the form also provides a resource in ordinary discourse. Glucksberg and McGlone (1999) cite "Cambodia is Vietnam's *Vietnam*," which appeared in several media commentaries on Vietnam's invasion of Cambodia in 1978. Here the trope refers to the problems the long involvement in the Vietnam war caused for the United States, and metaphorically transfers many of the entailments of the *US in Vietnam* schema to the topic, *Vietnam in Cambodia*. In a conversation among a group of homeowners about the conditions that make them feel that their neighborhood is safe relative to other close-in neighborhoods in Portland, the discussion turned to a habit of mutual watchfulness and one of the participants observed "You know everybody who's on the block ... an' so ... if there's *anything* ... that's *different* y'know ... and ... that's ... that's why ... um ... that's why *the block is the block*" (see Ritchie, 2011b). The first *block* refers to the geographic locale and metonymically to the social relationships among residents in that locale, and the second *block* refers to the participants' complex and positive feelings about these relationships and the feelings of pleasure and safety associated with them.

SOCIAL FUNCTIONS OF HUMOR AND PLAY

Humor often plays a complex role in social interactions. Recent research (see, e.g., Everts, 2003; Fine and De Soucey, 2005; Holmes and Marra, 2002; Plester and Sayers, 2007) has shown that group culture often includes a unique style and tradition of joking and teasing. Humor helps to define the group, distinguishing members from outsiders, building commitment to the group, and reinforcing acceptable behavior within the group. Humor is used to soften criticisms and negotiate differences of power and authority. In work groups humor can be used to challenge or subvert status hierarchies and to assert solidarity within subgroups.

Research in work settings (Holmes and Marra, 2002; Plester and Sayers, 2007) has sometimes emphasized the disruptive and distractive role of humor, the tendency of humor to distract attention from the business at hand. However, the use of humor to soften the expression of ideas that might otherwise meet resistance can also contribute to the accomplishment of group tasks. If a complex or morally ambiguous topic is under discussion, humor may be used to introduce sensitive ideas and express controversial views without taking direct responsibility for them.

HUMOR AS METAPHOR

Humorous quips as well as formal jokes often build on metaphors ("I didn't *pull any punches*") or depend on distortion of a familiar metaphorical idiom ("I've never *seen* the *ivory tower*"). There is also often a metaphorical element in narrative jokes. The kangaroo joke discussed earlier in this chapter provides a good example. The joke begins like a standard absurd joke ('a kangaroo walked into a bar'). But the punchline, 'at these prices, it's no wonder,' connects the joke to everyday experience and turns it into a metaphor for price inflation. The kangaroo maps onto tavern patrons, and the frame shift precipitated by the punchline implies, in effect, 'you may think it is absurd for a kangaroo to walk into a bar and order a beer, but it is not nearly as absurd as charging $10 for a beer!'

The joke about the hunter ('first, make sure that he's actually dead') is a *meta-communicative* metaphor. The panic-stricken hunter's confusion in the face of ambiguous instructions represents the confusion we all feel when faced with ambiguous instructions. The conversations analyzed in the next chapter include several other examples of both humorous distortions of familiar metaphorical idioms and metaphorical use of humorous anecdotes, quips, and jokes.

NARRATIVE ELEMENTS IN HUMOR AND SATIRE

Jokes often take the form of stories. This is exemplified by both the *kangaroo* joke and the *hunter* joke. However, even spontaneous quips and instances of wordplay often involve narratives, if only implicitly. In the exchange between the firefighters in Gamson's data, quoted in the preceding pages, "I didn't *pull any punches*" is a comment on the recalled narrative of the focus group discussion, but the response, "You didn't *throw any*, either" activates a narrative that is implicit in the metaphor vehicle, and contrasts it with the topic metaphor in a way that revises the implied narrative. The scientists' elaboration of the "*ivory tower*" metaphor not only takes the form of an extended narrative, which is transformed part-way through; it also invokes an underlying narrative about science funding, which is highly relevant to the overall topic of the conversation (Ritchie and Schell, 2009).

Schank and Abelson (1995) claim that memory works primarily in terms of narratives, that we remember events by telling others about them, and what we tell ends up being what we remember. Discussions of social and political issues such as public safety and homelessness often involve a sequence of narratives, including narratives embedded within narratives. These narratives are sometimes told for humorous effect, and sometimes even the stories told for serious purposes have bits of wordplay and humorous quips built in to them. It may be reasonable to extend Schank and Abelson's ideas about the memory function of narrative to embrace a social memory function of narratives that are told and retold; in effect, these narratives serve to construct a shared memory that comes to constitute the "history" of a group or of an entire culture.

CONCLUSION

Lakoff and Johnson (1980) claim that verbal metaphors express underlying conceptual metaphors, with the implication that the choice of words and phrases is constrained by the underlying conceptual metaphors. However, as Vervaeke and Kennedy (1996) point out, metaphorical expressions are often selected for rhetorical effect. Jokes and quips are also created and transformed for rhetorical effects, to accomplish task-oriented objectives (give information, and so on) as well as to accomplish social objectives, enhancing social bonds by generating shared pleasure (Norrick, 1993). In some cases, the play motive may be more important than the communicative intention. Metaphors and wordplay are often indulged simply to experience the pleasure of distorting language and subverting the communication process itself. The *absence* of interpretable '*content*' may contribute as much as anything else to the pleasurable, playful effect, and may in fact be the '*point*' of the utterance, as in "*fine as frog's hair*" and '*raining cats and dogs.*'

Metaphor and humor are frequently combined, and both of them frequently incorporate a good deal of language play. Both metaphor and humor rely heavily on narrative, and conversely, narratives often rely heavily on metaphor, humor, and other forms of wordplay.

It appears that most humor relies on an element of incongruity (Attardo, 2001; Martin, 2007) that either invokes a contrast between frames or forces an abrupt shift from one frame to another, radically different frame (Coulson, 2005). Metaphor also involves the juxtaposition of apparently incongruent frames, but in a way that seems to differ from the incongruity of humor or irony (Ritchie, 2005). However, the implied incongruity of many metaphors, like "*ivory tower*" or '*bulldozer*,' may provide ready material for conversion into a humorous story – and, like the Kangaroo joke, humorous stories often take the form of extended narrative metaphors. It appears that aggressive elements in humor can have an effect of social exclusion, when it is targeted at out-group members in a hostile manner. It can have an effect of social inclusion, when the aggression is playful. It can have an effect of simultaneously including in-group members and excluding out-group members. Sometimes, both speaker and listeners may be ambivalent as to whether the humor is to be taken as inclusive or exclusive.

DISCUSSION

Does the use of metaphors in a serious context such as a political speech or serious literature reflect a playful approach to language?

Work groups often engage in a bit of playful banter before a meeting. Is this a distraction or waste of time, or can it contribute to the group's productivity?

SUGGESTED READINGS

- Dunbar, R. (1996). *Grooming, gossip, and the evolution of language.* Cambridge, MA: Harvard University Press. Dunbar lays out the "grooming" theory of language in this very accessible and enjoyable book.
- Giora, R. (2003). *On our mind: Salience, context, and figurative language.* Oxford University Press. Giora is worth reading on both metaphor and humor. She proposes an approach that in my view almost certainly plays a role in both metaphor and humor use and comprehension – and her writing is clear and accessible to the non-specialist.
- Martin, R. A. (2007). *The psychology of humor: An integrative approach.* Amsterdam: Elsevier. This is an excellent and very accessible survey of contemporary theories of humor.

• Hurley, M. M., Dennett, D. C., and Adams, R. B., Jr. (2011). *Inside jokes: Using humor to reverse-engineer the mind.* Cambridge, MA: MIT Press. Here the authors develop an evolutionary cognitive account of humor. It is well written, very readable, and worth reading both for their theory itself and as a nice example of the evolutionary psychology approach to cognitive theory.

8 Metaphors in conversation

> Well that's the *journey* that I've – I've *been on* … the *journey*'s … been
> an *inner journey* … of *transforming* the – the feelings that were there at
> the beginning … the *pain* … and the *loss* … and the anger … and the
> grief … and … discovering that they can be *transformed*.
>
> (Jo Berry [Reconciliation Talks], quoted in Cameron [2007])

Cameron (2007; 2009) argues that our understanding of social interactions and the contexts in which they occur can be improved by
close attention to the pattern of metaphor use and storytelling,
and incorporates these elements into an analytic method, *Dynamic
Discourse Analysis*. Based on her research in elementary school class-
rooms, in the Reconciliation Talks, and in other conversational settings, Cameron has identified several patterns of thematic metaphor
use. In this chapter I will discuss several ways in which metaphors
are used in casual conversations, often in combination with humor,
irony, and storytelling. I will begin with a review of Cameron's (2007)
research on the Reconciliation Talks.

PATTERNS OF METAPHOR USE AND RE-USE

In October 1984 a bomb exploded in the Grand Hotel in Brighton,
England, where Prime Minister Margaret Thatcher and several
Members of Parliament were staying. Five people were killed by the
blast, including Sir Anthony Berry. Pat Magee, the Irish Republican
Army Operative who had planted the bomb several weeks earlier, was
later caught and imprisoned, then released under a peace agreement
in 1999. Soon after the bombing, Sir Anthony Berry's daughter Jo Berry
undertook what she described as "a *journey of healing*," attempting to
understand the motives behind the bombing and the events that led
to her father's death. This process led to a private face-to-face meeting
with Magee in late 2000, at Berry's request. That initial meeting led

to a series of further conversations between the two, some of which were video recorded, as well as to a series of joint public appearances and a television documentary. Through these conversations Berry and Magee became friends and collaborators in a peace-building project designed to bring about reconciliation in Northern Ireland and help other victims of the conflict.

Several of the conversations between Berry and Magee have been extensively analyzed by Cameron (2007; 2011). In her initial analysis of the Reconciliation Talks, Cameron focuses on four systematic groupings of metaphor, JOURNEYS, CONNECTION, SEEING MORE CLEARLY, and LISTENING TO A STORY (2007, p. 206). In this section I will summarize some key ideas from that initial analysis. I will generally follow Cameron's usage in which these groupings are analyzed as *thematic* metaphors, but I will also consider whether some of the metaphors used by Berry and Magee might also be analyzed as *conceptual* metaphors.

JOURNEY

Berry described an "*inner journey*" of "*healing*" as she sought to "*move on from*" her grief over the death of her father. She also described an "*outer journey*" in which she sought to understand the roots of violence and Magee's motives for his action, by "*walking in the footsteps of the bomber.*" This metaphorical "*outer journey*" involved an extended literal journey as Berry traveled around England and Northern Ireland to meet other victims, to meet with members of the Irish Republican Army, and eventually to meet with Magee. She used the JOURNEY metaphor to describe new challenges ("*there's another mountain to climb*") and the temporal sequence of the process ("*one step at a time*").

Berry's "*journey*" was a "*journey of discovery*" as well as of "*healing*." She described the purpose of her journey as "*to bring something – as much positive out of it as I could.*" According to Cameron this line characterizes the death of Berry's father as '*a place to move out of.*' At least one part of the "something *positive*" Berry "*brings back*" is "*transforming* her grief into compassion and empathy" and "*discovering* that they can be *transformed*" (Cameron, 2007, p. 208), which she later described as "the *gifts* that Brighton's *given me.*" All of this language is consistent with a JOURNEY OF EXPLORATION schema, but also with the HERO'S JOURNEY that appears in the mythology of many cultures and forms the core of many familiar fairy tales, in which the '*hero*' must accomplish some task, and usually bring back some valuable artifact (Campbell, 1949). These culturally shaped and shared schemas are available as discursive resources to everyone or virtually everyone in the culture, and they often appear in conversations and interviews about intense personal experiences (Taylor and Littleton, 2006).

The basic JOURNEY metaphor was elaborated in several ways, and connected with other groups of metaphors in several passages. In one passage, Magee characterized how he came to recognize the moral dimensions of his actions: "Magee … (2.0) but when you start *losing sight of* the … t- the – the fact that you're also harming a human being … (1.0) you *lose sight of* that, or ignore it, or you find it easier to ignore it … that's … always *had a price* … (1.0) and *some way*, well *down the line* … (1.0) you know, you're going to *come face-to-face with* that *price*" (Cameron, 2007, p. 209).

"*Seeing*" is often used as a metaphor for *understanding* but here it seems to refer more to *attention* or *awareness*. "*Price*" is a standard idiom for moral consequences of an action or decision, and fits within a more general MORALITY IS FINANCIAL ACCOUNTING metaphor group, which Lakoff (1996) identifies as a conceptual metaphor, and which was deployed in several other passages in the Reconciliation Talks. "*Come face-to-face with*" is metaphorical in the context of the passage, where it refers to a situation in which the forgotten or ignored facts can no longer be ignored, but as Cameron points out it is also metonymical, since the metaphorical event in which Magee "*comes face-to-face*" with the reality of his act, within the metaphorical JOURNEY OF UNDERSTANDING, was itself a result of coming physically face-to-face with Jo Berry. This literal/metaphorical idea of "*meeting face-to-face*" was repeated in several passages in other lexical forms, including "*sitting down and talking to the people who did it,*" "sitting in this wee kitchen, talking to this woman … whose father's dead," and "after all these decades we have *arrived at* a situation where we can now sit down across tables and talk to each other" (Cameron, 2007, pp. 210 and 211).

In another passage Magee used a different form of JOURNEY or MOTION metaphor, in combination with a variation on the SEEING vehicle, to express his own sense of moral responsibility in a different way: "I can't *walk away from* the fact that it was – I was directly responsible too for that. I can't *hide behind* the – you know the – sort of, *the bigger picture*" (Cameron, 2007, p. 210). "*Walk away from*" is a familiar metaphorical idiom for ignoring or evading responsibility for the consequences of an action, and "*hide behind,*" which entails MOTION TO ESCAPE SEEING OR BEING SEEN is a familiar metaphorical idiom for using an excuse to avoid moral responsibility. "*The bigger picture*" or "*the big picture*" is also a familiar idiom, used earlier in the conversations by Magee in reference to the political context of the bombing and his own political motives.

CONNECTION

In addition to *"meeting face-to-face"* and *"sitting down to talk,"* CONNEC-TION figured in another metaphor, first introduced by Berry when she read a poem she had written, in which she described reconciliation as *"building bridges."* As Cameron points out, this new metaphor initially "belonged to" (was introduced by) Jo, but Magee adopted it and reused it multiple times in the same and subsequent conversations. After Berry read the poem, Magee expressed appreciation for the poem, then transformed it to express his own thoughts: "in the er – the *journey, coming ... to a bridge,* you know, with *two ends,* er – that's – that's why this is so important" (Cameron, 2007, p. 213).

In a later conversation, Magee transformed the *"bridge"* metaphor even further, pointing out that bridges can also *"create distances"* and become *"barriers"* and *"exclusions."* Then he asserted that "if you *exclude anybody's voice,* you know, you're *sowing the seed* for later violence." Berry agreed, and Magee continued "the way to counter that is to *build bridges.* The way to ensure it doesn't happen is to *build bridges*" (Cameron, 2007, p. 214). Here, Magee began by transforming and virtually reversing the sense of Berry' s initial *"bridge"* metaphor by changing it from a metaphor of *"connecting"* to a metaphor of *"separating."* Then he elaborated the idea of *"barriers"* and explicated it in terms of *"excluding people's voices,"* and finally returned to the initial *"connection"* sense of the *"bridge"* metaphor. Each transformation indexes a different story (*"coming to a bridge,"* *"creating distances"* and *"excluding voices,"* then *"building bridges."* By connecting these stories with Berry's initial story of *"building bridges"* between communities, Magee drew attention to his own views regarding the social complexity of the process while supporting the process as a desirable step toward reconciliation.

SEEING

In earlier chapters I discussed several metaphors based on SEEING. Early in the series of conversations, Magee introduced the metaphor, asking Berry if she saw it as "the *big political picture.*" In passages previously quoted Magee referred to the danger of *"losing sight of"* the fact that human beings are involved. In the second talk, he expressed a similar thought: "if you're not *seeing* a human being *in front of you* ... if all you're *seeing* is an enemy." In the third talk, Magee referred to re-humanizing the Other as exchanging a *"deficient* or *distorted image"* for a "correct and *complete image*": "you *present* yourself in – in order, you hope, to *break down misrepresentations* because I – until we do *see each other in our true light,* we're always going to be dealing with some *reduction or a caricature*" Cameron (2007, p. 218). By extending and elaborating the SEEING metaphor, Magee added complexity to the topic, *understanding,* and elaborated on the cognitive obstacles to understanding, here expressed in terms of *"misrepresentation," "reduction,"* and *"caricature."*

Metaphors in the overall conversational context

Over the course of several conversations and interviews, the participants, Jo Berry and Pat Magee, developed a repertoire of metaphor vehicles that they drew on to express a range of ideas. The meanings attached to these vehicles in previous uses appears to have become part of their meanings for future uses within this sequence of conversations, and constitute something like a shared *interpretative repertoire* in the sense discussed by Taylor and Littleton (2006). Moreover, as Cameron points out, the re-use and transformation of each other's metaphors contributed to breaking down the *alterity* or emotional distance between them, and contributed to the development of empathic understanding.

The pattern of metaphor use across the entire series of conversations and the gradually changing nature of the relationship between Berry and Magee are important to understanding these metaphors, since they are used many times in different forms throughout the talks. In turn, as Cameron (2007) shows, the patterns of metaphor re-use and transformation are also crucial to understanding the content as well as the structure of the conversations. The shared cultural contexts and knowledge of other situations in which each of these metaphors has been used in the past also contribute to our understanding of their meaning in the context of these particular conversations.

Jo Berry's phrase, "the *gifts* that Brighton's *given me,*" has a form similar to Obama's characterization of "*carrying the blood of slaves and slave-owners*" as an "*inheritance*" that he and his wife "*pass on to*" their children, and poses some of the same interpretative challenges. *Brighton* stands metonymically for the murder of Berry's father by a terrorist bomb, which could render the use of the word "*gift*" ironic – but in the context of Berry' s utterance, "*gift,*" like Obama's reference to "*inheritance,*" was evidently *not* intended ironically. The meaning was explicated by Berry in the following sentences when she explained about learning to transform her grief into compassion and empathy. The event identified with *Brighton* and the emotional transformation described by Berry were separated by a long stretch of time; the metaphor requires the activation of a complex story, and invites the hearer to enter and participate in that story. In each example, it can be argued that the potential for ironic interpretation broadens and narrows the meaning of the phrases, *gift* and *inheritance* to refocus them on a very particular aspect of each concept.

From early in the talks, it appears that Berry and Magee engaged in a collaborative reconstruction of their understanding of the events that brought them together. They constructed their relationship with each other, consistent with their separate relationships with primary social groups; at the same time they collaborated to bring to the surface and partially resolve the tensions within their separate understanding of the bombing and its social and political context.

VEHICLE DEPLOYMENT AND TRANSFORMATION IN THE SCIENTISTS' CONVERSATION

Most of the key elements of metaphor use and development in the scientists' conversation have been discussed in earlier chapters. Here I will build on those earlier discussions to outline the thematic development of both metaphors and topics.

The scientists' conversation about communicating science to non-scientists (Ritchie and Schell, 2009) was part of a day-long conference on improving communication between scientists and members of the community affected by their work. The group of scientists had been talking about the fact that even a scientist doing basic research must continually seek funding, and Jack, one of the scientists in the group, summed it up by remarking, "Ya. There really is no more *ivory tower*." It appears that Jack used the phrase "*ivory tower*" in a strictly idiomatic way, to evoke an idealized situation in which a scientist or scholar is '*sheltered from*' the cares and concerns of ordinary life while conducting research and writing learned essays, in contrast to the situation faced by all of the scientists in the group. Although it may not be as familiar to members of the general public, "*ivory tower*" is a commonplace among academicians. Sometimes it is used (as it apparently was here) to describe an idealized research situation but it is often used to call attention to the fact that a particular line of inquiry has no apparent practical application by describing it as '*ivory tower research*.'

This kind of casual use of idiomatic metaphors is common in conversations, and often goes unremarked – compare "we'd be *swimming in* money," which appeared in the scientist's conversation just a couple of minutes before Jack's reference to the "*ivory tower.*" Participants in a conversation often do not appear even to notice that a phrase of this sort is metaphorical, and it is difficult to determine to what extent participants in the scientists' conversation processed the implicatures of these idiomatic metaphors. However, after the moderator unsuccessfully attempted to turn the conversation in a different direction (toward a metaphor of '*stewardship*' preferred by the conference organizers), one of the scientists picked up the phrase, and the following exchange ensued:

> LARRY: Jack said something, one way of ... of *capturing* part of that, ah, change of role is ah, no more *ivory tower*. It's probably, we're, we're *not there* now ... it's probably not too *far in* the future.
>
> JIM: I've never really *seen the ivory tower*. (Laughter)
>
> LARRY: You haven't. They never did *let you in* did they?
>
> JACK: Is that what you *dream about, in the night*, Jim? *Ivory tower* you just go to sleep, and the first thing you get is the seven million dollar grant from ... to do whatever you want ... from the MacArthur Foundation? and you *go up into the ivory tower*. What the, *open pit, unstable wall*.
>
> JAN: Ya the *unstable*.
>
> LARRY: Ya, instead of the *ivory tower*, we're in an *unstable foundation*.

Larry's initial repetition of Jack's phrase remained within the idiomatic sense of "*ivory tower*" as an idealized situation, but it appeared in a cluster of other idiomatic metaphors, including "*capture*," "we're *not there* now," and "not too *far in* the future." The last two of these may have activated the spatial metaphor, TIME IS DISTANCE, and drawn attention to the "*ivory tower*" as an OBJECT IN SPACE, specifically a certain kind of STRUCTURE. Jim's quip, "I've never really *seen the ivory tower*," connects the dual meaning of "*ivory tower*" as a *kind of structure* and an *idealized situation* with the dual meaning of another conceptual metaphor, EXPERIENCING IS SEEING. It seems likely that the laughing response to Jim's quip simultaneously expressed appreciation for his verbal cleverness and the audience members' recognition that his comment applied to them as well. This kind of wordplay in which metaphor vehicles are used and combined in ways that express surprising but readily recognized truths is quite common in conversation.

Larry's response, "They never did *let you in* did they?" continued the wordplay surrounding the dual meaning of "*ivory tower*" by activating another aspect of the STRUCTURE vehicle and blending it with a third conceptual metaphor, ACCEPTANCE IS ENTRY, thus emphasizing the sense of *privilege* and *exclusivity* associated with the "*ivory tower*" vehicle.

Among other entailments, this additional transformation of the initial metaphor also retroactively imbued Jim's quip with an element of pathos and complaining, as well as potentially implying that Jim had been found unworthy of "*entry*" into "*the ivory tower*." This kind of move, in which an instance of clever wordplay is extended and turned against the initial speaker in a teasing way, is fairly common in conversation (Norrick, 1993). In some situations it can have an aggressive tone that asserts power over the initial speaker or serves the function of social discipline directed against the initial speaker (Billig, 2005), but in a group of co-equal friends, like the scientists' group, it is more likely to serve a bonding function (Norrick, 1993).

Jack's extended turn began by reinforcing the jibe against Jim, "Is that what you *dream about, in the night*, Jim?" But then he developed the DREAM metaphor along with the STRUCTURE aspect of the "*ivory tower*" metaphor and combined it with a pun on *Foundation* to transform the initial metaphor into a comment on the group's *shared* situation, with the collaboration of Jan and Larry, who summed up the transformed metaphor: "instead of the *ivory tower*, we're in an *unstable foundation*."

Several things are noteworthy about this example. The participants began with an idiomatic metaphor that is quite conventional, at least among scientists and other academicians. Jim initially transformed the idiomatic metaphor as a humorous comment on his situation as a theoretical scientist who must continually search for funding. The others further transformed the metaphor as a humorously teasing insult, then elaborated it into a story that expresses the ambiguity of their shared roles as scientists working in a government-funded lab (coincidentally bringing Jim back into the group). Through this collaborative transformation and re-transformation of the "*ivory tower*" metaphor, the group members simultaneously described their actual situation and their response to it by contrasting it with the detailed implicatures of the "*ivory tower*," from which they are *all* excluded – and which, in any event, has an "*unstable foundation*."

Steen (2008) argues that standard accounts of metaphor recognition and interpretation are based on a model with two dimensions, language and cognition. He proposes that a third dimension, communication, should be explicitly recognized. Adding this third dimension facilitates distinguishing between metaphors that are used deliberately (with the intention that they be understood as metaphors) and metaphors that are not used deliberately. In Larry's initial statement from the scientist's conversation, "no more *ivory tower*," "*ivory tower*" may not have been used deliberately as a metaphor, but in Jim's quip,

"I've never really *seen the ivory tower,*" the humor depends on under-standing the phrase as a metaphor and focusing on the literal mean-ing of the vehicle, *ivory tower,* as something that can be seen. Larry's response, "they never *let you in,* did they?" carries this "literalization" (Cameron, 2007) of the metaphor vehicle further, focusing on *ivory tower* as a structure with an entrance that can be locked to exclude those deemed unworthy of entry.

In traditional approaches to metaphor theory, creative invention and uses of metaphors are typically associated with literature and the arts. As a consequence it is often assumed that metaphor use in conversation, especially ordinary casual conversation, is restricted to conventional (*'dead'*) metaphors or repetition of more colorful meta-phors that were originally encountered in literature or mass media. Certainly, Jack's initial comment, "there is no more *ivory tower,*" fits this account: Jack used "*ivory tower*" in a purely conventional way as a term designating an idealized situation, just as "*swimming in* money" was used, a few minutes earlier in the conversation, as a conventional expression for abundance. However, the ensuing transformation of "*ivory tower*" suggests a degree of creativity and wit that is quite at variance with the standard account; similar creative transformations of familiar idiomatic metaphors have been observed in many other conversational contexts. Even highly conventional metaphors are often used in original ways to accomplish particular effects.

Metaphors may be developed in several ways within a portion of a conversation, across the entire conversation, or sometimes across multiple conversations (Cameron, 2007; 2009). The "*ivory tower*" example illustrates several interesting forms of metaphor use in con-versations. In addition to the creative transformation of idiomatic metaphors, the "*ivory tower*" passage also illustrates the way conversa-tionalists sometimes play with the form of idiomatic metaphors for humorous effect as well as to express original meanings. Finally, it also illustrates how metaphors can be (and often are) developed into narratives that expand their expressive potential.

Metaphors and identity

Issues of scientific identity, the conflict between pure and applied sci-ence, and related issues of research funding were introduced early in the scientists' conversation, and reappeared in several guises before culminating in the creative language play in the "*ivory tower*" sequence. Scientific identity arose at the very outset, in the joking resistance to the label "*professionals,*" beginning the playful banter about "*geeks and nerds,*" and culminating in the use of the idiom "I've been called lots of things, but never *professional*" (Chapter 3). This ironically negative use of "*professional*" introduced the theme of the Platonic separation of the pursuit of knowledge from practical cares that was briefly reiterated in the passage about "*swimming in* money" and then developed more fully in the collaborative transformation of "*ivory tower*."

"*Ivory tower*" is a common idiom among scientists and academicians, and when it was first introduced, the linguistic context ("there really is no more *ivory tower*") is such that it may have been processed as a lexical unit and interpreted by activating the idiomatic meaning, with little or no further elaboration. However, the subsequent expansion, "it's probably, we're, we're *not there* now it's probably not too *far in* the future," by combining it with a TIME IS SPACE metaphor, demonstrates that at least one of the listeners processed it as a metaphor. The immediately following quip, "I've never really *seen the ivory towe*r," is almost certain to have activated the metaphor with its visual as well as emotional and introspective simulations, and these were richly exploited in the ensuing narration, in which the initial implicatures of "*an exclusive and protected place to do pure science*" were first exploited in an ironic tease, then developed into a metaphor for their current situation: "instead of the *ivory tower*, we're in an *unstable foundation*."

The "*ivory tower*" passage brought together the troubling themes of identity, pure versus applied science, and anxiety about funding and provided a kind of ironic resolution. It also advanced the stated purpose of the focus group itself, by exploring or at least setting the stage for exploring the role of scientists in communicating about their science to the lay public (Ritchie and Schell, 2009).

Throughout the first part, the participants collaborated in teasing each other and the moderator and in developing and transforming metaphors, in particular the "*ivory tower*" metaphor. The metaphor-based wordplay in the "*ivory tower*" passage appears to have been spontaneously generated, in part in response to the words themselves and in part in response to the foregoing conversation and especially to the underlying contrasts and contradictions between the group members' public roles as publicly funded scientists and their private identities as disinterested seekers of knowledge. This passage marked a transition from a playfully ironic, teasing, and occasionally resistant phase in which the group collectively came to understand then come to terms with its part in the larger event of which this one conversation is only a small part, to a more cooperative and ultimately highly productive discussion of the issues they were initially asked to address. As in the reconciliation dialogues analyzed by Cameron, these scientists collaboratively modified, combined, and transformed a set of stock metaphors, drawn from their common culture (Nerlich, 2003), in a way that expressed both their social relationships and their shared perception of their situations as "pure" scientists working on "applied" problems.

This example, like the Reconciliation Talks, underscores the importance of considering the broader social and cultural context of metaphors. As discussed in previous chapters, some of the metaphors can only be understood with reference to external and unstated cultural knowledge. The play on the word "*professional*" and the teasing about the "*ivory tower*" both make sense only in the context of knowledge about the higher prestige accorded, among scientists, to "*pure*" (theoretical) science over "*applied*" (professional) science, which dates back at least to the time of Plato.

COLLABORATIVE AND HUMOROUS TRANSFORMATION OF METAPHORS

Several interesting examples of metaphor play come from a conversation from the public safety and police–community relations study that took place among a group of young adults in Portland, Oregon (Ritchie, 2010a; 2010b). The participants in this conversation were all politically active in 'New Left' political protests, which often involve tense confrontations with riot police. All of them, particularly Tyler, seemed to nurture self-identities as marginally '*tough-minded*,' and existing at the fringes of the law, almost '*outlaws*.' This '*bad boy*' identity was expressed partly through joking and exaggeration and partly through deployment of outrageous and shocking images and metaphors.

At the very beginning of the conversation, Tyler introduced an implicit "*servant*" metaphor for the police: "I think they should be *like firemen, like letting cats out of trees.*" Michael made the metaphor explicit, "Would they be *civil servants* in that case, right?" After a brief discussion of the police use of non-lethal violence, Jordan returned to the "*public servant*" metaphor, leading to the following exchange:

> JORDAN: Police are *like garbage men*. They deal with a lot of things we don't want to deal with. That would be like drunk and disorderly parts of society.
>
> TYLER: Yeah. So do social workers, right? And doctors. I don't want to cut someone open and look at their guts. Well, okay I might. (Laughter) Fuck. Now everyone knows I'm a serial killer. And not

just the people in this room, but someone else I'm going to have to kill when they read this. This is great.

Jordan's *"garbage men"* metaphor was evidently intended seriously in that it rendered the meaning of the subsequent "things we don't want to deal with" in graphic terms. At the same time, by comparing police officers to garbage men, a stereotypically low-status occupation, Jordan appears to have intended to transfer the implication of low social status to police officers as well.

The denigration of police officers is somewhat standard rhetorical practice among political activist groups (cf. terms like *"pigs"* for the police), but it appears that Tyler intended to soften the effect by shifting the comparison to a higher-status group, social workers, and then to an even higher-status group, doctors. Bringing it back to the theme of "things we don't want to deal with," he explained, "I don't want to cut someone open and look at their guts," then seized on the comic potential of his own statement by adding, "Well, okay I might."

Jordan's comment was intended to illustrate "things we don't want to deal with" by activating aversive perceptual simulations of the smells, sights, and sounds associated with garbage trucks, then those associated with people who are "drunk and disorderly," then connecting them with the *police officer* schema. After extending this series of simulations by activating a surgeon schema, Tyler exploited the semantic connection and used the dramatic perceptual simulations it activated to enact a script familiar to all participants from popular movies. It appears that the incongruity of the simulations alerted him to the comic possibilities, motivating him to enact another, loosely connected story-world role, and to extend the fantasy story to a scenario in which his slip of the tongue would reveal his (imagined) criminal identity and force him to kill all the witnesses. The humor grew out of the incongruity of the progression of concepts and associated perceptual simulations, from police officers to garbage men to surgeons, then to autopsies, and finally to the *serial murderer* schema, strengthened by the incongruous contrast between those gruesome images and the present conversation. This is an example of thematic chaining in which the relevance is in the activated perceptual simulations rather than semantic meanings. This kind of playful chaining in which a serious comment is followed immediately by a humorously incongruous comment occurred repeatedly in this conversation.

Tyler pursued the implications of his mock confession that he might "want to cut someone open and look at their guts" by assuming the mass media-inspired role of a serial killer, forced to protect himself from exposure by killing all the current and potential witnesses to his "confession." At the surface level this can be characterized as the kind of media-inspired role playing that is common in friendly banter of this sort, but it also expresses, in an extremely exaggerated form, the 'bad boy' image Tyler projected repeatedly throughout the conversation. Capping the series of dramatic reframings, Tyler's comment "this is great" presents at least a double irony. Within the story-world (Tyler as master criminal) it is ironic in that having openly confessed to being a serial killer would be anything *but* "great." One level up, in the discourse world in which he has just reframed a serious discussion as a humorous media-inspired role play, "this is great" can be interpreted as an ironic comment on his own disruption of the conversation. Yet another level up, it could be interpreted as a literal self-congratulation on his successful role play.

Another example of identity reframing through role playing came about a minute later, when Tyler interrupted his own serious response to a serious remark from another participant, turned to Celeste, and remarked "You're awfully quiet, short one." The others laughed, and he asked Celeste: "Are you a cop? Are you a cop? Are you a cop?" Celeste replied, "no," and Tyler concluded "That's three times, okay. We're cool."

Here, Tyler enacted a script that is commonplace among political radicals, users of controlled substances, and others who regard themselves as potential targets for investigation by undercover police officers. The common belief is that a police agent who denies being a police officer three times cannot use any subsequent evidence in court. The humor stems from the incongruity of applying this test near the beginning of a thoroughly innocuous conversation that is being audio-recorded as part of a school assignment, and from applying it to a friend whom Tyler knows is not a police agent. In addition to teasing Celeste, the digression served to '*spice up*' the conversation by pretending that they were engaged in a conversation that might be of interest to an undercover agent, and to reinforce their shared identity. It also served to enact and reinforce Tyler's playful '*outlaw*' image.

Following Tyler's first '*master criminal*' digression, Michael returned to the "*public servant*" metaphor, and asserted that "there is a certain type of person that wants to be a policeman." Celeste replied, "Trash collector is much more important," reinstating both the "*public servant*" metaphor and the denigrating comparison to trash collectors, emphasized by asserting that it is even more important than policing.

In these passages, Tyler played with his own identity, and he and Celeste both played with the form of the conversation itself. This identity play and shifting of levels from serious to joking and from metaphorical role playing to reality continued throughout the conversation, and involved all the participants at one time or another. They apparently took the topic seriously, but whenever the conversation threatened to become *too* serious, one of them, usually Tyler or Celeste, would use language play or teasing to alleviate the seriousness and restore a mood of conviviality. The incongruous contrasts between the 'outlaw' play and the conversation itself contributed to maintaining the conversation as a fundamentally *social* event, in spite of its proximate *academic* purpose and *political* content.

These episodes also nicely illustrate shifting "*levels*" in conversation (Clark, 1996). The base level is a group of friends discussing public safety and the role of police officers. Jordan took the conversation up a level to a hypothetical world in which police officers are like garbage men. Tyler extended this hypothetical world to include surgeons, then shifted to a play frame and moved the conversation up another level to a world in which he is a serial killer who must kill all the witnesses to protect himself. The humor required crossing levels but maintaining both levels at the same time in order to contrast the fictional story world with the actual world. This easy movement among levels is frequently observed when stories are told in casual conversations, and is often a feature of humorous banter.

The "*public servant*" metaphor for the role of police officers was transformed again much later in the conversation into a "*food server*" metaphor. This began with a conversation about police officers who make mistakes or fail to follow procedures, often with lethal consequences such as shooting and wounding or killing innocent and often unarmed civilians. Tyler compared police in these instances to "a *servant*, like a *waiter or waitress*, right? So if they *fuck up*, they say, oh, I'm really sorry. You want to talk to my boss or manager?" Then he built on the incongruity of the comparison by using a commonplace but trivial mistake that a waitress might make and contrasting it with the sort of mistake a police officer might make. "If a waitress approached you with saying, oh I'm really sorry, you said 'over medium,' but I got you over easy. Cops just fucking *pepper sprayed your baby*, even more so, right?"

The "*breakfast order*" story potentially activates a familiar story script, and the "*baby doused with pepper spray*" potentially activates a very different and very intense set of simulations that contrast in an incongruous way with the blander simulations of the "*breakfast order*" story. This incongruity adds to the hilarity of the conversation but at the same time it also helps build the *serious* rhetorical point about the need to hold police officers more accountable when they make mistakes that cause intense pain and suffering to innocent civilians ("*your baby*").

Tyler built on the incongruity of the violent image introduced by "*pepper-sprayed your baby*" by developing the "*waitress*" metaphor in a bawdy, earthy direction: "If you're a waitress and you're not getting good tips and you think people hate you, then you should *quit pissing in their soup.*" This led to the following exchange, in which Celeste added to the incongruity by moving the conversation back from Tyler's fantasy world to the basic world of "here and now":

> MICHAEL: Of course, the fallacy of that assumption …
>   the waitress is doing something blatantly crazy unethical.
> CELESTE: Some places you get tipped more for that.
> MICHAEL: Like, I love that sauce. (Laughter)
> TYLER: You guys have the best soup. (Laughter)
> CELESTE: We do.

The obvious primary purpose of this sequence was to exploit the comic potential of Tyler's bawdy metaphor; it also continued and reinforced the group's identity as daring and outrageous, and maintained the conviviality of the interaction.

Virtually all of the analogies and metaphors used in this conversation were deliberately exaggerated. The exaggeration seems to have served at least three purposes at once. It emphasized the serious rhetorical point being made (if a waitress apologizes for bringing you the wrong eggs, a police officer should certainly apologize for causing grievous injury and suffering). It created incongruous images that enhanced participants' enjoyment of the conversation. The casual use of violent and earthy stories and metaphors ("*serial killer*," "*pepper spray your baby*," "*piss in your soup*") employed throughout the conversation provided much the same kind of pleasure that is associated with the horror movie and crime movie genres, and it expressed and reinforced the participants' individual and collective identities as tough-minded political activists operating outside or at least near the fringes of normal society.

AFFECTIVE IMPACT OF NON-METAPHORICAL LANGUAGE

Metaphors are often used to express or evoke particularly strong emotions, or to express particular qualities of emotions. At one point in the Reconciliation Talks, Jo describes her desolation as "*crying in the wilderness.*" In the New Left conversation about police discussed in the last section, the participants used intense metaphors such as "*pepper-sprayed your baby*" and "*pissing in your soup*" to express their horror and disgust at alleged police activities and attitudes.

As Cameron (2008, p. 203) points out, sometimes the *absence* of metaphor can be even more expressive. In one example from the Reconciliation Talks, Jo tells Pat about a conversation with her daughter prior to going to meet him:

> JO: Before I ... left this morning, I decided to tell my children ... that I was going to meet you.
> PAT: Hmh
> JO: ... and I told my seven-year-old.
> PAT: Yeah
> JO: ... and she said, I want to come ... I want to tell him... that it was a bad thing he did, to kill my mum's daddy.
> PAT: hmh
> JO: I want to tell him,
> PAT: hmh
> JO: ... can I come? She said, and I said, well no ... but you can write it *down*, or I'll tell him.

As Cameron points out, presenting the raw facts in the child's own words ("kill my mum's daddy") creates a particularly strong emotional impact on the audience. Its effect on Pat was demonstrated when he referred to it in subsequent conversations, a few weeks later and then again after the lapse of several years.

Another example comes from the African American men's conversation about police–community relations, when George tells a story that is clearly known to all of the participants:

> Tony Stevens was ex-Marine, Vietnam era. He had a guy came in. Robbed a gas station. Tony grabbed the guy and held him down. The police came in. In spite of what everybody in the surrounding area was telling them, the police *jumped on* Tony, and choked him to death. Why? The perpetrator was white and Tony was black. And this was a detective that did it. This was when Potter was chief of police. There are certain *patterns* that happen. (Ritchie, 2010a)

Here, George's use of short, direct sentences to set up the scene and relate the events enhance the impact of the story (which was almost certainly known to the other participants in the conversation, but may not have been known to the two graduate students who were facilitating and recording it). In this context, "*jumped on*," which is often used metaphorically, may be literally true. The almost dispassionate use of the metaphorical "*patterns*" in the coda (the last line) is strengthened by the raw factual language of the story itself: "There are certain *patterns* that happen."

META-COMMUNICATIVE USES OF METAPHORS IN CONVERSATION

In addition to their expressive functions, metaphors are often used to influence and shape the progress of a conversation and to influence how utterances are understood within a conversation (Cameron, 2008). As indicated in the preceding sections, once a metaphor (or a story) has been introduced into a conversation it provides a common discursive resource that is available to all participants. Metaphors and other linguistic devices may also be used to influence how metaphors and stories are understood ("*tuning*"), to manage the flow of a conversation, and influence how topics are understood or even how the conversation itself is understood ("*framing*").

"Tuning" metaphors in conversation

Cameron and Deignan (2003) describe a group of expressions they call "*tuning devices*" that are often used to qualify or constrain the way metaphors are interpreted. They initially identified these devices in data from Cameron's (2003) study of classroom discourse, and then used corpus-based analysis to find similar devices in a large body of discourse. Tuning devices may be used to direct the audience to a particular interpretation – "*a sort of nickname*"; "like *runny butter*"; "rock actually *melts*" (Cameron and Deignan, 2003, p. 253). Tuning devices may adjust or add to the strength of a metaphor – "just *make a little mental note*"; "you can't just *let it rip*." Tuning devices may be used to strengthen metaphor – "we need to really *polish it up*" (p. 154) or to draw attention to a metaphor – "So you can actually *switch off* and be in the country"; "He literally *went through the roof*" (p. 155).

Managing the conversation

Cameron (2008, pp. 204–205) provides several examples of the use of metaphors to manage the flow and direction of a conversation. Two examples of conversation-management metaphors come from the Reconciliation Talks: "a question that *comes to* my mind," and "[a question that] we've *covered before*." From talk between doctors and patients comes "let me just say something and *put it on the table*" and "let me *go back one step*." From Cameron's classroom data comes

"I'm going to ... *give you a little bit of* information *on* which we can *build* our understanding."

In the African American men's conversation about crime and public safety one of the facilitators introduced the topic as follows: "thank you for kind of *being a part of* this group ... We wanted to just to invite you To kinda tell the group about *what comes to mind.*" In the Latino Group discussion of crime and public safety, the facilitator's introduction included the following metaphors: "how do you *feel about* policing in your communities. We are also interested in *gathering* what are your thoughts *on* this topic, um views. Feel free to *share* any stories." Later in the same conversation one of the participants referred to a previous topic: "it's kind of *going back to* what we were talking about." In general, people often draw on metaphors of MOTION (A CONVERSATION IS A JOURNEY; A TOPIC IS A PLACE) and objectification (A STORY OR THOUGHT IS AN OBJECT) in conversation management meta-communication.

Framing and reframing

Chapter 6 explained how metaphorical language can be used to frame topics as well as interactions and social relationships. The conversations discussed in this chapter provide examples of each type of framing. In the Reconciliation Talks, Berry's metaphor of "*healing*" framed her grief and her attempts to come to terms with it by understanding the motivations of the bomber in terms of a "*wound*" that can be "*healed.*" Her use of a "*journey*" metaphor strengthened the implications that her grief was something to be actively encountered rather than simply accepted passively. When Magee adopted these same metaphors, later on, he accepted and endorsed this framing, and in effect committed himself to collaborating in the process.

When Magee spoke of "*losing sight of*" the humanity of his enemy, as something for which a "*price*" must be paid, then spoke of "*coming face-to-face with* that *price,*" he framed his earlier actions in terms of a kind of moral blindness, then reframed it in terms of moral accounting, a framing that committed him to accepting responsibility for the human (i.e. social and emotional) consequences of his actions. This was reinforced when he said "I can't *hide behind* the you know the – sort of, *the bigger picture.*" Here he activated a metaphorical frame, "*the big picture,*" that is often used to justify apparently immoral or inconsistent actions in terms of more inclusive concerns, only to reject it by reinforcing the moral accountability implications of the UNDERSTANDING IS SEEING frame. All of this, as Cameron (2007; 2009) shows, contributed to the growth of empathetic understanding and to reframing the relationship between Berry and Magee from one of adversaries to one of mutually empathetic collaborators in a process of peace-making. This reframing of their personal relationship also takes place within and has meaning within the broader political context of the somewhat uneasy peace process in Northern Ireland.

In the scientists' conversation, the early banter about "*geeks and nerds*" and "I've been called lots of things, but never *professional*" effectively rejected the event organizer's framing of the group members' identity and replaced it with a label that framed their roles in a way more to their liking. "*Swimming in* money" established a frame in which financial considerations are of paramount importance. The sequence in which "*ivory tower*" was transformed began with a teasing reframing of Jim's quip about not having "*seen the ivory tower*" into a kind of whining complaint ("*they never let you in, did they?*") Then it activated yet another frame, in which the crumbling of the "*ivory tower*" signifies the disappearance of the standard model of science, and broadens the jibe against Jim as a depiction of the condition they were all in.

In the political activists' discussion of police–community relations, Jordan's "*garbage men*" simile framed police officers not merely as *public servants* but also as *low status public servants*. Tyler's extension to *social workers* and *doctors* reduced the *low status* implication but left the *public servant* frame intact, and that was the dominant frame for the rest of the conversation. Tyler's segue into a "*serial killer*" play-frame was one of many instances in which wordplay and role enactment was used to reinstate or strengthen a *non-serious, convivial conversation* frame for the conversation itself. Celeste's re-lexicalization of the "*breakfast waitress*" metaphor for police officers derailed an ostensibly serious discussion centered around this metaphor and, by drawing the others into a story-world in which a waitress might actually urinate into a customer's soup – and the customer reward her with a larger tip – Celeste emphatically reinstated the playful, convivial conversation frame.

SUMMARY

Metaphors appear throughout some conversations, and only rarely in others. When they do appear, metaphors can serve a variety of conversational purposes, including purposes related to relationship development, social bonding, identity construction and identity reinforcement as well as the more conventionally recognized communicative functions related to informing and persuading. In her analysis of the Reconciliation Talks Cameron (2007) shows how a set of thematically related metaphors were deployed, repeated, and transformed both within individual conversations and across conversations, and contributed to developing the conditions for increased empathetic understanding between the participants. In the scientists' conversation and the New Left conversation, an even smaller set of thematically related metaphors served simultaneously to advance the purpose of the conversation, to express and develop the group's collective identity, and to reinforce and express group solidarity through metaphor-based teasing and joking. In each of these conversations the metaphors also serve to connect the internal themes within the conversation to broader themes in the surrounding political and social context.

Implications for conversation structure

In order to participate effectively in conversation, a speaker must sustain coherence by consistent and relevant activation of themes, semantic links, and perceptual simulations that are relevant both in the context of the immediate conversation and in broader contexts including relationships and socio-cultural background. It is also necessary to supply sufficient rewards to sustain attention and motivate processing (Abbott, 2008). In the storytelling literature, attention-sustaining is often discussed primarily in terms of *information* that improves listeners' representations of the world, but *enjoyment* is at least as important as information (Dunbar, 1996; Ritchie and Dyhouse, 2008). As Celeste's successful digression in the "*pissing in your soup*" example illustrates, the entertainment motivation may often be more important than the informational or persuasive motivation. Indeed, metaphors and stories often present information already well-known to other participants or, as in the New Left group conversation, pertain to invented fictional worlds based on attitudes and beliefs common to the participants.

All of these conversations present examples of metaphorical framing, both applied to topics and to the conversations themselves, and illustrate how metaphors and narratives can contribute to bringing frame conflicts and contradictions to the surface and resolving them. Each conversation also presents many examples of collaborative cognition, both in developing narratives and in representing complex ideas and relationships in stories and metaphorical form that render them more comprehensible.

DISCUSSION

Thibodeau and Boroditsky (2011) report experiments suggesting that clusters of thematically related metaphors do not necessarily increase framing effects. How might a similar research design be applied to understand the framing effects of thematic metaphors in other contexts, such as conversations?

How might researchers test whether thematic clusters enhance activation of perceptual simulations and stories, and transport hearers into a story world?

How closely do participants ordinarily keep track of metaphors and themes in a casual conversation?

How important is it in ordinary casual conversation that every utterance be clearly relevant to the context of what has gone before?

SUGGESTED READINGS

- Cameron, L. J. (2007). Patterns of metaphor use in reconciliation talk. *Discourse and Society, 18*, 197–222. Cameron, L. J. (2008). Metaphor and talk. In Gibbs, R.W., Jr. (ed.), *The Cambridge handbook of metaphor and thought*. Cambridge University Press, pp. 197–211. These two articles lay out Cameron's approach to dynamic discourse analysis in detail; although there is some repetition, both are well worth reading.
- Clark, A. (1997). *Being there: Putting brain, body, and world together again*. Cambridge, MA: MIT. This engaging book presents a very accessible discussion of extended cognition.
- Ritchie, L. D. (2010a). "*Everybody goes down*": Metaphors, stories, and simulations in conversations. *Metaphor and Symbol, 25*, 123–143. This article provides a more detailed analysis of the interaction of metaphors with storytelling, and their combined contribution to conversations.

9   Metaphors in politics

Where we know we can *make a difference* in the future, we *set out our stall* for the people with confidence. Because now they are thinking, reflecting – do we *go forward* with Labour, or *back to* the Tories. Our task is to persuade them to *go forward*.

(Tony Blair, 2005, address to the Conference of the Labour Party, Gateshead)

This was one of the tasks we *set forth* at the *beginning of this campaign* – to *continue the long march* of those who *came before us,* a *march* for a more just, more equal, more free, more caring and more prosperous America. I chose to *run* for the presidency *at this moment in history* because I believe deeply that we cannot solve the challenges of our time unless we solve them together – unless we *perfect our union* by understanding that we may *have different stories*, but we *hold common hopes*; that we may not look the same and we may not have *come from the same place*, but we all want to *move in the same direction* – *towards a better future* for our children and our grandchildren.

(Barack Obama, 2008, "A More Perfect Union," Philadelphia, PA)

Politics is about material needs and actions, repairing streets and bridges, educating children, protecting people from crime, war, and natural disaster, as well as about more abstract needs and values – freedom, justice, and dignity. Politics is also about the organization of social relationships, about power, influence, the balance between autonomy and community, about trade-offs between contradictory needs and values. All of this complexity is reflected, in political discourse, in the metaphors people use and the stories they tell.

In this chapter I will begin with a more detailed examination of the use of metaphors in Blair's Gateshead speech and Obama's Philadelphia speech. Then I will broaden the discussion to a more general consideration of conceptual and thematic metaphors that are widely used in political discourse. Finally I will review the findings of research on metaphors used in discourse about specific topics, including metaphors that have been used in discourse about local issues.

CONCEPTUAL METAPHORS IN CAMPAIGN SPEECHES
BY TONY BLAIR AND BARACK OBAMA

Although the Gateshead and Philadelphia speeches were given in very different situations, both Blair and Obama used phrases that draw on some of the same underlying conceptual metaphors, including POL-ITICS IS A JOURNEY and GOOD IS IN FRONT. Each developed these conceptual metaphors in different ways and combined them with other metaphors in different ways, reflecting the differences in their political situations, the political traditions of their respective nations, and their own personalities.

Tony Blair: "forward, not back"

(This section is based in part on the more detailed analysis in Ritchie, 2008a.)

For Blair, the SPATIAL ORIENTATION and JOURNEY metaphors had already been introduced by the Labour Party theme, "*forward, not back.*" As a political slogan, "*forward*" potentially activates perceptual simulations such as satisfaction and motion toward a desired goal. Conversely, "*back*" potentially activates simulations of frustration and motion away from a desired goal. Following conceptual metaphor theory, these metaphor vehicles can be identified with conceptual metaphors such as ACCOMPLISHMENT IS MOVEMENT TOWARD A GOAL and THE FUTURE IS IN FRONT. However, "*back*" is also identified with positive ideas, as in metaphors such as HOME IS BACK and SAFETY IS BACK. These contradictory entailments are commonly expressed in slogans like '*back* to the basics' and '*return* to fundamental values.' Blair exploited this ambiguity in his speech, using "*back*" several times, in a literal sense, then in a positive metaphorical sense, and finally in the negative sense implied by the Labour Party campaign slogan.

Blair began by listing the recent physical, economic, and social improvements in Gateshead and Tyneside, and then declared, "I'm back. And it *feels good.*" Here *back* apparently referred to his literal return to the geographic region, and was reinforced in the next line, "back in the North East." Immediately after this literal use, Blair used "*back*" in a metaphorical sense, "*back* with the Labour Party." This pairing implies a contrast: Blair did literally *leave* Sedgefield when he entered Parliament, but he did not *leave* the Labour Party, except perhaps in the view of some party dissidents who may have felt that Blair had '*left* the party *behind*' when he adopted conservative fiscal policies and supported the invasion of Iraq. Blair immediately followed with another metaphorical use of the vehicle, "*back* with a relentless *focus* on the job." These literal and figurative uses of "*back*" all carry a positive emotional valence, which contrast with the negative implications of the party slogan (FAILURE IS BACK).

Blair followed the ambiguous (literal/figurative) use of "*back*" with a second ambiguous JOURNEY metaphor: "In this second term, in particular after September 11th, events have sometimes *taken me far from home.*" The implication of "*far from home*" is both literally and figuratively true: Blair literally traveled to many world capitals on missions related to the Afghanistan and Iraq wars; figuratively, from the perspective of Labour Party dissidents Blair's preoccupation with the war had distracted him and "*taken him away*" from traditional Labour concerns of economics and social justice.

Immediately following this passage, Blair used "*I'm back*" in yet another metaphorical sense, to shift focus to the coming general election: "It is good to be *back in a fight* with the Tories." Then he introduced a negative sense of "*back.*" The Tories have a strategy, Blair asserted, to win power by entering, not through "*the front door*" but "*by the back.*" The "*front door*" versus "*back door*" metaphor extends the '*homecoming*' themes. However, entry by the "*back door*" (by the Tory party) also carries a sense of invasion and forced entry, which adds an ominously negative implication to "*back to the Tories,*" which Blair quoted in the next passage: "do we go *forward* with Labour, or *back* to the Tories?"

At this point, Blair reflected on his early years as Prime Minister and mused about his relationship with the British people, then summarizing these musings with the "*throwing crockery*" story discussed in previous chapters. This story ended with yet another cluster of "*journey*" metaphors: "And now you, the British people, have to *sit down* and decide whether you want *the relationship to continue.* If you decide you want Mr Howard, that is your choice. If you want to *go off with* Mr Kennedy, that's your choice too. It all *ends in the same place.* A Tory Government not a Labour Government." And, finally, he summarized with a paraphrase of the party slogan: "*Going back* not *moving forward.*"

Faced with intra-party discontent, disillusionment with his policies, and potential division on the eve of a national election, Blair used complex metaphors both to reframe and trivialize the internal policy disagreements as a '*domestic squabble,*' and frame power as a '*household*' and the Tory party as potential '*intruders.*' All of this contributed to shifting from a HOMECOMING frame ('*home is back*') to the PROGRESS frame implied by the Labour Party slogan ('*forward is progress; back is failure*'). At the same time he established himself firmly at the head of the party through the implications of the "*throwing crockery*" story ('the party leader is *the husband;* changing leaders is *running off with another man*'). By casting much of this in a humorously ironically, almost playful tone, he undermined the apparent grounds for disagreement without responding to the substance of the disagreement.

Barack Obama – "*Continuing the long march*"

In "A More Perfect Union" Obama combined a different set of JOURNEY metaphors, toward quite a different end. Obama began the speech with a brief recounting of the writing of the US Constitution by the "*founding fathers,*" referring to the more or less literal journey of: "statesmen and patriots who had traveled across an ocean to escape tyranny and persecution." Then, in the fourth paragraph of the text, he referred to those who "were willing to do their part – through protests and struggle, on the streets and in the courts, through a civil war and civil disobedience and always at great risk – to *narrow that gap between* the promise of our ideals and the reality of their time." In this passage he used repetition to link the *civil war* to the *civil rights* movement, and linked both of them to his own candidacy. With "*narrow that gap,*" based on DIFFERENCE IS PHYSICAL DISTANCE, he introduced a major theme of his speech. Finally, he referred to his own "*campaign,*" at the beginning of which he set the task to "*continue the long march* of those who *came before* us." The use of this metaphor linked Obama's *political* campaign to the *literal* freedom marches of the Civil Rights movement, to which the previous paragraph obliquely alluded, as well as to the more conventional MARCH OF PROGRESS metaphor.

The "*march*" metaphor is an important part of American culture, with its resonances of recent freedom marches as well as with Biblical accounts of the more historically remote exodus of the Israelites from Egypt – itself a powerful metaphor in African American culture for the "*deliverance*" from slavery and, more recently, from racist segregation laws and other forms of racial oppression. The JOURNEY metaphor also figures more broadly in US culture, as it echoes stories of immigration and of westward migration, which have been the subject of countless novels, movies, and television programs. Later in the speech, talking about the controversy over Reverend Wright's controversial sermons, Obama observed that "the politically safe thing would be to *move on from* this episode and just hope that it *fades into the woodwork.*"

Asserting the need for unity, Obama observes that "'we may not have *come from the same place,* but we all want to *move in the same direction – towards* a better future for of children and our grandchildren." "We may not have *come from the same place*" can be interpreted literally as well as metaphorically – Obama *comes from* Indonesia and Hawaii as well as Chicago, his mother and grandmother *came from* Kansas, and his father *came from* Kenya. His later reference to relatives "*scattered across* three continents" reinforces a literal geographic reading in parallel to a metaphorical reading. With these metaphors, he linked the previous uses of JOURNEY to the PROGRESS metaphor. Later in the speech, Obama returned to the themes of "*progress*" and "*barriers to progress.*" Referring to the temptation to ignore "the issues that have *surfaced* ... that we've never really *worked through,*" Obama asserted that "if we *walk away* now ... simply *retreat into our respective corners,* we will never be able to *come together* ...*" "Retreat into our respective corners*" is a BOXING metaphor as well as a MOTION and SEPARATION metaphor; as such it activates simulations of suspended strife and watchful wariness. These metaphors also connect the "*journey*" metaphor with a "*separation*" metaphor that figured throughout the speech.

Barack Obama – *"to narrow that gap"*

"*Unity*" has been an important political theme throughout US history, and it was a central theme in Obama's campaign. Unity implies its opposite, separation and division, and it was the risk of division because of controversy over remarks made by Obama's pastor, Reverend Jeremiah Wright, that led Obama to give the speech. Not surprisingly, metaphors of unity and division had a central place in the speech, beginning with "we may *have different stories,* but we *hold common hopes.*" Other examples: "the discussion of race in this campaign has *taken a particularly divisive turn,*" his characterization of Reverend Wright's remarks as "*divisive,*" with "the potential to *widen the racial divide.*"

An interesting aspect of the race issue in the United States is that White and Black Americans share the same history and pretty much the same culture – but they have experienced this shared history and shared culture in very different ways, '*seen*' them from '*different perspectives.*' In addition to using metaphors of "*separation*" and "*unification,*" Obama also used parallel constructions throughout much of the speech, telling the "*different stories*" side by side in order to emphasize their common elements.

"Fire" and *"blood"*

The somewhat oblique reference to "civil war and civil disobedience" was followed, early in Obama's speech, by mention of his wife: "I am married to a Black American who *carries within her the blood* of slaves and slave-owners." "Slaves and slave-owners" potentially activates an implicit contrast of economic classes that reinforces the overt contrast between Black and White, powerless and powerful. "*Blood*" is a stock idiom for both family and racial descent, and as such links readily to a network of related terms, including (in this context) terms related to *miscegenation* and *racial purity*. *Blood* also activates strong perceptions of violence and wounds, and "*within her*" activates a sense of identity or at least extreme intimacy. This phrase alludes to a story of sexual exploitation of slave women by their white owners and overseers (an exploitation that continued long after slavery was legally abolished, and well into the twentieth century), a story that was certainly experienced very differently by different groups within the audience. By referring to his wife not by name but as "a Black American," Obama generalized this duality to all African American women and by extension all African Americans. By referring to this mixed ancestry as an "*inheritance* we *pass on* to our two precious daughters" Obama negated the fear, anger, and shame associated with the history of racial violence and sexual exploitation and emphasized in its place the racial pride associated with the "Black empowerment" strain of the Civil Rights movement. This passage, appearing in a summary of his own biography, also strengthened his own connection with African American culture and history (possibly intended as an oblique refutation of the questions about whether he is "Black enough," and the even more basic issues about whether he is "a real American" that dogged his candidacy and have continued to dog his presidency).

Obama concluded this summary of his personal biography with the ironic understatement, "It's a story that hasn't made me *the most conventional* candidate" – probably the only bit of irony or humor in the entire speech. Then he reframed the story in terms of a fire metaphor that he developed in several later passages, and blended it with a conventional *unity* metaphor: "But it is a story that has *seared into my genetic makeup* the idea that this nation is *more than the sum of its parts* – that *out of many, we are truly one*." This final phrase, of course, is an almost literal translation of the slogan *E Pluribus Unum*, and connects the entire preceding story with the historical '*melting pot*' metaphor. Obama followed his personal story with several generic stories of economic struggles by African Americans, then connected them with similar stories of the economic struggles of European Americans, all in support of the underlying theme of DIFFERENCE/UNITY.

Obama made strong use of several other conceptual metaphors or metaphor groups, including several other expressions of the FIRE vehicle. When Obama characterized Reverend Wright's language as "*incendiary*" and referred to the ensuing controversy as a "*firestorm*," hearers may actually have experienced Wright's language *as* fire, based on the underlying conceptual metaphor, PASSION IS HEAT. This is a common and familiar metaphor, expressed in poetry and music as well as everyday usage (e.g. 'a *burning* desire'; 'that *burns me up*').

According to simulation theory these metaphors may only have partially activated neural circuits that would be fully activated by actual perceptions of intense fire. Either way, by repeating the metaphors based on FIRE and HEAT, Obama reinforced the underlying conceptual metaphor, intensifying and probably extending the experienced simulations. For some of his listeners, this phrasing may also have evoked other connections with *fire* (both semantic and perceptual). These connections may have included the Biblical allusion used as a title by African American writer James Baldwin, "*The fire next time*," as well as the race riots of the late 1960s that spawned the slogan, "*burn, baby, burn*." Similarly, the phrase "*seared into my genetic makeup*" has the potential to evoke emotionally intense connections with the practice of branding slaves (as well as convicted criminals) with red-hot iron. It is important to note that these metaphors, like many of the stories Obama told, refer to background knowledge that is almost certain to be very different for various groups within his audience, particularly for White Americans, African Americans, and immigrants who came to the country well after the passage of the civil rights laws of the 1960s.

It seems likely that the cognitive effects from processing the perceptual simulations associated with Obama's metaphorical language went beyond completing listeners' understanding of his ideas about the general topic, race, and the immediate topic of the speech, Reverend Wright's intemperate language. These cognitive effects also include potential changes in listeners' feelings and ideas about the social and political structure of US society, and about our shared history. Appearing in a major campaign speech by a man who was to become the nation's first Black President, these metaphors and the schemas and simulations they activate, including the stories, must also inevitably affect the context for future discourse on these and related topics. To encompass the full meaning of these metaphors and of the sequence of stories the comprised the bulk of Obama's speech, the notion of *context* needs to be broadened well beyond the context of preceding sentences to embrace the entire extended conversation about race. This approach may also help to link the analysis of specific texts, *discourse* in a micro-social sense, with the analysis of ideological modes of speaking and writing, discourse in a macro-social or cultural sense (see Koller, 2004).

Notable in Obama's speech is the use of both metaphors and stories to activate strong perceptual and emotional simulations alongside historical schemas. The language of BLOOD and FIRE activates multiple episodes from the history of race relations in the United States. The many references to JOURNEYS, both real and metaphorical, activate memories (for older listeners) and stories learned second-hand (for younger listeners) from the civil rights movement as well as other, earlier journeys that figure in US history. The powerful effect of the speech can be best understood by attending to the activation of a series of powerful simulations including the visual and visceral simulations activated by metaphors like "*seared into my genetic makeup*" as well as the more complex simulations of "*carries within her the blood of slaves and slave-owners.*"

Obama addressed an audience that included people with very different experiences of the same events, and these differences must be considered in any analysis of the effects of his language, either at the individual or the societal level. He acknowledged and addressed these differences repeatedly throughout the speech, using metaphors (like the JOURNEY metaphor) that are more likely to be experienced in similar ways by all members of the audience and by telling parallel stories in a way that emphasized their underlying similarity. For example Obama explained the anger of African Americans like Reverend Wright by referring to the lingering effects of discriminatory laws and employment practices in a series of powerful metaphors and mini-stories about blacks who "*scratched and clawed their way* to *get a piece of* the *American Dream* but were ultimately *defeated.*" He then acknowledged in a series of parallel metaphors and ministories that "a similar anger *exists within segments of* the white community," among working-class whites who have "worked hard all their lives, many times only to see their *jobs shipped overseas* or their pension *dumped.*"

Framing in political speeches ▬▬▬▬▬▬▬▬▬▬▬▬▬▬▬▬▬▬▬▬▬

Like Blair, Obama faced a situation of potential divisiveness and drew on multiple metaphors to reframe the underlying issues in a unifying way. However, Blair's objective was apparently to trivialize the Labour Party dissidents' complaints and criticisms and achieve sufficient unity to enable the party to win the coming election. It could be argued that his use of playful irony and deprecation, while successful in the short term (Labour won the 2005 election), left the underlying divisions unresolved and contributed to the subsequent party leadership struggle that led to his resignation in June 2007, followed by defeat of the Labour Party in the 2010 election.

Although Obama also faced an internal division within the Democratic Party, in contrast to Blair's approach Obama focused primarily on the historically grounded divisions within the nation. His immediate concern, of course, was the criticism of his own friendship and support for his long-time pastor and friend, Reverend Jeremiah Wright. His continued association with Wright had been characterized as evidence of his own poor judgment and, more seriously, as an implication that he shared Wright's allegedly unpatriotic opinions. However, by beginning with a reference to the history of the US Constitution and the parallel history of racism, which was initially embedded in the constitution itself, Obama framed Wright's controversial statements and the controversy over those statements as part of that more general history of racism. By emphatically condemning Wright's language and by characterizing it as "*incendiary*," Obama distanced himself from the radical views overtly expressed by Wright. Then he told the story of his own early encounters with Wright's church in a way that reframed his support of and friendship with Wright from *political* to *religious*. Finally, by telling the stories of race-based oppression and struggle experienced by African Americans of Wright's generation, he reframed Wright's language by placing it within that historic context and, implicitly, removing it from the present political context.

By his metaphorical allusion to his wife's (and by implication all African Americans') dual ancestry, and by subsequently telling the stories of racial oppression and class oppression as parallel and shared stories, Obama sought to reframe the shared history from one of DIVISION to one of UNITY. At the same time, he sought to establish his own presidential candidacy within this UNITY frame, resisting the RACIAL POLITICS frame that had been introduced by some of his opponents both within and outside the Democratic Party. Since unity and overcoming partisan and cultural differences was a major theme of Obama's candidacy, this reframing was of crucial importance to his electoral success.

SUMMARY: CONTRASTING USES OF METAPHORS IN TWO POLITICAL SPEECHES

These two speeches are very different in tone as well as purpose, but they have in common that they were produced at a time of political crisis. They also have in common the use of metaphors in thematic clusters. Given the strong association in Western culture between politics and change, it is not surprising that both speeches drew strongly on the JOURNEY conceptual metaphor, and on closely associated conceptual fields such as SEPARATION/UNITY. Blair also used or alluded to a number of religious metaphors (Ritchie, 2008a), and on two metaphors drawn from domestic life, a *'forcible entry'* metaphor and a *'domestic quarrel'* metaphor. Obama used several metaphors that are linked to the history of race relations in the United States, in particular to the civil rights movement, including FIRE and MARCH.

It can be argued that both Blair's and Obama's speeches were centrally focused on framing. However, after eight years as prime minister, Blair was primarily concerned with reframing the disputes over his record as prime minister, and did not address the framing of the underlying policy issues themselves. Obama also had to deal with an immediate crisis over Reverend Wright's comments and his own continuing relationship with Wright, but as a candidate for President he also needed to lay a foundation for future leadership, not just of his party but of his nation. We must leave it to history (and historians) to determine the ultimate effects of both politicians' metaphorical framing.

NATIONAL POLITICS IN ORDINARY DISCOURSE

I discussed Cameron's (2007) research on the Reconciliation Talks in some detail in Chapter 8, so I will touch on the topic only briefly here. The political issues behind the bombing that claimed the life of Jo Berry's father were alluded to frequently in the talks between Berry and Magee, but always with considerable delicacy and often metaphorically. Berry explained her motives for seeking the encounters in implicitly political terms, as wanting to "bring as much – … something – … as much *positive out of it* as I could" (referring to the bombing). Early on, Magee explained his motives for agreeing to the initial meeting in more explicitly political terms, using metaphors based on the theater and lecture hall (Cameron, 2007): "I felt obliged as a Republican to sit down and talk about that and *against the backdrop* of the political reasons *given a platform* for a Republican message that had been censored for decades."

Later, Magee referred to "the *big* … political *picture*, the IRA, or … the war," and then again, "it's never *the whole picture*." Berry read a poem that she had written about *"building bridges."* In subsequent sessions,

Magee adopted the metaphor, at first transforming it by pointing out that a bridge can also be a barrier. Then he introduced an agricultural metaphor: "if you exclude anybody's voice ... you know ... you're se – you're *sowing the seed* for later violence." Finally, he returned to the initial implicature of the "*bridge*" metaphor: "the way to counter that ... is to *build bridges*" and reinforced the message by repeating, "the way to ensure it doesn't happen, is to *build bridges.*"

The long history of troubled Anglo-Irish relations and IRA terrorism formed the backdrop for the Reconciliation Talks and had led to the murder of Jo Berry's father, the incident that instigated the talks. These conversations can only be understood in the context of that history, and the political implications of that history in both England and Ireland. Conversely, the talks and the consequent collaborative efforts of Berry and Magee to encourage a broader reconciliation have continuing implications for political discourse in both England and Ireland, and potentially in other divided societies as well. Many of the metaphors used by Berry and Magee were apparently drawn from a broader discourse about political reconciliation ("*building bridges,*" "*sowing the seed* for later violence," "*one step at a time,*" "*transforming,*" "*come face-to-face with,*" and so on). Conversely, these same metaphors and others they developed and used ("*journey of healing*"), as well as the discursive processes through which they reached a mutual understanding and empathy, are very relevant for other contexts in which reconciliation is needed (Cameron, 2011).

METAPHOR IN DISCOURSE ABOUT LOCAL ISSUES

Former US House of Representatives Speaker Tip O'Neill is quoted as having frequently said, "All politics is local." Local issues – land use planning, water and sewage services, schools, law enforcement – have an immediate impact on people's lives and are often more readily understood by ordinary citizens than national and international issues; hence, it is important to examine the metaphors used to discuss, debate, and frame these issues. In this section I will discuss metaphors that appear in talk about two of these issues, land-use planning and law enforcement.

Metaphors in debates about town planning

Schön (1993) provided a detailed analysis of how the choice of metaphors like '*disease*' versus '*community*' in discussions of urban slums can shape the debate over urban-planning policy and constrain the solutions that can be considered. Van Hulst (2008) followed up Schön's argument in a detailed analysis of a dispute about planning in a small Dutch town. At issue was whether to develop the traditional quaint historic district as the town center, or build a new vital shopping district to serve as the town center. The same metaphor, "*heart*," was used by advocates of both solutions but in very different senses, with very different entailments. Advocates of the new shopping district developed "*heart*" in a physiological sense as a source of life and vitality. Advocates for retaining and strengthening the quaint old historic district as the town center developed "*heart*" in an emotional sense as the (traditional) locus of affection and love for the town. Van Hulst argues that Schön's analysis was incomplete, in that it overlooks the possibilities of ambiguity and multiple interpretations of the same metaphor.

Metaphors in talk about police–community relations

In many cities in the United States (and in many other nations), relations between law enforcement agencies and the communities they serve are often fraught with misunderstanding and conflict. Not surprisingly, discourse about this topic is often laced with metaphors and metaphorical stories, including both novel metaphors and novel transformations of idiomatic metaphors. Several examples come from data I gathered in Portland, Oregon, in a study of how people talk about issues of crime, public safety and police–community relations. (Much of this section is adapted from Ritchie, 2010a; 2011a; see also Cameron and Ritchie, forthcoming.) In this study, small groups of people who already knew each other were invited to talk about the topic using a low-structure focus group approach (Gamson, 1992). In one of these conversations, among a group of four Black men, two of the participants repeatedly accused police officers of using excessive force against young Black males. Following this exchange, a third participant, Willard, responded with an extended critique of lax discipline in the community and in families. His critique included the following passage:

> Do you want the police officers to go and *handle* that kind of situation *with kiddie gloves*? ... *whisper poetry to them*? The momma and daddy, they *sweet talk* you they ... you know once you're *outside of their domain*, the society *lets you know* ... this is what's not gonna be tolerated ... it's like someone in a boat and saying, Well look I'm just gonna *put a hole in the boat* so I can *get me some water*. No, *everybody goes down. Everybody goes down.* (Ritchie, 2010)

In this passage Willard began with a sarcastic hypothetical story about how police officers might handle juvenile offenders more gently. He transitioned into a generic story about how parents supposedly coddle their children, then finished with a metaphorical story created by transforming the commonplace metaphorical idiom, '*we're all in the same boat.*'

The metaphor, "*sweet* talk," potentially activated simulations of emotional experience associated with previous uses of this idiom, along with the pleasure associated with consuming sweetened foods (PLEASANT IS SWEET). These simulations contrasted with the sarcasm conveyed by Willard's vocal tone and by the immediately preceding metaphors, "*handle* that kind of situation *with kiddie gloves*" and "*whisper poetry to them?*"

"*Handle with kiddie gloves*" modified the more conventional phrase, "*handle with kid gloves,*" in a way that emphasized Willard's sarcastic intention. The standard idiom refers to gloves made of a fine, soft leather that might be used to handle an extremely fragile object (TO OFFEND IS TO BREAK). By changing "*kid*" to "*kiddie,*" Willard blended the standard idiom with another idiom implying childishness, implicitly mocking the implied claim that young people who run afoul of the police are "*fragile.*" In his second metaphor, "*whisper poetry to them,*" Willard transformed the more idiomatic "*read poetry to them*" and blended it with "*whisper,*" more frequently encountered in idioms such as "*whisper sweet nothings,*" producing a blend that contrasts strongly with his subsequent characterization of the role of law enforcement as to "break things and kill people." Willard then developed the idiomatic metaphor "*we're all in the same boat*" (CONTAINER and JOURNEY) as a story about the consequences of lax child discipline. The hypothetical statement, "Well look I'm just gonna *put a hole in the boat* so I can *get me some water,*" represented antisocial behavior as both self-centered and short-sighted, activating visual and emotional simulations that emphasize the seriousness of the conclusion: "No, *everybody goes down. Everybody goes down.*"

Another example comes from a conversation in the same research project, among a group of four middle-class urban homeowners (Ritchie, 2011c). One of the participants raised the issue of alleged police profiling, and referred to a series of incidents in which unarmed African Americans had been fatally shot by police officers during routine traffic stops. A second participant, Todd, responded, "I definitely think it happens here … and I … my personal *view* is that they need to … the police need to … to kill fewer people during routine traffic stops." Following this ironic use of overstatement, Todd brought up the explanation, often given by police officers involved in shooting incidents, that "I felt my life was in danger."

whenever I hear a an officer say ... it seems like the *magic words* ... like the *get out of jail free card* ... is ... 'I felt ... that ... my life was in ... that I was being threatened or ...' like these *magical phrases* that police officers it's like ... they're trained that's the word like if anything bad ever *goes down* say ... 'I felt you know I felt that my life was in jeopardy.'

Todd established an ironic frame with his suggestion that "the police need to ... to kill fewer people during routine traffic stops." "*Magic words*" potentially activates schemas of stage magic along with memories of childhood play and magic shows, along with the associated emotions and perceptual simulations. These might include a sense of wonder mixed with cynical skepticism. The cynical skepticism attaches to the police officer in the discourse world. "*Get-out-of-jail-free card*" refers to the popular board game, *Monopoly*™, in which "*jail*" represents a penalty that can be avoided by producing the card. This metaphor is likely to have activated simulations of the game board and emotions associated with playing the game.

"*Get-out-of-jail-free card*" has become a common idiomatic metaphor, used at least in the United States to refer to any situation in which a person evades ordinary expectations or penalties by invoking some apparently irrelevant status. "*Magic word*" is also commonly used as an idiomatic metaphor for an utterance through which some logically unrelated objective is accomplished. Memories of these idiomatic uses of the metaphors are likely also to have been activated for the other participants, contributing to a sense that police officers who use the excuse are non-serious, "*playing a game*" to evade the consequences of their actions.

Frame conflicts in a public meeting

In yet another discourse sample, analyzed in detail in Ritchie (2010a) and Cameron and Ritchie (forthcoming), city and police officials met with a group of citizens in a public meeting held after a young African American woman, Kendra James, was shot and killed by police officers subsequent to a routine traffic stop. Although Ms. James was wanted on an outstanding drug use warrant, neither she nor any of the other occupants of the vehicle were armed. Because the incident seemed to support long-standing concerns about alleged ethnic "profiling" and excessive use of force by the police, members of the community requested an open inquest into the shooting. Mayor Vera Katz decided against the requested public inquest, and instead agreed to hold an informal meeting with concerned members of the community to discuss the case.

The meeting began with brief and informal introductory speeches by Mayor Katz, Police Chief Mark Kroeker, and District Attorney (DA) Mike Schrunk. All three public officials used idiomatic metaphors that downplayed the possibility of conflict between community members and public officials and implied a shared understanding of the shooting incident and of the underlying conditions in the community. Mayor Katz promised *"transparency"* and hoped that everyone could *"open up our minds and our hearts,* and … accept each other." Chief of Police Kroeker, following Mayor Katz, used similar metaphors. He described his *"heart of gratitude"* toward the audience, "who have come here tonight to *spend this evening* with us," and followed the mayor's lead in referring to the meeting as "an example of community policing, a moment that *brings us all together."* District Attorney Schrunk began in an informal, friendly tone, "let me just *chat with you* just briefly," but proceeded with a short, factual, and detailed account of his own actions. Schrunk echoed several tropes from the mayor (*"open/closed," "movement," "visual"*), replaced *event* with *situation,* and used tropes that reinforced *tragic,* for example in "one of the things that are *going down that path* of *making something positive come out of* a real tragic situation".

All three officials used colloquial metaphors that framed the meeting as a frank discussion among people with equal status. The metaphors used by the public officials also imply a common understanding between public officials and members of the community and seemed to deny any deep disagreement or conflict between police and community. The public officials' remarks also imply that they had already achieved an empathetic understanding of the community members' experiences and concerns.

After a few minutes in which the chair of the meeting and the professional facilitators hired by the city set forth the ground rules for the meeting, the chair introduced Reverend Hardy, a member of the community organization's investigating committee, who was going to *"make a presentation."* It appears Hardy was expected to summarize the investigating committee's findings, but he addressed most of his remarks as a response to the public officials.

Hardy began by declaring "I am frustrated," and then acknowledged the public officials' overt cooperation with his committee with a few polite remarks. Then he returned to the topic of his frustration "But let me *flip the coin.* I am frustrated … *I'm irritated with the double talk, the smoke and the mirrors, the perception* that we are *in agreement with the performance,* the process, and the proceedings that have *brought us* here tonight."

"*Smoke and mirrors*" is a common metaphor for deception or obfuscation. It is often used to describe deceptive accounting practices, and may activate related schemas. It is also likely to activate schemas associated with the underlying vehicle, stage magic, in which smoke is used to obscure the performer's actions and mirrors are used to create optical illusions. Hardy repeated this metaphor several times, and several other speakers also used it. "*Double-talk*" draws on a different vehicle, and is often used in reference to deliberately ambiguous language, as in a sales pitch or deceptive contract. The use of these metaphors creates a discourse world that contrasts with that created by the opening statements of the three public officials in a way that potentially created a powerful ironic negation.

Hardy criticized the District Attorney for failing to obtain an indictment against the police officer who shot Ms. James, and contrasted the District Attorney's neutral presentation of the facts of the James shooting with the more aggressive way he presents the facts in other criminal investigations. Hardy then linked this with the city's failure to prosecute any officers in recent excessive force cases, and transformed a familiar idiomatic metaphor to comment on this sequence of events. "Somebody said that 'justice *is blind*,' but we as Portland citizens, we need to know, or I need to know, that our elected and sworn officials are not *taking advantage of her or us* just because *she's blind*." In the conventional idiom, '*blind justice*' means that justice disregards irrelevant individual characteristics. In Hardy's transformed version, "*blind*" activates an equally common idiomatic meaning, *being oblivious to obvious faults or crimes*.

The city officials' metaphors presented the shooting in an *episodic* frame (Iyengar, 1991) as an isolated event, a "*tragedy*," and framed the meeting as an "*open*" and frank discussion among fellow citizens who share a common view of the situation. Hardy's metaphors challenged both the episodic and the "open and frank" frame and substituted a *thematic* frame for the shooting (Iyengar, 1991), and framed the meeting in more contentious terms as a meeting in which public officials were to be held accountable by members of the community. (For a more detailed discussion, see Cameron and Ritchie, forthcoming.)

A third example, in which a group of young political activists discuss police–community relations, is discussed in some detail in earlier chapters. Of particular interest here is the way the political activist group began with a metaphorical comparison in which the duties of a police officer are compared to those of a waitress, and a police officer's use of excessive force is compared to a waitress making a mistake on a breakfast order. The metaphorical comparison was clearly intended as a kind of demonstration by exaggeration, similar to a *reductio ad absurdum* argument, but the group found it sufficiently entertaining that they developed it into an elaborate narrative, leading to a vulgar metaphor for a deliberate violation of customer expectations, which was then literalized to enhance the humor even more – without undermining the basic metaphorical point.

Summary

Each of these samples presents many instances in which conventional metaphors are transformed, turned into narratives, or blended with other, apparently incompatible metaphors for ironic or comic effect. Some of them, like the "*smoke and mirrors*" and "*get-out-of-jail-free card*" metaphors, appear in other conversations in the same series that are not analyzed here. These data suggest that the process of ideology formation and transformation discussed by Harris-Lacewell (2004) works at the level of local politics as well as at the level of national and international politics. They also support another aspect of Harris-Lacewell's argument, the fundamental creativity of language use among ordinary citizens, who draw on the same cultural resources as the "elites" of standard ideology theory and use them to great effect, and who may in many instances develop the metaphorical resources that are drawn on by the political elites.

OTHER VEHICLES FOR POLITICAL METAPHORS

Obama and Blair both drew on the JOURNEY and FRONT/BACK metaphors, although they used them in different ways. They both also made liberal use of metaphors drawn from ordinary life. Blair's metaphors include "we *set out our stall* for the people" (POLITICS IS A MARKETPLACE), "the *swirl* of what passes for political debate," "*Where we have lost old friends, we try to persuade them to come back to the fold*" (LEADER AS GOOD SHEPHERD), "I could *feel the warmth growing*, the expectations *rising*," "the *steady hard slog* of decision-*making* and *delivery*," and of course the metaphorical "*throwing crockery*" story. In addition to the central SEPARATION/UNION metaphors, Obama used BLOOD and FIRE metaphors. All of these appear frequently in political discourse, both in formal speeches and in political commentary and ordinary conversations about political issues.

In addition to these examples, researchers have identified a wide range of other metaphors for political processes, issues, and activities as well as for nations and governing bodies. Metaphor vehicles are often drawn from the human body: 'head of state,' 'body politic,' 'arm of government,' 'commerce is the life-blood of society,' 'an agency flexes its muscles' (Carver and Pikalo, 2008; Ringmar, 2008). The industrial era brought the use of machines as metaphor vehicles in metaphors: 'levers of power,' 'the mill of justice.'

In an extension of the machine metaphor, the state is conceptualized as a cybernetic device, like a thermostat or the 'governor' on a steam engine. In this metaphor, the state is a 'self-balancing mechanism' that, left to itself, will right itself whenever it becomes out of balance. Diversity is beneficial to the state, and the citizens are able to run their affairs and settle their differences by themselves as long as the economic and political systems are left to operate freely without interference (Ringmar, 2008, p. 65). Adam Smith's oft-quoted metaphor of the 'invisible hand' expresses this idea by combining a body metaphor with the cybernetic device metaphor.

Plato referred to the "ship of state" in The Republic (Carver and Pikalo, 2008), and Longfellow wrote a patriotic poem with the same title. More recently, Melanie Haider (2011) wrote an article for IPS titled "Ship of State Needs More Women at the Helm." Walter Brasch (2007) wrote a book titled Sinking the Ship of State: The Presidency of George W. Bush and Mary Papenfuss (2011) wrote an article for Newser about the electoral victory of a new German political party titled Pirate Party Storms German Ship of State. Political opponents often accuse a government of being 'rudderless' or 'adrift,' and editorialists may discuss the difficulty of 'navigating,' or the risk that a policy will 'founder' or 'go aground' on fiscal 'shoals,' and so on.

Winston Churchill coined the metaphor "iron curtain" for the "cold war" Soviet domination of Eastern Europe; this was later modified and extended to Chinese domination of Asia as the 'bamboo curtain.' During the Cold War, allies of the USSR were referred to as 'satellite nations' and the world was divided into 'spheres of influence,' drawing on an astronomical metaphor dating at least back to Tom Paine's analysis of relations between England and America (Arkivoulis, 2008). Other metaphors drawn from physics describe the geopolitical system as a structured, interacting 'system,' based on a 'balance of power,' and, later in the Cold War era, discussions about a 'multipolar' versus 'bipolar' political order (Arkivoulis, 2008, p. 21).

THE NATION IS A FAMILY: a conceptual
metaphor applied to politics ▬▬▬▬▬▬▬▬▬▬

Probably the oldest form of government is the tribe, based on kinship groups. Quite naturally, family and kinship terms provide many vehicles for political metaphors. The leader is a '*patriarch*' (or, in some cultures, '*matriarch*'). In more modern societies, a historically important leader (such as George Washington in the United States) is often called 'the *father* of his country,' and a nation may be called either the '*fatherland*' or the '*motherland*' (with somewhat different implications).

In his analysis of US politics, George Lakoff (1996) extends this basic NATION IS A FAMILY metaphor to incorporate two quite different underlying approaches to morality, and argues that political life in the United States is organized around two competing versions of the FAM-ILY metaphor. Lakoff grounds his discussion of the FAMILY metaphor in a broader discussion of the metaphorical basis of morality that is worth reviewing on its own merits. Lakoff argues that moral ideas are grounded in the literal experience of wellbeing, which is associated with health, material abundance, physical beauty, comfort, light, and social inclusion. Health includes cleanliness, upright stature, and freedom from disease and disfigurement. Social inclusion includes being cared for, belonging to a community, experiencing social relationships. These literal experiences of wellbeing provide vehicles for many of the metaphors we use to express moral qualities ('*clean living*' and '*dirty tricks*'; "*stained by* the *original sin* of slavery" from Obama's speech, "*A More Perfect Union*").

Combining the experience of material abundance with the principle of reciprocity, we get what Lakoff calls a "metamoral metaphor" of MORAL ACCOUNTING. MORAL ACCOUNTING includes reciprocation of favors, retribution and restitution for wrongdoing, and so on, and is expressed in common metaphors such as '*pay one's debt to society*' and "*balance the scales of justice.*" Because the welfare of children is often dependent on obedience to their parents, Lakoff argues that *obedience* itself becomes a moral duty. Combining obedience with moral accounting, failure to pay a debt or to take positive action when it is warranted are moral crimes; conversely, failing to punish wrongdoers is also a moral crime.

According to Lakoff's analysis, the moral role of the parents is to protect and provide for the family, and to prepare the children to thrive as independent adults. This role is actualized in two very different ways, according to the parents' underlying view of reality. Lakoff discusses two archetypal models of the family, and argues that these models of the family have become models for competing visions of politics and government.

According to Lakoff, conservative political views are based on a STRICT FATHER morality. The *strict father* believes that life is difficult and the world is dangerous. The father must set strict rules to protect the family in a harsh world. In order for children to develop independence and '*stand on their own two feet*' they must be rewarded when they do right, punished when they do wrong, and not coddled or indulged. Lakoff argues that conservative views on issues such as law and order, welfare, and education all derive from extending these views and applying them to the government's responsibility toward its citizens.

According to Lakoff, political liberalism is based on a NURTURANT PARENT model of the family. The NURTURANT PARENT view sees the world as less dangerous and more promising than the STRICT FATHER view, and emphasizes cooperation more than competition and conflict. In this model, children are more likely to become responsible and self-reliant if they are cared for and respected, and if they are encouraged to care for and respect others. This view of morality emphasizes empathy, nurturance, compassion, self-nurturance (to build ability to nurture others), fairness, happiness, and self-development.

Musolff (2004) identifies several extensions of the basic FAMILY/ MARRIAGE metaphor to international relations, for example in news stories and editorials referring to "*the fate of the EU couple*" and in the dialogue between Gorbachev and Weizsäcker about "the *common European house.*" However, when Tony Blair (2005) characterized himself as an errant husband and the voters/disaffected party members as an angry wife "*throwing crockery*" and threatening to "*run off with*" another partner, the tone was more playful and ironic. Gorbachev and Weizsäcker used the metaphor to frame east–west relations in domestic terms and highlight the importance of resolving differences peaceably. Blair used the metaphor to frame the discontent of many party members with his policies as a petty domestic quarrel and trivialize the criticisms of his policies.

Legitimation and delegitimation

Based on research in four western democracies, Schneider (2008) identifies four broad categories of metaphors in discourse about the legitimacy of governments. In addition to social relations, such as the family, these include metaphors based on the animate world, metaphors based on the inanimate world, and orientational and spatial metaphors. Metaphors that draw on the animate world as source include metaphors discussed in the preceding paragraphs based on the human body, biology and medicine, including evolution, the life cycle of organisms, mental disorders and diseases, for example, "a spreading cancer of dishonesty ... has corrupted large parts of the

British state" (quoted in Schneider [2008, p. 92]). In addition to other family metaphors, Schneider cites the *'nanny state'* as another example of a political metaphor based on social relations. Metaphors based on spatial orientation, travel and motion include "gives the people 'room to decide and leeway to make mistakes' and 'casting adrift of democratic politics from its anchor in rational argument'" (quoted in Schneider, 2008, p. 93).

From the inanimate natural world comes examples like 'Washington's *fog* of secrecy' (Schneider, 2008, p. 94). Another example from Schneider combines the inanimate natural world with the machine metaphor: "Our *stagnant* first-past-the-post electoral system had no *escape valve* for *pent-up* frustration" (*Guardian*, 2004, 6 June, 'Would-be voters need to *get a grip on* reality,' quoted in Schneider, 2008, p. 94). Schneider also cites metaphors of legitimacy based on a "*chain*" (e.g. *'chain of command'* and *'flow from a source'*), which imply that the legitimacy of a political order or institution can originate with one and only one source, just as a river originates from only one source.

During the 2012 Republican primary election in the United States, candidate Rick Perry accused George Romney of "*vulture* capitalism," a pun on Romney's career as a *venture* capitalist. Vultures are attracted to dead or dying animals, where they feed on the remains. Reputedly vultures sometimes hasten the animal's death, beginning their feast before the animal is completely dead. Romney's firm bought over-capitalized or faltering firms and restructured them, often adding to their debt burden and siphoning off substantial amounts of capital in the process (*'feeding on the remains'*). The restructuring process usually leads to the elimination of many well-paying jobs and occasionally culminates in the dissolution of the firm (*'hastening the animal's death'*). Perry's metaphor invited the audience to experience Romney's relationship to weak companies in terms of a vulture's relationship to weak or sick animals. In nature, actual vultures play a crucial role in ecosystems by disposing of rotting carcasses that might otherwise be a source of infection for healthy animals, and by facilitating the return of nutrients into the ecosystem. Oddly enough, the Romney campaign neglected the opportunity to develop or exploit this more positive entailment of the "*vulture*" metaphor.

Metaphors of political argumentation

Citing familiar expressions such as *'win'* or *'lose'* an argument, *'attack'* and *'defend a position,'* Lakoff and Johnson (1980) claim that much of our thinking about argumentation is based on the conceptual metaphor

ARGUMENT IS WAR. Lakoff and Johnson claim that using these metaphorical expressions lead us to think about and experience argument in terms of war, and make it more difficult to think about (or conduct) arguments, including political arguments, in terms of cooperation or collaboration.

Stenvoll (2008) analyzes a different set of expressions, such as '*slippery slope*,' which "constitutes politics as a world of physical objects, where predictable laws of physics rule instead of complex and unpredictable social factors" (p. 28). Like a physical object such as a vehicle on an icy hill or a hiker on a steep, gravel-strewn path, the political entity that moves from a state of safety and rest by allowing even one small change in policy (a single '*step*' onto the '*slope*') will risk losing control and '*sliding downhill*,' ultimately ending in a state of danger or ruin. The '*slippery slope*' argument transfers the physical laws of gravitational cause and effect to the realm of politics and policies, and leads us to experience the end state of a policy-making process in terms of the danger associated with an unrestrained slide down a steep hill. Other expressions that draw on a similar metaphorical logic include '*be on slippery ground*,' '*stand at the edge of the precipice*,' '*domino effect*,' '*quagmire*,' '*sliding scale*,' '*downhill*,' '*backslide*,' '*pitfall*,' '*last bulwark*.' Most of these imply risk of '*loss of control*' and '*downward movement*,' consistent with the conceptual metaphors UP IS GOOD / DOWN IS BAD.

The claims of inevitable '*descent into ruin*' associated with the '*slippery slope*' are sometimes countered by other metaphors from the same conceptual realm. Details of a proposed policy may provide a '*foothold*' or a '*line*' to control further progression. The policy may include a '*hedge*' against unwanted side-effects or a '*bulwark*' that will prevent the slide from the instant case to the danger case. But in some cases, Stenvoll points out that those favoring the proposed "instant case" policy may also favor the potential end state about which opponents warn. In this case, the argument becomes more complex: proponents may simultaneously argue that there are '*bulwarks*' or '*footholds*' that will prevent uncontrolled further policy changes, and that in any event the potential end state is to be desired rather than feared. For example, it is often argued that gay marriage does not necessarily lead to gay adoption but even if it does, gay adoption itself is not a problem.

'*Slippery slope*' is an example of a more general class of '*threshold metaphors*.' Other examples include '*camel's nose under the tent*' (based on a hypothetical story about travels in the desert), '*thin edge of the wedge*' (wood-splitting), and '*foot in the door*' (from a reputed practice of insistent sales agents). From a study of '*designer babies*' (Nerlich, Johnson, and Clarke 2003) comes '*crossing a line*,' '*taking one step too far*,' and '*opening Pandora's Box*,' a metaphor based on a familiar Greek myth.

SUMMARY

Sometimes political metaphors are carefully crafted by speech writers, but it appears that speakers, both public orators and ordinary conversationalists, also draw on the stock of metaphors and metaphorical idioms that are available in their culture, and then transform these in ways that give them new vitality. Metaphors are transformed into stories, and stories are told with metaphorical effect. Metaphors are blended in ways that create deliberate irony or sarcasm, and contrasted in ways that emphasize differences between political positions. Examining the metaphors that appear in political discourse provides insights into the way speakers understand their situation, and how they seek to accomplish their ends. In addition to examining the metaphors in the "official" discourse of political speeches and commentary, it is important to examine the metaphors that appear in casual discourse of ordinary people as they talk about the political issues that confront them – and, eventually, to compare the metaphors used by ordinary people with those used by political leaders.

DISCUSSION

Obama's metaphors and stories drew on and resonated with themes in US political and cultural history that date back to Revolutionary War days – some of these themes Obama directly alluded to in the opening passages of his speech. It also seems likely that some of these themes were experienced in quite different ways by members of different groups within Obama's audience. To what extent do people when hearing or reading this speech or others like it really think of these broader contexts? Do the broader contexts influence people's responses and reactions to the metaphors and stories, even when people are not consciously aware of them? In terms of differences among audience members, do members of different groups within US culture experience references to the same events in different ways? And, again, if they do, how do these differences influence their responses to the message?

Harris-Lacewell (2004) argues that ideologies are transformed and transmitted at the level of ordinary discourse as well as at the level of policy elites. How do the metaphors used by political elites interact with the use of metaphors in ordinary conversations? To what extent do political leaders pick up and adopt metaphors that originate in or are commonly used in ordinary talk? How do the metaphors used by political leaders influence ordinary talk? Under what circumstances are they picked up or ignored by ordinary citizens?

To what extent might members of various groups within Obama's audience have been aware of the historical and cultural contexts of his various metaphors and stories? Is it likely that people who were not aware of these contexts were nonetheless influenced by them?

To what extent were members of Blair's audience aware of the implications of his "*throwing crockery*" story? To what extent might they have been aware of and influenced by his transformations of the "*back*" metaphor?

Many of the students in my metaphor classes did not recognize the vehicle "*kid gloves*," and many had not previously heard of "*kid-skin*." It seems likely that other metaphors that are commonly used and transformed in political discourse may be unfamiliar to many members of the audience. How does the use of archaic or unfamiliar metaphor vehicles affect the outcome of political discourse?

SUGGESTED READINGS

- Charteris-Black, J. (2005). *Politicians and rhetoric: The persuasive power of metaphor*. Basingstoke, Hants: Palgrave Macmillan. This book addresses metaphorical framing in a broad way, using discourse analysis of a wide range of texts.
- Harris-Lacewell, M. V. (2004). *Barbershops, Bibles, and BET: Everyday talk and Black political thought*. Princeton University Press. Harris-Lacewell applies sociological methods, including survey research, in-depth interviews, and ethnographic observation to identify four dominant African American ideologies (related to ethnicity and race relations), and to show that these ideologies are not merely "top-down" (handed down by intellectual leaders) but also emerge from everyday conversations, such as those that take place in barbershops and beauty salons, churches, and in Black media outlets like BET. The introductory chapters are particularly important but the entire book is well worth the read.
- Lakoff, G. (1996). *Moral politics: What conservatives know that liberals don't*. University of Chicago Press. In this classic text George Lakoff applies CMT to US political rhetoric in a broad way. He

does not analyze actual samples of discourse, rather basing his analysis on examples from his own memory – but for all that, his examples seem realistic and his analysis is well worth reading.

- Musolff, A. (2004). *Metaphor and political discourse: Analogical reasoning in debates about Europe.* Basingstoke, Hants: Palgrave Macmillan.

10   Metaphors in literature

> But, soft! What light through yonder window breaks?
> It is the east, and Juliet is the *sun*.
>
> *(Romeo and Juliet*, Act 2, Scene 2)

"Juliet is *the sun*" has been frequently discussed in debates about metaphor theory, often without any reference to the scene in which it appears (e.g. Searle, 1993). Ignoring the context leaves the imaginations of theorists free to invoke whatever characteristics of *the sun* they wish as a basis for interpretation – usually its *light* or its *heat*. Even the immediate lines in which "Juliet is *the sun*" appears provide sufficient evidence to rule out *heat* and focus the interpretation on *light*, but it is important to look beyond just these two lines. In Scene 1, Romeo's friends Benvolio and Mercutio find Romeo in the Capulets' garden, remind him of his passionate love for Rosaline, and tease him about it. They depart, and Romeo speaks:

> He jests at *scars* that never *felt a wound.*
> But, soft! What *light* through yonder window *breaks*?
> It is the east, and Juliet is *the sun.*
> *Arise, fair sun,* and *kill the envious moon,*
> Who is already *sick and pale* with grief
> That thou her maid art far more fair than she.

From these lines it is apparent that what is transferred from *sun* to *Juliet* is much more than either *"heat"* or *"light."* More important to understanding these lines is the celestial relationship of *sun* and *moon*. By transferring this astronomic relationship onto the comparison of *Juliet* with *Rosaline*, Romeo answers his friends' teasing about his previous infatuation with Rosaline, compares Rosaline unfavorably to Juliet, and entreats Juliet (*the sun*) to *"kill the envious moon"* (overcome his previous infatuation with her rival, Rosaline). In the following lines Romeo further develops the metaphorical mapping of *Juliet* onto *light*.

> Two of the fairest stars in all the heaven,
> Having some business, do entreat her eyes

To twinkle in their spheres till they return.
What if her eyes were there, they in her head?
The brightness of her cheek would shame those stars,
As daylight doth a lamp; here eyes in heaven
Would through the airy region stream so bright
That birds would sing, and think it were not night.

These lines can be analyzed in terms of attribute transfer or categorization theories, but the systematic development of the metaphor calls for the more complex mapping, such as that provided by structure-mapping theory. However, "*light*," "*twinkle*," and "*bright*" all invite further metaphorical interpretation. Conceptual metaphor theory helps – many pleasant emotions are associated with x is light, including happiness, wisdom, and importance. The comparison to the "*envious moon*" also suggests important is the sun, which is consistent with Romeo's reaction to his friends' teasing about Rosaline. Many metaphors, both in English and in other languages and cultures, are based on x is light, including religious metaphors such as "the *light of the world*," and Shakespeare could count on his audience's familiarity with this metaphorical field.

In terms of perceptual simulations, the line "What *light* through yonder window *breaks*" seems likely to activate visual simulations associated with dawn, but "*Arise, fair sun,* and *kill the envious moon*" seems more abstract and may have the effect of activating more semantic connections than perceptual simulations. The fanciful little story about the stars asking Juliet's eyes to stand in for them while they take care of other business also seems more likely to activate primarily semantic processing. At first, the fanciful story that immediately follows, about the "*brightness* of her cheek" overwhelming the stars, also seems more likely to be processed semantically, but the closing line, "birds would sing, and think it were not night" may activate perceptual schemas that interact with the semantic networks activated by the celestial metaphors from the previous lines, and activate relevant *night sky* schemas with the associated perceptual simulations.

In summary, although these metaphors, including "*Juliet is the sun*" can be interpreted in the local context of the lines in which they appear, they are much more meaningful when interpreted in the broader context of Act 2, the entire play, and cultural conventions associated with the metaphor field, x is light.

At first glance, Carl Sandburg's poem "Fog," briefly discussed in previous chapters, seems more straightforward.

The fog comes
on little cat feet.

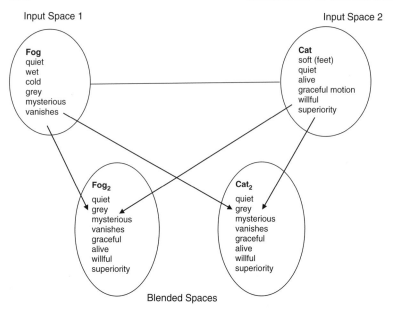

Figure 10.1 Conceptual integration theory applied to *fog*

It sits looking
over harbor and city
on silent haunches
and then moves on.

According to attribute-transfer theory, the attribute of *silence* is transferred from *cat* to *fog*; categorization theory would say that a superordinate category of *things that are silent* is established, and fog placed into it. Neither approach seems quite adequate for explaining the effect of the poem – or why the second stanza is needed at all. Structure-mapping theory is more satisfying: the first stanza sets up a comparison, "*fog is a cat*," and the next stanza fills out and maps onto each other some of the other parts of both concepts. Perceptual simulation theory and conceptual integration theory (CIT) also seem to have something to contribute, although CIT will require some modification. The opening stanza activates two distinct schemas, *fog* and *cat*, each with intense perceptual simulations, and blends them. However, upon closer analysis it appears that the poem may be as much about the cat as it is about the fog, in which case we need to posit *two* output schemas, one for both concepts. However, upon closer analysis it appears that the poem may be as much about the cat as it is about the fog, in which case we need to posit *two* output schemas, one for both concepts (see Figure 10.1).

The *fog* schema activates qualities such as *grey, damp, cold, appears and disappears silently and mysteriously*, and the visual disorientation and sense of mystery that comes with dense fog. The *cat* schema activates qualities such as *soft feet, quiet, alive, graceful motion, willful*, and the sense of calm superiority cats often exhibit. The first stanza refers to a familiar brief story of fog developing (or *arriving*), and links it to another familiar story of a cat arriving. The second stanza elaborates and blends the stories, describing the fog as a cat sitting on its haunches – its *silent* haunches – looking out over harbor and city. This stanza invests the fog schema with the *life* of a cat as well as with the kind of willful air of superiority that is part of the *cat* schema. However, the first line of the second stanza, "It sits looking," is ambiguous: "it" can also refer to the cat, a reading that is reinforced by the peculiarly cat-like behavior described in this stanza. Thus, the second stanza reinforces the impression that the story is actually about a cat arriving then departing. It seems likely that this leads to a new *cat* output schema, that includes some of the qualities from the *fog* input schema, as well as a new *fog* output schema that includes relevant qualities from the *cat* input schema. Thus, contrary to the standard view that metaphors always map in only one direction, the metaphor established by "Fog" seems to map in both directions. The way the poem sets up a brief but dramatic little story may contribute to this reverse/parallel mapping.

Fauconnier and Turner, in their original exposition of CIT (Fauconnier and Turner, 1998; 2002), claim that a *generic space* is needed to connect the two input spaces or schemas, and in the example of Tony Blair's "*throwing crockery*" narrative metaphor, a generic space was easily identified. However, it is quite difficult to determine any generic space that could reasonably connect *fog* and *cat* schemas prior to some kind of metaphorical interpretation (Ritchie, 2004; 2006).

CONTRASTING METAPHORS (LEONARD COHEN)

Many writers use contrasting metaphors and similes, sometimes for ironic effects and sometimes to bring out or strengthen the effects of both. Poet and songwriter Leonard Cohen provides several examples. "Bird on the Wire" (Cohen, 1969) begins with a contrasting pair of similes:

Like a bird on the wire
Like a drunk in a midnight choir
I have tried *in my way to be free*

Here, "*free*" is characterized in two senses – the physical lack of constraint associated with the "*bird*" and the lack of social constraint associated with the "*drunk*," who presumably sings offkey or otherwise does as he pleases. Two stanzas later comes another contrasting pair of similes:

> Oh, like a baby, stillborn
> Like a beast with his horn
> I have *torn* everyone who *reached out for* me

The first line of the stanza describes the heartbreak of a parent who is "*torn*" emotionally by the stillborn baby. The second literalizes the metaphor as a beast whose sharp horn might literally *tear* a person's flesh. Then the third line returns to the emotional metaphor, which is rendered all the more poignant by the literalization in the second line, which is blended with the metaphorical "*tearing*" in the first line. These contrasts (along with others in the first part of the song) amount to an intense apology, leading to the promise, "I will make it all up to thee."

In another of Cohen's songs, "One of Us Cannot Be Wrong" (1967), each stanza sets up a small, self-contained story to exemplify his love for the subject of the song, and the distress the love causes him (and others who have encountered her). The first stanza opens with a metaphorical reference to voodoo (or other practices in which magic is used to influence a lover):

> I lit a thin green candle, to make you jealous of me.
> But the room just filled up with mosquitoes,
> they heard that my body was free.

The first line activates a black magic script, then ironically contradicts it: The spirit summoned is not a demon or a god, but a swarm of mosquitoes! The third line also uses two senses of *free* – *unclaimed* and *liberated*. This stanza carries through the voodoo metaphor, then closes with what could be voodoo or merely a lover's spite:

> And then I confess that I tortured the dress
> that you wore for the world to look through.

This couplet raises several interesting ambiguities. Did she wear the dress for the world to look through or did he torture it (twist it or cut holes in it) for the world to look through? Tortured again calls up voodoo practices – torturing an item connected with the victim, but "for the world to look through" makes it clear the writer is the one who is tortured. The entire voodoo narrative is metaphorical of the unrequited lover's yearning and attempts to will the object of affection into compliance.

The second stanza begins with a visit to a doctor who counsels that he "quit," and then becomes addicted to the same "*drug*," the woman who is the topic of the song. Then in the third stanza, the singer learns of a "*saint* who had loved you" and journeys to learn from this "*saint*."

> He taught that the duty of lovers
> is to *tarnish the golden rule*.

These lines strongly evoke the Romantic tradition of the idealized and unattainable woman as goddess/muse. "*Saint*" can be understood ironically or in the sense of an adept in spiritual discipline, which would apparently include the discipline to withstand the sexual wiles of any woman, even a woman as emotionally potent as the topic of the song. The final line, "*tarnish the golden rule*," turns the most familiar religious truth upside-down and invests the entire script with bitter irony. Then the saint's own susceptibility to the *femme fatale* becomes evident:

> And just when I was sure that his teachings were pure
> he drowned himself in the pool.

Another metaphorical narrative carries the mystical quest script forward ironically, unites it with the drug abuse script in a very different form of "*ruin*." The second couplet distorts the goddess/muse script and renders it pathetic.

The final stanza begins with a story about an Eskimo who took a movie of the lady: the Eskimo "froze when the wind took your clothes" and "never got warm." This turns the conventional PASSION IS HEAT metaphor upside down; here the identity of the stricken would-be lover as an Eskimo (presumably inured to extreme cold) underscores the intensity of the passion aroused by the lady. Note also that she did not take her clothes off, but the wind – the "*storm*," which is explicitly mentioned in the next line, stripped them off, leaving her naked and apparently oblivious to the cold (implying that she generates her own inner heat). This activates another conventional love metaphor, PASSION IS A STORM, which provides the vehicle to the singer's final plea to his love object:

> But you stand there so nice, in your blizzard of ice,
> oh please let me come into the storm.

Like *Bird on a Wire*, this song builds a story-world through a series of contrasting metaphors, each of them activating powerful perceptual, emotional, and interoceptive simulations and blends all of these into an account of the lady, the subject of the song, as extremely desirable and emotionally potent. The plea to be allowed to "*come into the storm*" in the final stanza poses an ironic contrast with the singer's helpless and inept attempts at voodoo in the first stanza. The song is apparently motivated by much the same emotional script as Keats' *La Belle Dame Sans Merci* (1962, p. 248), a script that also figures in many folk ballads such as "Dance with Me" (Steeleye Span, 1975), about a knight who encounters an elf-king's daughter who attempts to seduce him, then when he refuses her offered love curses him – "A *plague of death shall follow thee.*" However, Cohen's ironic and self-deprecating variation on this ancient theme achieves its effects by way of a very different series of metaphorical contrasts and stories.

"SEASCAPE" (STEPHEN SPENDER)

A complex example of metaphor development is provided by Stephen Spender's (1939) "Seascape." The poem opens with a personification metaphor, "*happy* ocean" and a rather odd simile that sets up an important metaphorical theme:

> There are some days the happy ocean lies
> Like an unfingered harp, below the land.

"*Happy* ocean" activates emotional simulations and connects them with sensory simulators activated by "ocean." The ocean is positioned "below the land," suggesting a point of view from above the water, as on a headland looking down, with sun reflecting off the waves. Indurkhya (1999) analyzed these lines as an example of "perceptual blending," based on a combination of perceptual simulation theory (Barsalou, 1999) with conceptual-blending theory (Fauconnier and Turner, 2002). "As the simulators of both the harp and the ocean are activated, they try to build a simulation together" (Indurkhya, 1999, pp. 621–622). Indurkhya argues that the way the rays of the sun reflect on the ripples of a calm ocean "resonate[s] with" the way the light reflects off the parallel lines of harp-strings, thus creating a new representation of the ocean, and perhaps also of the harp, a totally new "confluence of features."

Indurkhya emphasizes that the context suppresses other features associated with the "*harp*" concept, but "unfingered" seems likely to *activate* the negated music simulations (sounds of a strummed harp and the image of a harpist seated at the harp) associated with *harp*, along with simulations of *silence* and *latency* or *potential action*. Even within the first two lines, this simile goes far beyond a mere blended visual image. As the poem develops, it becomes apparent that the *harp* is not *blended into* the ocean swells, but rather kept separate, part of an independent source of introspective and emotional simulations.

The title and the first line have already activated the *ocean* schema, with an associated *person gazing at the ocean from above* schema as the dominant frame. Everything that follows, including the harpist, who appears in lines 9 and 10 ("And a sigh, like a woman's from inland / Brushes the instrument with shadowy hand"), interacts with and connects new perceptual elements to previously activated elements of these schemas to build a complex cognitive context.

The second and third lines fill in the blended *ocean/harp* schema with the golden color of late afternoon, and activate the *sound* aspects of the *harp* schema:

> Afternoon *guilds* all the *silent wires*
> Into a *burning music for the eyes*

At the most direct level, "*burning*" simply emphasizes the intensity of the sunlight reflected off the swells, but the combination with "*music for the eyes*" is likely to activate more complex emotional and introspective simulations, possibly even interoceptive simulations of the physical pain and squinting associated with looking too near the sun. These simulations are strengthened by the fifth line, "*On mirrors flashing between fine-strung fires*," which connects the foregoing depiction of the ocean in the late afternoon sun with a brief reference to the shore in the last two lines of the stanza. At the same time, "*between fine-strung fires*" may activate, at least weakly, a *signal fire* schema with its implications of ancient history and war, which is picked up in the last stanza.

In the second stanza, the "sigh" like a "shadowy hand" draws from the ocean/harp some sounds characterized as "some gull's sharp cry / Or bell, or shout, from distant, hedged-in, shires." These strengthen the connection to the shore briefly opened at the end of the first stanza, activating schemas of ordinary domestic life, but in the final line of the second stanza, "these, deep as anchors, the hushing wave buries." This effectively separates the poet (and reader) from the brief little story of village life and returns to the ever-darkening mood of "*shadowy* hand." The third stanza briefly activates simulations of the liveliness and gaiety of the rural scene once more with a brief story of two butterflies who dance across the waves – then fall into the water and drown, a "*ritual sacrifice*" which "fishermen understand."

The final stanza builds on the somber theme of the "*ritual sacrifice*" of the butterflies, referring to "legends of undersea, *drowned* cities," activating semantic links to Atlantis and its voyager heroes, "*flamed like pyres*," who "the seas engulfed." Then the poem concludes by connecting "the *cruel* waves" above with the eyes of the drowned heroes, which

> *Glitter with coins* through the tide scarcely scanned,
> While, far above, *that harp assumes their sighs.*

The poem as a whole tells a story that begins with a serene afternoon, standing on a bluff or headland above a "*happy* ocean" and ends with the somber image of drowned voyager-heroes beneath these same waves, ultimately described as "*cruel.*" In the final line, "*that harp assumes their sighs*" echoes and explains the "*unfingered harp*" from the first stanza and the "*sigh*" that "*brushes the instrument with shadowy hand*" in the second stanza. In between, the brief tragic (and familiar) story of the "*butterflies*," symbols of beauty and light-hearted joy, who drown in "*ritual sacrifice*" echoes the overall movement of the poem from serenity and beauty to somber grief. Both the brief little story of the butterflies and the overall story of a poet's transition from serene happiness ("the *happy* ocean lies") to grief (Their eyes / Distorted to the *cruel waves* desires) activate story schemas that stand in metaphorical relation to an ambiguous topic, alluded to in the dedication ("*In memoriam M.A.S*") but also perhaps more broadly in metaphorical relation to a tragic view of life in which any joy or happiness is destined to end in "*sighs.*"

The poem begins with a description of "some days" on which "the happy ocean lies ... below the land," reinforcing the schema activated in cognitive context by the title, "Seascape." The dedication, "*In memoriam M.A.S.,*" also activates a contrary schema of mourning. Metaphors and images activate new emotions, perceptual simulations, and introspections that progressively expand with the initial *ocean* schema, and others that build and strengthen the *mourning* schema, until these two are blended in the small story of the butterflies in the third stanza; this blend is then strengthened by the indexed story of the lost city of Atlantis with its drowned voyager-heroes in the final stanza. These blends are consistent with conceptual integration theory, although too complex to capture in a diagram small enough to fit on a printed page. The images, emotions, and introspections activated are fully consistent, as Indurkhya argues, with perceptual simulation theory, although they are much more complex than this brief discussion captures.

The conceptual neural system includes simulations of preconscious, preverbal affective stimuli and responses. Since they are preverbal, these experiences cannot be named or described; they are simply *experienced*. The best we can do is to evoke similar responses through communicative actions and the simulations they activate. Words like *harp* activate proprioceptive, introspective, and emotional experiences that are both more subtle and more complex than what could be expressed in direct, "literal" language. Simulation builds upon simulation throughout the poem: "*burning music*," "*sigh*," "*shadowy hand*," "gull's sharp cry," "distant, hedged-in shire." "Ocean" is introduced in the first line as an almost generic schema; it provides a framework on which the poet builds a complex story-world that develops, from the quietly rapturous experience of looking out at the ocean from a high bluff in the late afternoon sun, toward a deep, abiding grief. The poem builds images that can be described in literal language, and at least some of the phrases are very probably processed through semantic connections ("zig-zag butterflies" and "drowned cities," for example). The poem also builds intense, prelinguistic simulations of emotions, physical sensations, and nuances of perception.

In its progression from the commonplace experience of viewing a calm ocean to an expression of profound grief of temporality, mortality, and loss, "Seascape" also demonstrates what Seanna Coulson (2001) calls *frame shifting* or *frame blending*. Much of the poem's effect is achieved by the gradual shift from the "*happy* ocean" frame to the more melancholy frame evoked by "a sigh, like a woman's from inland, / Brushes the instrument with shadowy hand," and finally to a historical, epic, and tragic frame in the final stanza, with its drowned voyager-heroes. All three frames are blended together in the poem's final lines, which echo the intense visuality of the opening lines, while maintaining the emotional tone of the intervening lines: "Glitter with coins through the tide scarcely scanned, / While, far above, that harp assumes their sighs." Spender's metaphors and stories, some brief and others, like Atlantis, merely hinted, activate a series of perceptual, proprioceptive, and emotional simulations and visual images, and link them to the seascape; they also activate and fully develop distinct cognitive frames and blend these frames themselves in a way that enables each frame to transform the others, just as *fog* and *cat* are mutually transformed in Sandburg's poem. And through this frame shifting and eventual blending as the poem unfolds, Spender accomplishes a more abstract introspective and emotional simulation of the passage of time itself, and links the melancholy and grief of time and mortality with his own personal grief.

THE POWER OF PLAIN LANGUAGE

In previous chapters I mentioned two situations when metaphors are *not* often used. One is in purely informative interactions, as when giving directions or arranging a future meeting. Another is when the experience to be expressed is so intense, so raw and immediate that metaphors would only serve to distance the speaker and hearer from it, as when Jo, in the Reconciliation Talks, describes how she had to tell her half-sister about their father's death in the parking lot of her school. Another example occurred when George, in the African American men's conversation about police–community relations, told a story (which was almost certainly familiar to the other participants) in straightforward, factual language. Yet a third example appears somewhat frequently in literature, when an author chooses to describe an experience in simple language such that the reader (or hearer) will enter directly into the experience, without the intermediation of metaphorically activated simulations.

For example, in "Pine Tree Tops," Gary Snyder (1969, p. 33) recounts a night-time hike in the forest. The poem begins by invoking a "blue night" with a "frost haze," describes the moon over pine tree tops and the sound of boots on cold snow. Snyder selects bits of sensory experience that directly activate simulations (especially but not exclusively for readers who have experienced similar scenes). Most of the images are visual, but *frost haze* evokes a simulation of cold air, and the one reference to sound, *the creak of boots*, evokes not merely the mentioned sound but also the surrounding silence and the intense cold. Only the final line, *what do we know*, might possibly lend a metaphorical meaning to the poem as a whole, with an implicit reference to Zen practice of "mindlessness." The introspective simulations activated by this line are likely to reinforce thoughts of mystery and quiet reflection associated with walking through woods on a cold night.

In another poem in the same volume, "The Wild Mushroom" (1969, p. 47), the poet begins by setting the stage:

> Well the sunset rays are shining
> Me and Kai have got our tools
> A basket and a trowel
> And a book with all the rules

There follows a series of verses setting out rules for what to gather and where to find them, all set as the kind of thoughts and conversation one might actually have during a mushroom-gathering expedition, including a description of poisonous and psychedelic mushrooms ("some *bring you close to God*") and ending in a toast:

> So here's to the mushroom family
> A far-flung *friendly clan*

The only metaphors in the entire poem, "*bring you close to God*" and "far-flung *friendly clan*," appear at the end, in an ironic voice that highlights the playful, almost sardonic tone of the entire poem. The meter, almost sing-song, evokes the kind of didactic poems and songs familiar from elementary school, but also familiar from many other satirical poems and songs in Anglo-American culture. The final lines reinforce this sense of playful satire, more effective because the poem also works as a description of a commonplace outdoor activity.

Snyder sometimes avoids metaphors almost entirely: like "Pine Tree Tops," many of his poems can be read either as straightforward evocations of experiences for their own sake or as metaphors of spiritual quest. In other work he uses them sparingly, as in "Rain in Allaghany" (Snyder, 1969, p. 60), which has just one metaphor, joined to a metaphorical simile: "it's a *skinny awkward* land / *like a workt-out miner's hand*." Set in an otherwise straightforward account of having a beer after a long drive through the woods, this juxtaposition evokes a contrast that lends meaning and emotional impact to the preceding, sparse, description of the drive. "*Skinny awkward* land" activates a schema associated with a young adolescent, but "*workt-out miner's hand*" contrasts that schema with a schema of youth and awkwardness to one of aging and weakness that communicates a clear understanding of the landscape. In still other poems, like "Avocado" (Snyder, 1969, p. 61), in which the *Dharma* is compared to *an avocado*, Snyder uses metaphors more profusely, often in a playfully teasing way.

Ernest Hemingway is known for a more pointed avoidance of metaphor, seeking intensity in plain language descriptions of ordinary events, as in his brief description of a wartime evacuation in Greece, that closes with "There was a woman having a kid with a young girl holding a blanket over her and crying. Scared sick looking at it. It rained all through the evacuation" (Hemingway, 1987, p. 70). *Scared sick* is often used idiomatically as a metaphor, but here it seems literal: The girl was certainly scared and probably sick. The closing statement about the weather is ironically commonplace, but it activates a vivid set of perceptual simulations that reinforce the misery and sadness of everything that has gone before. The passage is quite short, with only a few sentences and no metaphors or similes, but it creates a vivid story-world into which the reader enters almost unwillingly, drawn into the misery and fear of the evacuees, the young girl and the woman, probably her mother. The matter-of-fact tone of the statement, "having a kid," followed by the terse weather report, "It rained all through the evacuation," underscores the evacuees' desperation and misery through the way it minimizes the act of childbirth itself.

In "Big Two-Hearted River Part I" (1987, pp. 161–170), Hemingway uses similar declarative literal statements, descriptions and actions, to create a very different story-world. We are not told the back-story, where Nick was before this story, although from its positioning in the original short story/novel collection (*In Our Time*, 1924) among stories of Nick in battlefield scenes, we can surmise that he may be home from war. (If so, that would invite a metaphorical reading of the burnt-out landscape, scorched by a recent forest fire – but Hemingway's sparse prose resists such a reading.) The writer describes Nick gazing at a fire-ruined landscape, "There was no town, nothing but the rails and the burned-over country," then watching fish in the river, "keeping themselves steady in the current with wavering fins." One phrase might be construed metaphorically, "Nick's heart *tightened* as the trout moved. He felt all the old feeling." "Nick's heart *tightened*" is presented as a physiological description, and probably requires a metonymic reading (*heart* for *chest muscles*). "He felt all the old feeling" indexes a story that may or may not be familiar to the reader, but provides no further details. Otherwise the story is a long series of direct literal statements, including characterization of Nick's mood when he has his tent set up. "Already there was something mysterious and homelike. Nick was happy as he crawled inside the tent. He had not been unhappy all day. This was different though. Now things were done. There had been this to do. Now it was done." The contrast (*happy* with *not unhappy*) and repetition of *done* serve to evoke an emotion and an underlying mood, but neither emotion nor mood is otherwise enhanced or elaborated. It is left to the reader to fill in the emotional and proprioceptive simulations.

After describing how Nick opened and cooked two cans of food, a solitary bit of discourse appears: "'I've got a right to eat this kind of stuff, if I'm willing to carry it,' Nick said. His voice sounded strange in the darkening woods. He did not speak again." The brief statement serves to evoke a schema of back-packer purism, and alludes to a tension within the story and, by extension, within Nick's own intentions and feelings, that is never resolved. "His voice sounded strange ... He did not speak again" emphasizes the solitude and quietness that has been implicit in all that went before.

The story ends a couple of pages later with "He curled up under the blanket and went to sleep." The entire story simply recounts the first day of a camping and fishing trip, apparently to a countryside Nick knew from "before" – before whatever he came from. Aside from the metonymic reference to a tightening heart, there is no figurative language, just a description of the country and Nick's actions and responses, including the utilitarian actions of setting up camp, making a camp-fire, cooking and eating a simple meal as well as aesthetically motivated actions of watching the fish, gazing at the river through the woods beyond the burned-over country, and gazing at the camp-fire. This plain-language style relies heavily on the reader to activate the schemas and simulations that will fill out the story-world. Even readers who have never experienced camping in the woods can draw on other fiction, movies, and so on for the requisite schemas and simulations, but readers who have direct personal experience to draw on are likely to experience Hemingway's story-world more vividly. The style also foregrounds actual experience over interpretation, simulations of sensory and physiological perceptions over introspection.

SUMMARY

Metaphor is commonly associated with literature, and most writers use metaphors, but with quite different styles. A few writers follow Hemingway's approach and avoid metaphors in order to concentrate on the evocative power of plain, direct language. Many writers use metaphors playfully, as Gary Snyder often does, or sprinkle in a summative metaphor near the end of a passage or poem that otherwise relies on direct language, as Snyder does in many of his wilderness poems. Others develop complex metaphorical schemes, sometimes relying on one or a handful of thematically developed metaphors, as Stephen Spender does in "Seascape," but sometimes using contrasting metaphors in an ironic way, as Leonard Cohen does in much of his work.

DISCUSSION

As with the topics discussed in earlier chapters, there is need for experimental research to test the degree to which these and other poetic metaphors and story indexes activate complex schemas in readers, and stimulate readers' transportation into a story-world they create. How does the terse "plain language" used by a writer like Hemingway, or in many of Gary Snyder's poems, compare to more metaphorical language in terms of its power to activate complex schemas and perceptual simulations? Additionally, as with "Seascape" and Snyder's poetry, how much of the broader historical and cultural context is activated for a typical reader, and how does that broader context affect the activation of schemas, scripts, and perceptual simulations?

How much of the effects of the poems and stories discussed in this chapter – or of other familiar literary passages – can be explained by the more traditional property attribution and categorization models?

In the examples discussed in this chapter, are the metaphors primarily *ornamental*, as Aristotle argued, or do they add to the meaning of the passages to create meaning that could not be achieved without metaphors?

Conversely, could Hemingway's stories discussed in this chapter express more if he had used a few well-chosen metaphors?

SUGGESTED READINGS

- Lakoff, G., and Turner, M. (1989). *More than cool reason: A field guide to poetic metaphor*. University of Chicago Press. This book makes a case for applying conceptual metaphor theory to poetry and provides many interesting examples.

11   Closing reflections

'The question is,' said Alice, 'whether you can make words mean so
many different things.'

'The question is,' said Humpty Dumpty, 'which is to be master –
that's all.'

Alice was too much puzzled to say anything; so after a minute
Humpty Dumpty began again. 'They've a temper, some of them –
particularly verbs: they're the proudest – adjectives you can do
anything with, but not verbs – however, I can manage the whole lot
of them! Impenetrability! That's what I say!'

'Would you tell me please,' said Alice, 'what that means?'

'Now you talk like a reasonable child,' said Humpty Dumpty,
looking very much pleased. 'I meant by "impenetrability" that we've
had enough of that subject, and it would be just as well if you'd
mention what you mean to do next, as I suppose you don't mean to
stop here all the rest of your life.'

'That's a great deal to make one word mean,' Alice said in a
thoughtful tone.

'When I make a word do a lot of work like that,' said Humpty
Dumpty, 'I always pay it extra.'

(Lewis Carroll, Through the Looking Glass)

Words can be made to do a lot of work, and carry a lot of meanings.
Some of the tools for putting them to work include using metaphors,
storytelling, and wordplay. As Humpty Dumpty suggests, we can get
a lot more work out of a metaphor vehicle if we pay extra. In particular, we need to pay extra attention to contexts, and pay extra in
processing effort.

SOME OF THE WORK METAPHORS DO

One way to think of metaphor analysis is in terms of understanding
how speakers and writers put words to work when they use them
as metaphor vehicles. Metaphors are often used to express ideas

and feelings in more interesting or more compelling ways. Even if it adds no new meaning, "we'd be *swimming in* money" is more interesting than "we'd have lots of money" and "*incendiary* language" is both more interesting and more compelling than "controversial language." Metaphors also provide a means for expanding available vocabulary to express new concepts or new ways of understanding familiar concepts, as when "world-wide *web*" was coined to describe a new medium of communication.

A metaphor may also activate a particular conceptual structure that will contribute to hearers' or readers' understanding of a topic. "*Web*" and "*net*" both activate conceptual structures related to systems of connection that lack a defined center. "*Incendiary* language" activates a conceptual structure related to FIRE and HEAT, which connects with other FIRE metaphors in Obama's speech and in religious and political discourse more generally, and may have helped shape his listeners' understanding of his response to Reverend Wright's controversial sermons. "Some of you *throw a bit of crockery*" potentially activates a complex script with immediate comic overtones as well as an underlying theme of emotional and physical violence that contributed to listeners' understanding of Blair's attitude toward his critics within the Labour Party, as well as to their understanding of the options facing party members as they prepared for the coming election.

Both "*incendiary* language" and "*throw a bit of crockery*" gain extra strength and are able to do more work because of the way they are connected with other metaphors in the immediate context of the speech as well as with broader themes in the culture. "*Incendiary* language" is connected with several other FIRE metaphors within Obama's speech, and also has the potential to activate stories about the urban riots of the Civil Rights era in the United States (it may also have activated stories of the Ku Klux Klan cross burnings and bombings of Black churches that continued well past the middle of the twentieth century). "*Throw a bit of crockery*" connects more loosely with other DOMESTICITY metaphors in Blair's speech, including his allusions to *homecoming* early in the speech as well as his accusation that the Tories want to "*enter by the back door.*" "*Throw a bit of crockery*" also activates a schema of comic violence familiar from popular culture, including comic strips, TV sitcoms, and other cultural texts, and may have activated for some listeners a darker schema of actual marital discord and actual violence.

In both of these examples from major political speeches, the metaphors served to express complex ideas as well as to '*frame*' the topic of the speech in a particular way, thereby influencing the way in which listeners and subsequent readers respond to it, the thoughts it might generate, and the resolutions that would seem '*natural*' and right. Similarly, in the public meeting following the shooting death of Kendra James in Portland, Oregon (Chapter 9), metaphors were used to express conflicting frames for both the topic of the meeting (the death of Ms. James) and the nature of the meeting. The public officials used language like "*transparency,*" "*open up our minds and our hearts,*" "*heart of gratitude,*" and "*spend this evening* with us" to frame the meeting as an informal and unstructured conversation among equals, a problem-solving conversation among people who understand the situation in much the same way. They referred to the shooting as a "*tragedy,*" "a moment that *brings us all together,*" both reinforcing the *conversation among equals* frame and establishing an *episodic* frame (Iyengar, 1991) for the shooting itself.

In the Kendra James meeting, various members of the community challenged both of these frames, using metaphors and stories as well as literal language. A member of the community's ad hoc investigating committee, Reverend Hardy, challenged the official framing of the meeting with a series of *oppositional* metaphors: "*double talk, the smoke and the mirrors, the perception* that we are *in agreement with the performance,* the process, and the proceedings that have *brought us* here tonight." He challenged the *episodic* frame with a play on the idiomatic metaphor, "*blind justice,*" expressing his hope "that our elected and sworn officials are not *taking advantage of her or us* just because *she's blind.*" Other members of the community challenged the public officials' framing with stories about the deaths of other unarmed citizens at the hands of the police, as well as with personal stories of incidents they characterized as racial "*profiling*" and harassment.

Yet another function of metaphors is to reinforce social structure. Clever wordplay exhibits intelligence and verbal ability, and thus can contribute to raising the speaker's social status. Language play, including invention and distortion of metaphors as well as storytelling, is often a source of shared pleasure and amusement in a group, and thus contributes to reinforcing social bonds. It can also contribute to reinforcing social bonds by emphasizing the common ground, the shared familiarity with the idioms and cultural practices that underlie a bit of metaphor play. Hardy's play on "*blind justice*" was no doubt appreciated by members of the audience for the clever way it transformed a standard idiomatic metaphor, even though Reverend Hardy may not have been the first to use this bit of wordplay. Indeed, use of a familiar metaphor transformation often contributes to the audience's enjoyment. The audience's enjoyment of the "*blind justice*" metaphor was also likely to have been enhanced by its effectiveness in this particular context, where it served to undermine the status of the public officials (who are expected to represent and enforce "*blind justice*"). Similarly, when Willard transformed idioms including "*sweet talk*," "*handle with kid gloves*," and "*all in the same boat*," in the Black men's conversation (Chapter 9), it increased the effectiveness of his sarcastic rejoinder to George's complaints about the police's excessive use of force, and may have raised Willard's status in the group.

In the urban homeowners' group (Chapter 9, when Todd referred to the common excuse for police shootings ("I felt that my life was in danger") as a "*get-out-of-jail-free card*" he activated common knowledge of the game *Monopoly*™ in a way that framed the police excuse as '*a move in a game*,' and thus not to be taken seriously. He also reinforced common ground both through the assumption that everyone present was familiar with the game and through the implicit assumption that they were all sufficiently politically liberal to share his cynical view of the police bureau. The wordplay itself, as in the other examples, is also likely to have contributed to the mutual enjoyment of the conversation and thus strengthened bonds of friendship. The extended playful distortions of "*ivory tower*" in the scientists' group and "*public servant*" in the New Left group (Chapter 8) similarly served complex functions by framing the topic and at the same time providing for shared enjoyment. The collaborative wordplay in these examples are also likely to have contributed to group solidarity through the collaborative interaction itself, as an exercise of ad hoc teamwork.

Cameron (2007; 2011) describes a more extended and complex kind of collaboration in her detailed examination of the Reconciliation Talks (Chapter 8). Berry and Magee collaborated, in successive turns as well as across conversations, in constructing some metaphors, such as the "*bridge*" metaphor first introduced in a poem by Berry. In other instances, when Magee picked up and used a metaphor such as "*healing*" that was first introduced by Berry, it signaled an important change in their relationship. In different ways, all of these examples support the idea, forcefully advanced by Cameron, that researchers need to attend to the pattern of metaphor use, re-use, and transformation in discourse.

Poets and writers often develop metaphors in complex structures, as exemplified by "*All the world's a stage*" (Chapter 1) and "Seascape" (Chapters 1 and 10), but they also use metaphors, including idiomatic metaphors, in playful ways. One example is Emily Dickinson's combination of two personification metaphors in "Death *kindly stopped for me*" (Chapters 1 and 10). The lyrics to Leonard Cohen's song, "One of

Us Cannot Be Wrong" (Chapter 10) provide another example. In each stanza Cohen activates a different metaphor, usually a metaphor that implies a story, then distorts it in an ironic way: The lover's use of "*magic*" that summoned mosquitoes instead of spirits, the "*heart doctor*" who advised his patient to "*quit*," then prescribed the same "*medicine*" to himself and became fatally addicted, and so on. A large part of the enjoyment of this song comes from the merging of clever wordplay, irony, and commentary on obsessive love into highly evocative images.

HOW DO METAPHORS DO THEIR WORK? THEORIES OF METAPHOR INTERPRETATION

Many theories have been advanced to explain how metaphors are understood, how they create (or activate) meanings. Over the past thirty years or so, increasingly sophisticated research methods have been applied to compare and test these theories, and where necessary to elaborate or supplement them. Although the accumulated results of this research have contributed greatly to our understanding and appreciation of metaphors, they have been somewhat inconclusive. Some theories explain certain metaphors in some contexts, but either fail to account for other metaphors altogether, or fail to account for the effect of context. At least for the present it appears that no one theory is sufficient to explain all aspects of metaphor use and understanding in all situations (Gibbs, 2006). As a practical matter, the best approach may be to apply the theory that seems to account for the observed use and effects of metaphors in a particular communicative context with the least amount of complexity. On the other hand, if more complex theories add to understanding of particular metaphors in particular contexts, the results may justify the added complexity.

Simple nominative and adjective metaphors such as 'Achilles is *a lion*,' 'the lad is a *beanpole*,' '*flaming* red hair,' and '*turned beet-red*' can be readily explained by property attribution (Chapter 2). Nothing seems to be added to the meaning of the topic beyond one or two properties commonly associated with the vehicle. The more complex mapping of structure-mapping theory (Chapter 2) may be needed to explain metaphors like 'computer *virus*' and 'that man is *a wolf*,' in which not only attributes but also relationships among attributes are potentially mapped from the vehicle onto the topic.

For some metaphors category theory may provide unique insights (Chapter 3). With stock examples like 'Achilles is *a lion*' and 'the lad is a *beanpole*,' it is not evident what category theory adds to property attribution theory (Vervaeke and Kennedy, 1996), and property attribution seems to provide a more straightforward explanation of '*beet-red*.' However, for other metaphors like '*shark*' and '*time-bomb*' (Glucksberg and Keysar, 1990), as well as '*bulldozer*' and '*princess*' (Wilson and Carston, 2006; Wilson and Sperber 2004) it seems reasonable to claim that the metaphor either activates a pre-existing category or establishes an ad hoc category with the vehicle as the prime exemplar. The case is strengthened by the observation that each of these metaphor vehicles, '*shark,*' '*time-bomb,*' '*bulldozer,*' and '*princess,*' is used with many topics, and hence might be classified as a *generic metaphor*. However, with the exception of '*bulldozer*,' when applied to a bodyguard or a lineman in American football, creation of a category exemplified by each of these that can include topics like *lawyer*, *cigarettes*, *my boss*, and *my sister*, respectively, all require further metaphorical interpretation (Chapter 3). In the case of this sort of abstract metaphor, category theory may contribute to our understanding of the comprehension process, but it cannot supply a complete explanation.

Lakoff and Johnson (1980; 1999) claim that verbal metaphors express underlying conceptual metaphors (Chapter 4), and sometimes two or more conceptual metaphors are blended to form a more complex conceptual metaphor. According to this view, '*bulldozer*' expresses a combination of underlying conceptual metaphors that might be summarized as INSISTING IS PHYSICALLY PUSHING and NON-COMPLIANCE IS A PHYSICAL OBSTACLE. Perceptual simulation theory (Barsalou, 2007; Gibbs, 2006) helps fill in details of how metaphors add to meaning over and above purely linguistic connections. Consistent with conceptual metaphor theory, at least in some cases metaphors activate partial simulations of muscular action, perceptions, and emotional responses associated with the vehicle (Gibbs, 2006), and these perceptual simulations help to explain how abstract metaphors achieve their effects (Chapter 5). A possible cognitive mechanism for combining conceptual metaphors and creating compound metaphors is provided by conceptual integration theory (Chapter 6), which also provides a useful notation for analyzing complex conceptual metaphors.

In "*steady hard slog* of decision-*making* and *delivery*" (Chapters 1 and 9), several conceptual metaphors are combined, including DECISIONS ARE OBJECTS, DECIDING IS A JOURNEY, and INTELLECTUAL DIFFICULTY IS PHYSICAL DIFFICULTY. "Decision-*making*" is a familiar idiom and may have activated perceptual simulations only weakly. "*Steady hard slog*" may have been less familiar to many of those who heard and read the speech, and may have activated more elaborate and more intense simulations. It is impossible to determine the extent to which these or other metaphors in the speech actually activated perceptual simulations in audience members, so the discourse analyst can at best assess the potential responses of audience members. However, it might be at least possible to test the analyst's interpretation, for example by looking at the results of public opinion polls after the speech.

Metaphors are often developed into stories (*"ivory tower," "all in the same boat"*), and stories often have a metaphorical function (*"throw a bit of crockery," "a kangaroo walked into a bar"*). Even when they are not developed into a complete narrative, metaphors may activate story scripts (*"carries within her the blood of slaves and slave-owners," "enter by the back door, not the front," "get-out-of-jail-free card"*). If they are extensively processed, metaphors may contribute to the cognitive and persuasive effects of a story by enhancing the listener's '*transportation into the story-world*' (Green and Brock, 2000).

METAPHORS AS CULTURAL AND RHETORICAL RESOURCES

As metaphors are invented, used, transformed, and re-used, they enter into the culture's shared *interpretative repertoire* (Taylor and Littleton, 2006) as a resource for speakers and writers to draw on in the future. The idiomatic metaphor *"ivory tower"* provided a readily recognized resource in the scientists' conversation first for some light-hearted teasing, then for an ironic depiction of the scientists' shared situation as theoretical scientists dependent on public money to support their work. "Public *servant*" served a similar purpose in the New Left conversation. Berry and Magee, in the Reconciliation Talks, drew on several familiar idiomatic metaphors and shaped them in ways that expressed their own complex thoughts. In both of these conversations it appears that the collaborative re-use and transformation of familiar metaphors contributed to shaping the participants' relationships as well.

Harris-Lacewell (2004) argues that political ideologies are not simply transmitted from political elites to ordinary citizens, but are also shaped and transformed in the everyday conversations that take place in barber shops, beauty salons, churches, and so on. Political elites are held to account in these everyday conversations, in part according to their use of metaphors and stories. Harris-Lacewell also claims that ordinary citizens as well as political and cultural elites display considerable creativity in their language use, draw on the same cultural resources as the "elites" of standard ideology theory, and are actively engaged in developing these cultural resources. The conversations analyzed in this book provide many examples of this cultural and linguistic creativity.

The discourse samples analyzed in this book present many instances in which conventional metaphors are transformed, turned into narratives, or blended with other, apparently incompatible metaphors for ironic or comic effect. Some of them, like *"smoke and mirrors"* and *"get-out-of-jail-free card,"* appeared in other conversations in the same series. It is likely that few if any of them were invented on the spot by the speaker. Clever bits of wordplay, amusing or shocking stories, distorted metaphors, and other linguistic bits circulate widely through society and are shaped and reshaped by speakers to fit the context of a particular conversation. Politicians, poets and writers, and journalists draw on these same resources, reshape them and feed them back into the culture, where they may be picked up, repeated, and reshaped yet again, in an endless cycle of collective and collaborative linguistic creativity.

SUMMARY

Metaphor use, like storytelling and humor, is part of language use, but metaphor use is also part of conversation, speech-making, politics, issue framing, cultural transformation, and communication processes generally. I have focused on metaphor use in conversation, political communication, and literature: Metaphors also play an important role in religion, philosophy, science, and many other fields, all of which reward closer investigation. A central claim of this book is that analyzing metaphors and patterns of metaphor use in any communication context will contribute both to our understanding of metaphor and to our understanding of the contexts in which metaphors are used. These claims are supported by a rapidly growing research literature that includes both research on how metaphors are understood and research using metaphors to understand other domains. I have been able to provide but a limited sample of this literature; I hope the reader's appetite will have been whetted for more. In closing, let me quote poet and linguist John Ciardi (from his weekly National Public Radio broadcast): "Good words to you!"

Glossary

Ad hoc category: A category formed on the spot for a particular situation.

Analogical models: Theories that treat metaphors as a type of analogy.

Broadening: In relevance theory, extending the range of objects, events, or ideas included within a concept.

Candidate inferences: In Structure-mapping theory, secondary topic–vehicle mappings that can be inferred from previously established mappings.

Career of metaphor: A theory that metaphors begin as novel metaphors and gradually come to be lexicalized.

Category inclusion statement: A statement that assigns a thing, event, or concept to a more inclusive or general category.

Circularity: The claim that metaphor interpretations often call upon other metaphors that require interpretation. Wilson and Carston (2006) call this phenomenon "metaphor within metaphor."

Cognitive context: In relevance theory, a coherent set of ideas and knowledge that is active and salient. A cognitive context can represent very local knowledge or very general knowledge about the world. See *context*.

Cognitive effects: In relevance theory, the changes to the mutual cognitive environment (the thoughts that are salient to both speaker and listener) that result from processing an utterance.

Comparison: A theory that treats metaphors as implicit comparisons or similes, with the word *like* omitted.

Conceptual metaphor: A word or phrase that expresses an underlying relationship between a more abstract concept and a more physical experience.

Conceptual metaphor theory: A theory that verbal metaphors express underlying conceptual relationships, such that the topic is experienced *as* the vehicle.

Context: Generally, the situation in which communication occurs. *Context* can be described at a very general level such as mutual cultural knowledge, relationships, and so on, or at a very specific level such as the immediately preceding utterances. See *cognitive context*.

Dead metaphor: In traditional metaphor theory, a metaphor that has become so thoroughly lexicalized that it is no longer recognized as metaphorical.

Dual reference: The idea that idiomatic metaphor vehicles refer to two categories, a superordinate category and a more specific category named by the vehicle. For example, SHARK is said to refer both to vicious and merciless beings and to a certain species of PREDATORY FISH.

Embodied metaphor: In conceptual metaphor theory, the claim that the topic becomes associated with the vehicle through repeated correlation with physical experience of the vehicle.

Emergent entailments: Entailments of a metaphor that are not prominently identified with either vehicle or topic but *emerge* from the interaction of vehicle and topic.

Entailment: A quality or relationship that may be inferred from a metaphor vehicle and consequently attributed to the topic.

Functional Magnetic Resonance Imaging (fMRI): A technique for discerning which areas in the brain are most actively engaged at a given time.

Generic metaphor: A metaphor vehicle that can be used with many different topics.

Graded salience hypothesis: The claim that meanings that are more conventional, more familiar, more frequently encountered, or more prototypical are more salient; hence they are likely to be accessed more rapidly and become activated more quickly than less salient ones.

Ground: The attributes that provide a basis for comparing a metaphor vehicle to its topic.

Idiom: An expression that is commonly used within a speech community to express a consistent idea or experience.

Implicature: An idea or concept that can be inferred from or is implied by a word or phrase.

Inter-coder reliability: How closely two or more members of a research team agree about the identification of metaphors.

Interpretive repertoire: A set of themes and ideas that are available to members of a speech community or other group, that serve to express key ideas, for example about personal identity.

Lexical information: Information about word meanings and usage.

Lexicalized metaphor: A common metaphor in which an originally metaphorical meaning has come to be regarded as one of the word's basic definitions.

Literal: Use of words or phrases in such a way that they are mapped onto specific primary meanings.

Mapping: A process in which particular words are connected with meanings; a process in which certain attributes of a metaphor vehicle are associated in a systematic way with attributes of the topic.

Meta-communication: Communication about communication; for example, discussing how eye contact helps people to take turns in speaking.

Metaphor: seeing, experiencing, or talking about something in terms of something else.

Metonym: Use of a word to reference another closely related concept.

Narrowing: In relevance theory, constricting the range of objects, events, or ideas included within a concept.

Ostensive: Obtrusively noticeable. In relevance theory, an *ostensive* act is performed in a manner that calls attention to itself as having communicative intent.

Processing set: A tendency to process newly encountered phrases in the same way as previously encountered phrases; for example, as literal versus metaphorical.

Property attribution: The theory that a metaphor works by attributing or transferring certain topics ordinarily associated with the vehicle to the topic.

Relevance: In relevance theory, the degree to which the cognitive effects of processing an utterance are sufficient to justify the mental effort required.

Salience: The degree to which a property or idea is likely to be noticed.

Structure-mapping theory: A theory based on the idea that metaphor interpretation begins by aligning representations of topic and vehicle in a one-to-one mapping that can be extended to multiple features of the topic and vehicle.

Substitution: The theory that a metaphor is created when a word or phrase from an apparently different area of experience is substituted for a word that expresses some attribute of the topic.

Superordinate category: A category that includes several other categories: ANIMAL is a superordinate category that includes DOG as well as HUMAN.

Thematic metaphors: In dynamic discourse analysis, metaphors with vehicles that represent a common theme but are not necessarily processed as conceptual metaphors.

Topic: The concept that is described or expressed by the metaphor

Trope: A word or phrase that is used in a figurative or non-literal sense.

Truth conditions: A set of assumptions or conditions such that a specified utterance is true if and only if all of the conditions are true.

Tuning devices: Words or phrases used to qualify or constrain the way in which metaphors are interpreted; for example, *sort of* or *metaphorically speaking*.

Vehicle: The metaphorical word or phrase.

Bibliography

Abbott, H. P. (2008). *The Cambridge introduction to narrative* (2nd edn.). Cambridge University Press.

Al-Zahrani, A. (2008). Darwin's metaphors revisited: Conceptual metaphors, conceptual blends, and idealized cognitive models in the theory of evolution. *Metaphor and Symbol*, 23, 50–82.

Anka, P. (1969). My way, first performed by Frank Sinatra on the album *My Way*. Music by Claude Francois and Jacques Revaux. Reprise Records.

Apter, M. J. (1991). A structural phenomenology of play. In Kerr, J. H., and Apter, M. J. (eds.), *Adult play: A reversal theory approach*. Amsterdam: Swets & Zeitlinger, pp. 13–30.

Arkivoulis, D. E. (2008). The ways of stargazing: Newtonian metaphoricity in American foreign policy. In Carver, T., and Pikalo, J. (eds.), *Political language and metaphor: Interpreting and changing the world*. London and New York: Routledge, pp. 15–27.

Armstrong, L., and Middleton, V. (1949). Baby it's cold outside. Lyrics by Frank Loesser (1944). Recorded live; currently available on *Louis Armstrong: Christmas Through the Years*. Los Angeles, CA: Delta Records.

Attardo, S. (1994). *Linguistic theories of humor*. Hawthorne, NY: Mouton de Gruyter.

    (2001). Humorous texts: A semantic and pragmatic analysis. New York: Mouton de Gruyter.

Barsalou, L. (1999). Perceptual symbol systems. *Behavioral and Brain Sciences*, 22, 577–609.

    (2007). Grounded cognition. *Annual Review of Psychology*, 59, 617–645.

    (2008). Grounding symbolic operations in the brain's modal systems. In Semin, G. R., and Smith, E. R. (eds.), *Embodied grounding: Social, cognitive, affective, and neuroscientific approaches*. Cambridge University Press, pp. 9–42.

Berra, Y. (2011). Quoted in *The Baseball Almanac*. www.baseball-almanac.com/quotes/quoberra.shtml. Last accessed April 9, 2011.

Billig, M. (2005). *Laughter and ridicule: Towards a social critique of humour*. London: Sage.

Biria, E. (2012). Figurative language in the immigration debate: Comparing early 20th century and current U.S. debate with the contemporary

European debate. Thesis presented in partial fulfillment of the requirements for the degree of Master of Arts in Communication. Portland, OR: PSU.

Black, M. (1993). More about metaphor. In Ortony, A. (ed.), *Metaphor and thought*, (2nd edn.). Cambridge University Press, pp. 19–41.

Blair, T. (2005). A fight we have to win. A speech to Labour's Spring Conference. Gateshead: Sage Centre. http://politics.guardian.co.uk/speeches/story/0,,1412459,00.html. Last accessed September, 2006.

Blasko, D. G., and Connine, C. M. (1993). Effects of familiarity and aptness on metaphor processing. *Journal of Experimental Psychology: Learning, Memory and Cognition*, 19, 295–308.

Bobrow, D., and Bell, S. (1973). On catching on to idiomatic expressions. *Memory and Cognition*, 1, 343–346.

Boroditsky, L., and Ramscar, M. (2002). The roles of body and mind in abstract thought. *Psychological Science*, 13, 185–189.

Bortfeld, H., and McGlone, M. S. (2001). The continuum of metaphor processing. *Metaphor and Symbol*, 16 (1 and 2), 75–86.

Bowdle, B. F., and Gentner, D. (2005). The career of metaphor. *Psychological Review*, 112, 193–216.

Bowen-Hassel, E. G., Conrad, D. M., and Hayes, M. L. (2003). *Sea raiders of the American Revolution: The continental navy in European waters.* Washington, DC: Naval Historical Center, p. 47. Online quote in the Naval Historical Center home page, www.history.navy.mil/bios/jones_jp_did.htm. Last accessed April 9, 2011.

Boyed, R. (1979). Metaphor and theory change: What is a metaphor for? In Ortony, A. (ed.), *Metaphor and thought*. Cambridge University Press.

Brasch, W. (2007). *Sinking the ship of State: The presidency of George W. Bush.* North Charleston, SC: Booksurge.

Brock, T. C., Strange, J. J., and Green, M. C. (2002). Power beyond reckoning: An introduction to narrative impact. In Green, M. C., Strange, J. J., and Brock, T. C. (eds.), *Narrative impact: Social and cognitive foundations*. Mahwah, NJ: Lawrence Erlbaum, pp. 1–15.

Brône, G., and Feyaerts, K. (2004). Assessing the SSTH and GTVH: A view from cognitive linguistics. *Humor – International Journal of Humor Research*, 17, 361–372.

Bruner, J. (2002). *Making stories: Law, literature, life.* New York: Farrar, Straus, & Giroux.

Burke, K. (1945). *A grammar of motives.* Berkeley: University of California Press.

Cameron, L. J. (principal investigator). (2006). Procedure for metaphor analysis. *The Metaphor Analysis Project.* Milton Keynes, Bucks: Open University Centre for Research in Education and Educational Technology. http://creet.open.ac.uk/projects/metaphor-analysis/procedure.cfm?subpage=discourse-data. Last accessed December 15, 2010.

(2003). *Metaphor in educational discourse.* London: Continuum.

(2007). Patterns of metaphor use in reconciliation talk. *Discourse and Society*, 18, 197–222.

(2008). Metaphor and talk. In Gibbs, R.W., Jr. (ed.), *The Cambridge handbook of metaphor and thought*. Cambridge University Press, pp. 197–211.

(2009). *Metaphor and reconciliation*. New York: Routledge.

(2011). *Metaphor and reconciliation*. New York: Routledge.

Cameron, L. J., and Deignan, A. (2003). Using large and small corpora to investigate tuning devices around metaphor in spoken discourse. *Metaphor and Symbol*, 18, 149–160.

Cameron, L. J., and Ritchie, L. D. (forthcoming). Learning from failure: Deliberative empathy in a police–community meeting.

Campbell, J. (1949). *The hero with a thousand faces*. Princeton University Press.

Campbell, J. D., and Katz, A. N. (2006). On reversing the topics and vehicles of metaphor. *Metaphor and Symbol*, 21, 1–22.

Cannon, C. J. (1923). Selecting citizens. *The North American Review*, 217, 325–333.

Carroll, L. (1872). Jabberwocky, from *Through the Looking-Glass and What Alice Found There*. www.jabberwocky.com/carroll/jabber/jabberwocky. html. Last accessed April 9, 2011.

Carston, R. (2002). *Thoughts and utterances: The pragmatics of explicit communication*. Oxford: Blackwell.

Carter, R. (2004). *Language and creativity: The art of common talk*. New York: Routledge.

Carver, T., and Pikalo, J. (2008). Editors' introduction. In Carver, T., and Pikalo, J. (eds.), *Political language and metaphor: Interpreting and changing the world*. London and New York: Routledge, pp. 1–11.

Chiappe, D. L., and Kennedy, J. M. (2001). Literal bases for metaphor and simile. *Metaphor and Symbol*, 16, 249–276.

Chiappe, D. L., Kennedy, J. M., and Smykowski, T. (2003). Reversibility, aptness, and the conventionality of metaphors and similes. *Metaphor and Symbol*, 18, 85–105.

Channell, J. (1994). *Vague language*. Oxford University Press.

Charteris-Black, J. (2005). *Politicians and rhetoric: The persuasive power of metaphor*. Basingstoke, Hants: Palgrave Macmillan.

Chomsky, N. (1957). *Syntactic structures*. The Hague and Paris: Mouton.

Cienki, A. (2008). The application of conceptual metaphor theory to political discourse: Methodological questions and some possible solutions. In Carver, T., and Pikalo, J. (eds.), *Political language and metaphor: Interpreting and changing the world*. London and New York: Routledge, pp. 241–256.

Cienki, A., and Müller, C. (2008). *Metaphor and gesture*. Amsterdam: John Benjamins.

Clark, A. (1997). *Being there: Putting brain, body, and world together again*. Cambridge, MA: MIT.

Clark, H. H. (1996). *Using language*. Cambridge University Press.

Cohen, L. (1967). One of Us Cannot Be Wrong. In *Songs of Leonard Cohen*. New York: Columbia Records.

  (1969). *Songs from a room*. New York: Columbia Records.

Coleman, C. L., and Ritchie, L. D. (2011). Examining metaphors in bio-political discourse. *Lodz Papers in Pragmatics*, 7, 29–59.

Conan Doyle, A. (1984). The case of the copper beeches. In Coyle, A. C., *Great cases of Sherlock Holmes*. Franklin Center, PA: Franklin Library, pp. 205–233.

Cook, G. (2000). *Language play, language learning*. Oxford University Press.

Coulson, S. (2001). *Semantic leaps: Frame-shifting and conceptual blending in meaning construction*. Cambridge University Press.

Darlington, T. (1906). The medico-economic aspect of the immigration problem. *The North American Review*, 576, 731–740.

Davenport, J., and Cooley, E. (1956). *Fever*. Fort Knox Music.

Deignan, A. (2005). *Metaphor and corpus linguistics*. Amsterdam: John Benjamins.

Deignan, A., and Semino, E. (2010). Corpus techniques for metaphor analysis. In *Metaphor analysis: Research practice in applied linguistics, social sciences and the humanities*. London: Equinox.

Dickinson, E. (1960). Because I could not stop for Death. In Williams, O. (ed.), *Immortal poems of the English Language*. New York: Washington Square Press, p. 443.

Dunbar, R. (1996). *Grooming, gossip, and the evolution of language*. Cambridge, MA: Harvard University Press.

Edwards, D. (1997). *Discourse and cognition*. Thousand Oaks, CA: Sage.

Everts, E. (2003). Identifying a particular family humor style: A sociolinguistic discourse analysis. *Humor: International Journal of Humor Research*, 16, 369–412.

Fagen, R. (1995). Animal play, games of angels, biology, and Brian. In A. D. Pellegrini (ed.), *The future of play theory: A multidisciplinary inquiry into the contributions of Brian Sutton-Smith*. Albany, NY: State University of New York Press, pp. 23–44.

Fauconnier, G. (1994). *Mental spaces: Aspects of meaning construction in natural language*. Cambridge University Press.

Fauconnier, G., and Turner, M. (1998). Conceptual integration networks. *Cognitive Science*, 22(2), 133–187.

  (2002). *The way we think: Conceptual blending and the mind's hidden complexities*. New York: Basic Books.

Feldman, J. A. (2006). *From molecule to metaphor: A neural theory of language*. Cambridge, MA: MIT Press.

Fine, G. A., and DeSoucey, M. (2005). Joking cultures: Humor themes as social regulation in group life. *Humor: International Journal of Humor Research*, 18, 1–21.

Flor, M., and Hadar, U. (2005). The production of metaphoric expressions in spontaneous speech: A controlled-setting experiment. *Metaphor and Symbol*, 20, 1–34.

Frost, R. (1923). Stopping by woods on a snowy evening. In Lathem, E. C. (ed.), *The Poetry of Robert Frost*. New York: Henry Holt.

(1960). The road not taken. In Williams, O. (ed.), *Immortal poems of the English language*. New York: Washington Square Press, p. 504.

Gamson, W. A. (1992). *Talking politics*. Cambridge University Press.

Gentner, D. (1983). Structure-mapping: A theoretical framework for analogy. *Cognitive Science*, 7, 155–170.

Gentner, D., and Bowdle, B. F. (2001). Convention, form, and figurative language processing. *Metaphor and Symbol*, 16, 223–247.

Gentner, D., and Clement, C. (1988). Evidence for relational selectivity in the interpretation of analogy and metaphor. In G. Bower (ed.), *The psychology of learning and motivation*. San Diego, CA: Academic, pp. 307–358.

Gernsbacher, M. A., Keysar, B., Robertson, R. W., and Werner, N. K. (2001). The role of suppression and enhancement in understanding metaphors. *Journal of Memory and Language*, 45, 433–450.

Gerrig, R. J. (1993). *Experiencing narrative worlds: On the psychological activities of reading*. New Haven, CT: Yale University Press.

Gibbs, R. W., Jr. (1994). Figurative thought and figurative language. In Gernsbacher, M. A. (ed.), *Handbook of Psycholinguistics*. New York: Academic Press, pp. 411–446.

(2000). Making good psychology out of blending theory. *Cognitive Linguistics*, 11, 347–358.

(2006). Metaphor interpretation as embodied simulation. *Mind and Language*, 21, 434–458.

(2008). Metaphor and thought: The state of the art. In Gibbs, R. W., Jr. (ed.), *The Cambridge handbook of metaphor and thought*. Cambridge University Press, pp. 3–16.

Gibbs, R. W., Jr., and Matlock, T. (2008). Metaphor, imagination, and simulation: Psycholinguistic evidence. In Gibbs, R. W., Jr. (ed.), *The Cambridge handbook of metaphor and thought*. Cambridge University Press, pp. 161–176.

Gibbs, R. W., Jr., and Tendahl, M. (2006). Cognitive effort and effects in metaphor comprehension: Relevance theory and psycholinguistics. *Mind and Language*, 21, 379–403.

Giora, R. (1997). On the priority of salient meanings: Studies of literal and figurative language. *Journal of Pragmatics*, 31, 919–929.

(2003). *On our mind: Salience, context, and figurative language*. Oxford University Press.

Giora, R., Fein, O., Kronrod, A., Elnatan, I., Shuval, N., and Zur, A. (2004). Weapons of mass distraction: Optimal innovation and pleasure ratings. *Metaphor and Symbol*, 19, 115–141.

Glucksberg, S. (2001). *Understanding figurative language*. Oxford University Press.

(2008). How metaphors create categories – quickly. In Gibbs, R. W., Jr. (ed.), *The Cambridge handbook of metaphor and thought*. Cambridge University Press, pp. 67–83.

Glucksberg, S., Gildea, P., and Bookin, H. A. (1982). On understanding nonliteral speech: Can people ignore metaphors? *Journal of Verbal Learning and Verbal Behavior*, 21, 85–98.

Glucksberg, S., and Haught, C. (2006). On the relation between metaphor and simile: When comparison fails. *Mind and Language*, 21, 360–378.

Glucksberg, S., and Keysar, B. (1990). Understanding metaphorical comparisons: Beyond similarity. *Psychological Review*, 97, 3–18.

(1993). How metaphors work. In Ortony, A. (ed.), *Metaphor and thought* (2nd edn.). Cambridge University Press, pp. 401–424.

Glucksberg, S., Keysar, B., and McGlone, M. S. (1992). Metaphor understanding and accessing conceptual schema: Reply to Gibbs (1992). *Psychological Review*, 99, 578–581.

Glucksberg, S., and McGlone, M. S. (1999). When love is not a journey: What metaphors mean. *Journal of Pragmatics*, 31, 1541–1558.

Glucksberg, S., McGlone, M. S., and Manfredi, D. (1997). Property attribution in metaphor comprehension. *Journal of Memory and Language*, 36, 50–67.

Glucksberg, S., Newsome, M. R., and Goldvarg, Y. (2001). Inhibition of the literal: Filtering metaphor-irrelevant information during metaphor comprehension. *Memory and Symbol*, 16, 277–294.

Goffman, E. (1959). *The presentation of self in everyday life*. New York: Anchor Books.

Grady, J. E. (1997). THEORIES ARE BUILDINGS revisited. *Cognitive Linguistics*, 8, 267–290.

Grady, J., Taub, S., and Morgan, P. (1996). Primitive and compound metaphors. In Goldberg, A. (ed.), *Conceptual structure, discourse and language*. Stanford, CA: CSLI Publications, pp. 177–187.

Graesser, A. C., Olde, B., and Klettke, B. (2002). How does the mind construct and represent stories? In M. C. Green, J. J. Strange, and T. C. Brock (eds.), *Narrative impact: social and cognitive foundations*. Mahwah, NJ: Lawrence Erlbaum, pp. 229–262.

Green, M. C. (2004). Transportation into narrative worlds: The role of prior knowledge and perceived realism. *Discourse Processes*, 38, 247–266.

Green, M. C., and Brock, T. C. (2000). The role of transportation in the persuasiveness of public narratives. *Journal of Personality and Social Psychology*, 79, 701–721.

(2002). In the mind's eye: Transportation-imagery model of narrative persuasion. In Green, M. C., Strange, J. J., and Brock, T. C. (eds.), *Narrative impact: social and cognitive foundations*. Mahwah, NJ: Lawrence Erlbaum, pp. 315–342.

Grofman, B. (1989). Richard Nixon as Pinocchio, Richard II, and Santa Claus: The use of allusion in political satire. *The Journal of Politics*, 51, 165–173.

Gruner, C. W. (1997). *The game of humor: A comprehensive theory of why we laugh*. London: Transaction.

Haider, M. (2011). Ship of state needs more women at the helm. http://ipsnews.net/news.asp?idnews=105172. Last accessed December 7, 2011.

Harris-Lacewell, M. V. (2004). *Barbershops, Bibles, and BET: Everyday talk and Black political thought.* Princeton University Press.

Haught, C., and Glucksberg, S. (2004). When old sharks are not old pros: Metaphors are not similes. Paper presented at the annual meeting of the Psychonomic Society, Minneapolis, MN.

Hemingway, E. (1924). *In our time.* Paris: Three Mountains Press. [Subsequently reissued by Scribners' in 1959 and 1969.]

    (1987). *The complete short stories of Ernest Hemingway.* New York: Charles Scribners'.

Holmes, J., and Marra, M. (2002). Over the edge? Subversive humor between colleagues and friends. *Humor: International Journal of Humor Research*, 15, 65–87.

Honohan, I. (2008). Metaphors of solidarity. In Carver, T., and Pikalo, J. (eds.), *Political language and metaphor: Interpreting and changing the world.* London and New York: Routledge, pp. 69–82.

Howe, J. (2008). Argument is argument: An essay on conceptual metaphor and verbal dispute. *Metaphor and Symbol*, 23, 1–23.

Huizinga, J. (1955). *Homo ludens; a study of the play-element in culture.* Boston, MA: Beacon Press.

Hurley, M. M., Dennett, D. C., and Adams, R. B., Jr. (2011). *Inside jokes: Using humor to reverse-engineer the mind.* Cambridge, MA: MIT Press.

Indurkhya, B. (1999). Creativity of metaphor in perceptual symbol systems. *Behavioral and Brain Sciences*, 11, 621–622.

Iyengar, S. (1991). *Is anyone responsible? How television frames political issues.* University of Chicago Press.

Katz, A. N., and Taylor, T. E. (2008). The journeys of life: Examining a conceptual metaphor with semantic and episodic memory recall. *Metaphor and Symbol*, 23: 148–173.

Keats, J. (1962). *Poems and selected letters.* New York: Bantam.

Kerr, J. A., and Apter, M. J. (eds.) (1991). *Adult play: A reversal theory approach.* Amsterdam: Swets & Zeitlinger.

Keysar, B., and Bly, B. M. (1999). Swimming against the current: Do idioms reflect conceptual structure? *Journal of Pragmatics*, 31, 1559–1578.

Keysar, B., and Glucksberg, S. (1992). Metaphor and communication. *Poetics Today*, 13(4), 633–658.

Kintsch, W. (1998). *Comprehension: A paradigm for cognition.* Cambridge University Press.

    (2008). How the mind computes the meaning of metaphor: A simulation based on LSA. In Gibbs, R.W., Jr. (ed.), *The Cambridge handbook of metaphor and thought.* Cambridge University Press, pp. 129–142.

Klatsky, R. L., Pellegrino, J. W., McCloskey, B. P., and Doherty, S. (1989). Can you squeeze a tomato? The role of motor representations in semantic sensibility judgments. *Journal of Memory and Language*, 28, 56–77.

Koller, V. (2004). *Metaphor and gender in business media discourse: A critical cognitive study.* Basingstoke, Hants: Palgrave Macmillan.

Kövecses, Z. (1990). *Emotion concepts.* New York: Springer.

(2002). *Metaphor: A practical introduction.* Oxford University Press.

(2005). *Metaphor in culture: Universality and variation.* Cambridge University Press.

Kruskal, J. B., and Wish, M. (1981). *Multidimensional scaling.* Beverly Hills, CA and London: Sage Publications.

Lakoff, G. (1993). The contemporary theory of metaphor. In Ortony, A. (ed.), *Metaphor and thought* (2nd edn.). Cambridge University Press, pp. 202–251.

(1996). *Moral politics: What conservatives know that liberals don't.* University of Chicago Press.

Lakoff, G., and Johnson, M. (1980). *Metaphors we live by.* University of Chicago Press.

(1999). *Philosophy in the flesh: The embodied mind and its challenge to western thought.* New York: Basic Books.

Lakoff, G., and Kövecses, Z. (1987). The cognitive model of anger inherent in American English. In Holland, D., and Quinn, N. (eds.), *Cultural models in language and thought.* Cambridge University Press, pp. 195–221.

Lakoff, G., and Nunez, R. E. (2000). *Where mathematics comes from: How the embodied mind brings mathematics into being.* New York: Basic Books.

Lakoff, G., and Sweetser, E. (1994). Forward to Fauconnier, G., *Mental spaces: Aspects of meaning construction in natural language.* Cambridge University Press.

Lakoff, G., and Turner, M. (1989). *More than cool reason: A field guide to poetic metaphor.* University of Chicago Press.

Landauer, T. K., and Dumais, S. T. (1997). A solution to Plato's problem: The latent semantic analysis theory of acquisition induction, and representation of knowledge. *Psychological Review,* 104, 211–240.

Lear, E. (1871). The owl and the pussy-cat. Available online on the Edward Lear homepage, www.nonsenselit.org/Lear/ns/pussy.html. Last accessed April 9, 2011.

Lieber, J., and Wheeler, B. E. (1963). *Jackson.* Nashville, TN: Kapp Records.

Louwerse, M. M. (2007). Symbolic or embodied representations: A case for symbol interdependency. In Landauer, T. K., McNamara, D. S., Dennis, S., and Kintsch, W. (eds.), *Handbook of latent semantic analysis.* Mahwah, NJ: Lawrence Erlbaum, pp. 107–120.

Maalej, Z. (2004). Figurative language in anger expressions in Tunisian Arabic: An extended view of embodiment. *Metaphor and Symbol,* 19, 51–75.

MacArthur, F. (2005). The competent horseman in a horseless world: Observations on a conventional metaphor in Spanish and English. *Metaphor and Symbol,* 20, 71–94.

Maeda, E., and Ritchie, L. D. (2004). The concept of *shinyuu* in Japan: A replication of and comparison to Cole and Bradac's study on U.S. friendship. *Journal of Social and Personal Relationships,* 20, 579–598.

Mansbridge, J. (1999). Everyday talk in the deliberative system. In S. Macedo (ed.), *Deliberative politics: Essays on democracy and disagreement.* New York: Oxford University Press.

Martin, R. A. (2007). *The Psychology of humor: An integrative approach.* Amsterdam: Elsevier.

McCanlies, T. (Director) (2003). *Second-hand lions.* New Line Cinema.

McLaughlin, A. J. (1903). The American's distrust of the immigrant. *Popular Science Monthly*, 62, 230–236.

Meier, B. P., and Robinson, M. D. (2005). The metaphorical representation of affect. *Metaphor and Symbol*, 20, 239–257.

Meyrowitz, J. (1985). *No sense of place: The impact of electronic media on social behaviour.* New York: Oxford University Press.

Müller, C. (2008). *Metaphors dead and alive, sleeping and waking: A dynamic view.* University of Chicago Press.

Musolff, A. (2004). *Metaphor and political discourse: Analogical reasoning in debates about Europe.* Basingstoke, Hants: Palgrave Macmillan.

Nerlich, B. (2003). Metaphor, science and the media [online]. www.medrad. org/Panacea?Actual/n13–14tribuna-metafora.pdf. Last accessed September, 2008.

Nerlich, B., Johnson, S., and Clarke, D. D. (2003). The first 'designer baby': The role of narratives, cliches and metaphors in the year 2000 media debate. *Science as Culture*, 12, 471–498.

Niedenthal, P. M., Barsalou, L. W., Winkielman, P., Krauth-Gruber, S., and Ric, F. (2005). Embodiment in attitudes, social perception, and emotion. *Personality and Social Psychology Review*, 9, 184–211.

Nishishiba, M., and Ritchie, L. D. (2000). The concept of trustworthiness: A cross-cultural comparison between Japanese and U.S. business people. *Journal of Applied Communication Research*, 28(4), 347–367.

Norrick, N. R. (1993). *Conversational joking: Humor in everyday talk.* Bloomington: Indiana University Press.

(2003). Issues in conversational joking. *Journal of Pragmatics*, 35, 1333–1359.

Obama, B. (2008) "A More Perfect Union," Philadelphia, PA, March 18, 2008.

O'Brien, G. V. (2003). Indigestible food, conquering hordes, and waste materials: Metaphors of immigrants and early immigration restriction debate in the United States. *Metaphor and Symbol*, 18, 33–47.

Obst, P. (2003). *Grief as a journey.* www.helphorizons.com/care/search_details.htm?id=455. Last accessed May 10, 2011.

Ortony, A. (1993). Metaphor, language, and thought. In Ortony, A. (ed.), *Metaphor and thought* (2nd edn.). Cambridge University Press. pp. 1–18.

Pan, Z., and Kosicki, G. M. (1997). Priming and media impact on the evaluations of the president's performance. *Communication Research*, 24, 3–30.

Papenfuss, M. (2011). *Pirate party storms German ship of State.* www.newser. com/story/128956/pirate-party-storms-german-ship-of-state.html. Posted September 20, 2011. Last accessed December 7, 2011.

Perlmutter, D. D. (2002). On incongruities and logical inconsistencies in humor: The delicate balance. *Humor: International Journal of Humor Research,* 15, 155–168.

Pierotti, J. (1973). President Richard Nixon as Pinocchio – cartoon drawing. *New York Post,* June 8. The Granger Collection, Image No. 0085370. www.granger.com/results.asp?inline=trueandimage=0085370andww wflag=1andimagepos=32andscreenwidth=984. Last accessed October 29, 2011.

Pinker, S. (2011). *The better angels of our nature: Why violence has declined.* New York: Viking.

Plester, B. A., and Sayers, J. (2007). "Taking the piss": Functions of banter in the IT industry. *Humor: International Journal of Humor Research,* 20,157–187.

Pragglejaz Group (2007). MIP: A method for identifying metaphorically used words in discourse. *Metaphor and Symbol,* 22, 1–39. [The letters stand for the first names of the ten co-authors.]

Price, V., Tewksbury, D., and Powers, E. (1997). Switching trains of thought: The impact of news frames on reader's cognitive responses. *Communication Research* 24, 481.

Raskin, V. (1985). *Semantic mechanisms of humor.* Boston, MA: D. Reidel.

Raskin, V., and Attardo, S. (1994). Non-literalness and non-bona-fide in language: An approach to formal and computational treatments of humor. *Pragmatics and Cognition,* 2(1), 31–69.

Reddy, M. J. (1993). The conduit metaphor: A case of frame conflict in our language about language. In Ortony, A. (ed.), *Metaphor and thought* (2nd edn.). Cambridge University Press, pp. 164–201.

Richards, I. A. (1936). *The philosophy of rhetoric.* London: Oxford University Press.

Ringmar, E. (2008). Metaphors of social order. In Carver, T., and Pikalo, J. (eds.), *Political language and metaphor: Interpreting and changing the world.* London and New York: Routledge, pp. 57–68.

Ritchie, L. D. (1986). Shannon and Weaver: Unravelling the paradox of information. *Communication Research,* 13, 278–298.

(1991). *Communication concepts 2: Information.* Newbury Park, CA: Sage.

(2003a). Categories and similarities: A note on circularity. *Metaphor and Symbol,* 18, 49–53.

(2003b). "ARGUMENT IS WAR" – Or is it a game of chess? Multiple meanings in the analysis of implicit metaphors. *Metaphor and Symbol,* 18, 125–146.

(2004). Lost in *"Conceptual Space"*: Metaphors of Conceptual Integration. *Metaphor and Symbol,* 19, 31–50.

(2005). Frame-shifting in humor and irony. *Metaphor and Symbol*, 20, 275–294.

(2006). *Context and connection in metaphor*. Basingstoke, Hants: Palgrave Macmillan.

(2008a). Gateshead revisited: The integrative function of ambiguous metaphors in a tricky political situation. *Metaphor and Symbol*, 23, 24–49.

(2008b). *X IS A JOURNEY*: Embodied simulation in metaphor interpretation. *Metaphor and Symbol*, 23, 174–199.

(2009a). Relevance and simulation in metaphor. *Metaphor and Symbol*, 24, 249–262.

(2009b). Distributed cognition and play in the quest for the double helix. In H. Pishwa (ed.), *Language and social cognition*. Berlin: Mouton de Gruyter, pp. 289–323.

(2009c). Review of *Metaphor and Gesture* edited by Alan Cienki and Cornelia Mueller. *Metaphor and Symbol*, 25, 121–123.

(2010a). *"Everybody goes down"*: Metaphors, stories, and simulations in conversations. *Metaphor and Symbol*, 25, 123–143.

(2010b). Metaphors and simulations in conversational storytelling. Presented at the 8th International Conference on Researching and Applying Metaphor (RaAM), Amsterdam, June 30 – July 3, 2010.

(2011a). *"Justice is blind"*: A model for analyzing metaphor transformations and narratives in actual discourse. *Metaphor and the Social World*, 1, 70–89.

(2011b). "You're lying to Jesus!" Humor and play in a discussion about homelessness. *Humor* 24, 481–511.

(2011c). Why the block is *the block*: Reinforcing community through casual conversation. *Metaphor and the Social World*, 1, 240–261.

(2012). Metaphor and stories in discourse about personal and social change. In Wagoner, B., Jensen, E., and Oldmeadow, J. (eds.), *Culture and social change: Transforming society through the power of ideas*. A volume in *Advances in Cultural Psychology*, J. Valsiner (series ed.). Charlotte, NC: Information Age Publishers.

Ritchie, L. D., and Dyhouse, V. (2008). FINE AS FROG'S HAIR: Three models for the development of meaning in figurative language. *Metaphor and Symbol*, 23, 85–107.

Ritchie, L. D., and Schell, C. (2009). *"The ivory tower"* on an *"unstable foundation"*: Playful language, humor, and metaphor in the negotiation of scientists' identities. *Metaphor and Symbol*, 24, 90–104.

Roberts, K. (1924). Slow poison. *The Saturday Evening Post*, 196(31), 8–9, 54, 58.

Sandburg, C. (1919). Fog. http://carl-sandburg.com/fog.htm. Last accessed April 15, 2011.

Sasson, T. (1995). *Crime talk: How citizens construct a social problem*. New York: Aldine De Gruyter.

Schank, R. C., and Abelson, R. P. (1995). Knowledge and memory: The real story. In Wyer, R. S. (ed.), *Advances in social cognition*, vol. VIII: *Knowledge and memory: The real story*. Hillsdale, NJ: Lawrence Erlbaum, pp. 1–86.

Schank, R. C., and Berman, T. R. (2002). The pervasive role of stories in knowledge and action. In Green, M. C., Strange, J. J., and Brock, T. C. (eds.), *Narrative impact: Social and cognitive foundations*. Mahwah, NJ: Lawrence Erlbaum, pp. 287–314.

Schneider, S. G. (2008). Exploring the metaphorical (de-)construction of legitimacy: A comparison of legitimation discourses in American and British newspapers. In Carver, T., and Pikalo, J. (eds.), *Political language and metaphor: Interpreting and changing the world*. London and New York: Routledge, pp. 83–101.

Schön, D. A. (1993). Generative metaphor: A perspective on problem-setting in social policy. In Ortony, A. (ed.), *Metaphor and thought*, (2nd edn. [1st edn. 1979]). Cambridge University Press, pp. 137–163.

Schubert, T. (2005). Your highness: Vertical positions as conceptual symbols of power. *Journal of Personality and Social Psychology*, 89, 1–21.

Schubert, T. W., Waldzus, S., and Seibt, B. (2008). The embodiment of power and communalism in space and bodily contact. In Semin, G., and Smith, E. R. (eds.), *Embodied grounding: Social, cognitive, affective, and neuroscientific approaches*. (Chapter 7.) Cambridge University Press.

Searle, J. R. (1993). Metaphor. In Ortony, A. (ed.), *Metaphor and thought* (2nd edn. [1st edn. 1979]), pp. 83–111. Cambridge University Press.

Semino, E. (2008). *Metaphor in discourse*. Cambridge University Press.

(2010). Descriptions of pain, metaphor, and embodied simulations. *Metaphor and Symbol*, 25, 205–226.

Shakespeare, W. (1961). When forty winters shall besiege thy brow (Sonnet 2). In Bush, D., and Harbage, A. (eds.), *Shakespeare's sonnets*. New York: Penguin, p. 24.

Shapiro, L. (2010). *Embodied cognition*. Hoboken, NJ: Taylor & Francis.

Sharifian, F., Dirven, R., Yu, N., and Neiemier, S. (eds.) (2008). *Culture, body, and language: Conceptualizations of internal body organs across cultures and languages*. New York: Mouton De Gruyter.

Shelley, M. W. (1969). *Frankenstein; or The modern Prometheus*. London: Oxford University Press.

Sherzer, J. (2002). *Speech play and verbal art*. Austin: University of Texas Press.

Snyder, G. (1969). *Turtle Island*. New York: New Directions.

Spender, S. (1955). *Seascape. Collected poems, 1928–1953*. New York: Random House. Available online: www.nbu.bg/webs/amb/british/6/spender/seascape.htm. Last accessed April 15, 2011.

Sperber, D., and Wilson, D. ([1986] 1995). *Relevance: Communication and cognition*. Cambridge, MA: Harvard University Press.

(2008). A deflationary account of metaphors. In Gibbs, R.W., Jr. (ed.), *The Cambridge handbook of metaphor and thought*. Cambridge University Press, pp. 84–105.

Steeleye Span (1975). Dance with me. (Traditional folk ballad.) From the album *All Around My Hat*, London: Chrysalis Records.

Steen, G. (2008). The paradox of metaphor: Why we need a three-dimensional model of metaphor. *Metaphor and Symbol*, 23: 213–241.

Stenvoll, D. (2008). Slippery slopes in political discourse. In Carver, T., and Pikalo, J. (eds.), *Political language and metaphor: Interpreting and changing the world*. London and New York: Routledge, pp. 28–40.

Stephenson, W. (1967). *The play theory of mass communication*. University of Chicago Press.

Sutton-Smith, B. (1995). Conclusion: The persuasive rhetorics of play. In Pellegrini, A. D. (ed.), *The future of play theory: A multidisciplinary inquiry into the contributions of Brian Sutton-Smith*. Albany: State University of New York Press, pp. 275–296.

Taylor, S., and Littleton, K. (2006). Biographies in talk: A narrative-discursive research approach. *Qualitative Sociology Review*, 2(1), 22–38.

Thibodeau, P. H., and Boroditsky L. (2011). Metaphors we think with: The role of metaphor in reasoning. PLoS ONE 6(2): e16782. doi:10.1371/journal. pone.0016782. www-psych.stanford.edu/~lera/papers/. Last accessed May 3, 2011.

Thomas, D. (2011). "Go not gentle into that good night." www.poets.org/viewmedia.php/prmMID/15377. Last accessed May 11, 2011.

Torreano, L. A., Cacciari, C., and Glucksberg, S. (2005). When dogs can fly: Level of abstraction as a cue to metaphorical use of verbs. *Metaphor and Symbol*, 20, 259–274.

Tourangeau, R., and Rips, L. (1991). Interpreting and evaluating metaphors. *Journal of Memory and Language*, 30, 452–472.

Tracy, K. (1997). Interactional trouble in emergency service requests: A problem of Frames. *Research on Language and Social Interaction*, 30, 315–343.

Vaid, J., Hull, R., Heredia, R., Gerkens, D., and Martinez, F. (2003). Getting a joke: The time course of meaning activation in verbal humor. *Journal of Pragmatics*, 35, 1431–1449.

Van Hulst, M. J. (2008). Love and life in Heart-less Town: Or, the use of metaphor in local planning. In Carver, T., and Pikalo, J. (eds.), *Political language and metaphor: Interpreting and changing the world*. London and New York: Routledge, pp. 212–224.

Veale, T., and O'Donoghue, D. (2000). Computation and Blending. *Cognitive Linguistics*, 11, 253–281.

Vega Moreno, R. E. (2007). *Creativity and convention: The pragmatics of everyday figurative speech*. Amsterdam: John Benjamins.

Vertessen, D., and de Landtscheer, C. L. (2008). A metaphorical election style: Use of metaphor at election time. In Carver, T., and Pikalo, J. (eds.), *Political language and metaphor: Interpreting and changing the world*. London and New York: Routledge, pp. 271–285.

Vervaeke, J., and Kennedy, J. M. (1996). Metaphors in language and thought: Falsification and multiple meanings. *Metaphor and Symbolic Activity*, 11(4), 273–284.

Watson, J. D. (1968). *The double helix*. New York: Penguin.

Werth, P. (1999). *Text worlds: Representing conceptual space in discourse*. London: Longman.

Williams, L. E., and Bargh, J. A. (2008). Temperature to temperament: Warm objects alter personality impressions. Unpublished manuscript, New Haven, CT: Yale University Press.

Wilson, D., and Carston, R. (2006). Metaphor, relevance and the 'emergent property' issue. *Mind and Language*, 21, 404–433.

Wilson, D., and Sperber, D. (2004). Relevance theory. In Horn, L. R., and Ward, G. (eds.), *The handbook of pragmatics*. Oxford: Blackwell, pp. 607–632.

Wilson, N., and Gibbs, R. W., Jr. (2007). Real and imagined body movement primes metaphor comprehension. *Cognitive Science*, 31, 721–731.

Yanow, D. (2008). Cognition meets action: Metaphors as models of and models for. In Carver, T., and Pikalo, J. (eds.), *Political language and metaphor: Interpreting and changing the world*. London and New York: Routledge, pp. 225–237.

Yus, F. (2003). Humor and the search for relevance. *Journal of Pragmatics*, 35, 1295–1331.

Zhong, C.-B., and Leonardelli, G. J. (2008). Cold and lonely: Does social exclusion literally feel cold? *Psychological Science*, 19, 838–842.

Zhong, C.-B., and Liljenquist, K. (2006). Washing away your sins: Threatened morality and physical cleansing. *Science*, 313: 1451–1452.

Zillmann, D., and Cantor, J. R. (1976). A disposition theory of humor and mirth. In Chapman, T., and Foot, H. (eds.), *Humor and laughter: Theory, research, and applications*. London: Wiley, pp. 93–115.

Zwaan, R. A., and Taylor, L. (2006). Seeing, acting, understanding: Motor resonance in language comprehension. *Journal of Experimental Psychology: General*, 135, 1–11.

Index

226